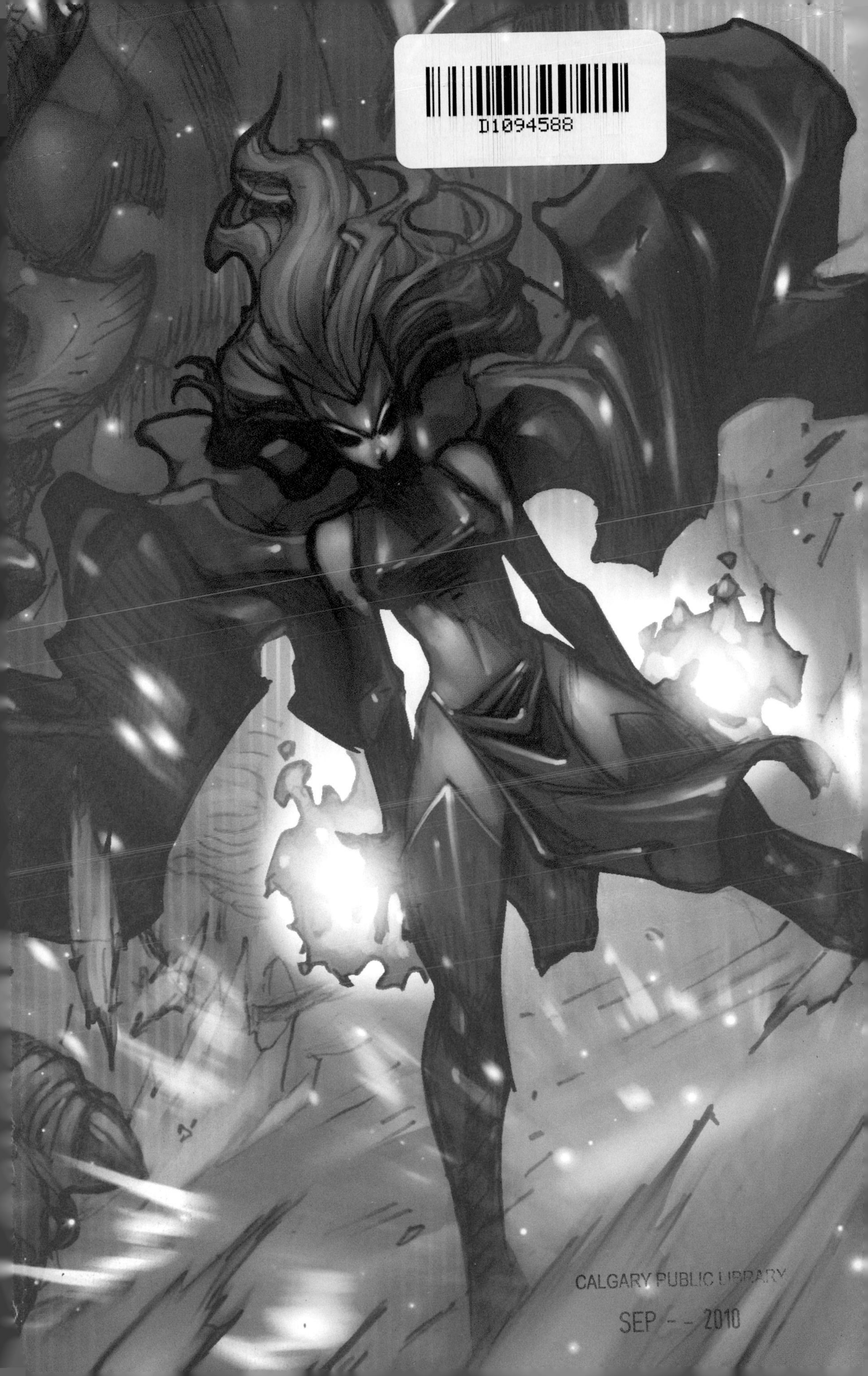

Iron Man. Thor. Captain America. The Wasp. Hawkeye. The Earth's Mightiest Heroes assembled together to handle situations no other team could. Once kept under the thumb of the United States government, billionaire playboy Tony Stark (a.k.a. Iron Man) decided to take the team on their own, housing them in his private Manhattan mansion on Fifth Avenue.

Joined now by the Black Panther, Valkyrie, Quicksilver and the Scarlet Witch, the team deals with conflicts that are both internal and external. Until six weeks ago, Valkyrie was an ordinary 19-year-old groupie, dreaming of being a super hero, yet she now possesses the powers of a goddess. The ever-silent Black Panther keeps to himself, with the exception of a yet unexplained bond with Captain America.

And that's just the beginning.

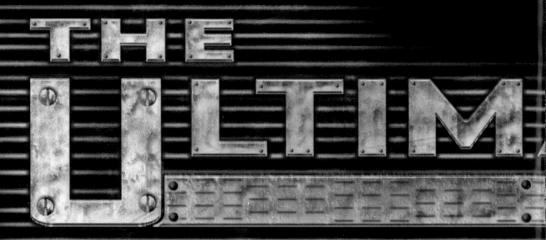

THE ULTIM[A

WHO KILLED THE

JEPH LOEB
STORY

CHRISTIAN LICHTNER
DIGITAL PAINTS

ATES 3

SCARLET WITCH?

JOE MADUREIRA
ARTWORK

RICHARD STARKINGS
LETTERING

JOHN ROSHELL
OF COMICRAFT
BOOK DESIGN

BILL ROSEMANN
LAUREN SANKOVITCH
LAUREN HENRY
ASSISTANT EDITORS

RALPH MACCHIO
EDITOR

JENNIFER GRÜNWALD
COLLECTION EDITOR

ALEX STARBUCK
EDITORIAL ASSISTANT

CORY LEVINE
JOHN DENNING
ASSISTANT EDITORS

MARK D. BEAZLEY
EDITOR, SPECIAL PROJECTS

JEFF YOUNGQUIST
SENIOR EDITOR, SPECIAL PROJECTS

DAVID GABRIEL
SENIOR VICE PRESIDENT OF SALES

JERRY KALINOWSKI
PRODUCTION

JOE QUESADA
EDITOR IN CHIEF

DAN BUCKLEY
PUBLISHER

ULTIMATES 3: WHO KILLED THE SCARLET WITCH? Contains material originally published in magazine form as ULTIMATES 3 #1-5. First printing 2008. ISBN# 978-0-7851-3037-6. Published by MARVEL PUBLISHING, INC., a subsidiary of MARVEL ENTERTAINMENT, INC. OFFICE OF PUBLICATION: 417 5th Avenue, New York, NY 10016. $24.99 per copy in the U.S. and $26.50 in Canada (GST #R127032852); Canadian Agreement #40668537. **Printed in Canada.** ALAN FINE, CEO Marvel Toys & Publishing Divisions and CMO Marvel Characters, Inc.; DAVID GABRIEL, SVP of Publishing Sales & Circulation; DAVID BOGART, SVP of Business Affairs & Talent Management; MICHAEL PASCIULLO, VP of Merchandising & Communications; JIM O'KEEFE, VP of Operations & Logistics; DAN CARR, Executive Director of Publishing Technology; JUSTIN F. GABRIE, Director of Editorial Operations; SUSAN CRESPI, Editorial Operations Manager; STAN LEE, Chairman Emeritus. For information regarding advertising in Marvel Comics or on Marvel.com, please contact Mitch Dane, Advertising Director, at mdane@marvel.com. For Marvel subscription inquiries, please call 800-217-9158.

10 9 8 7 6 5 4 3 2 1

ONE

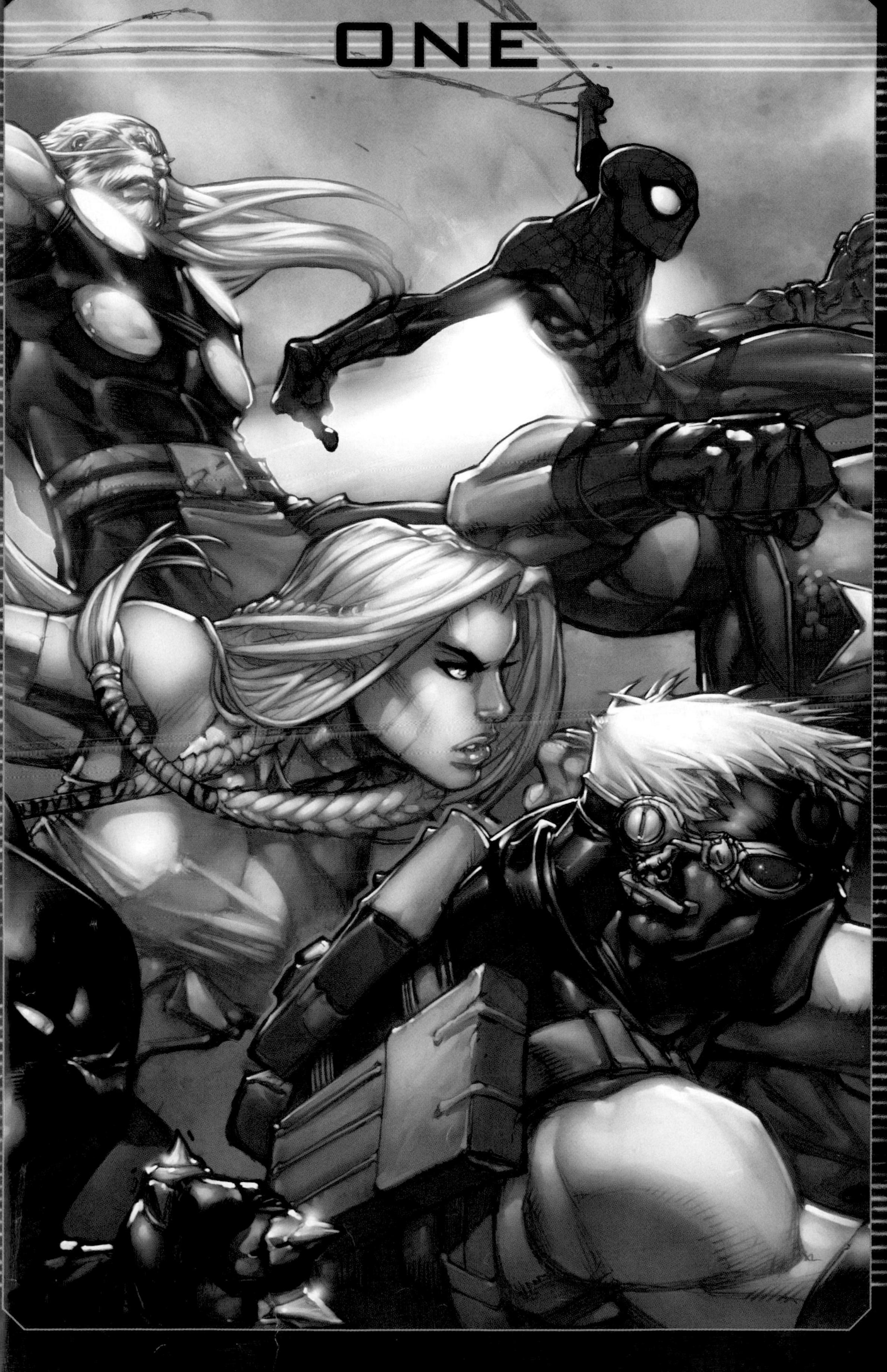

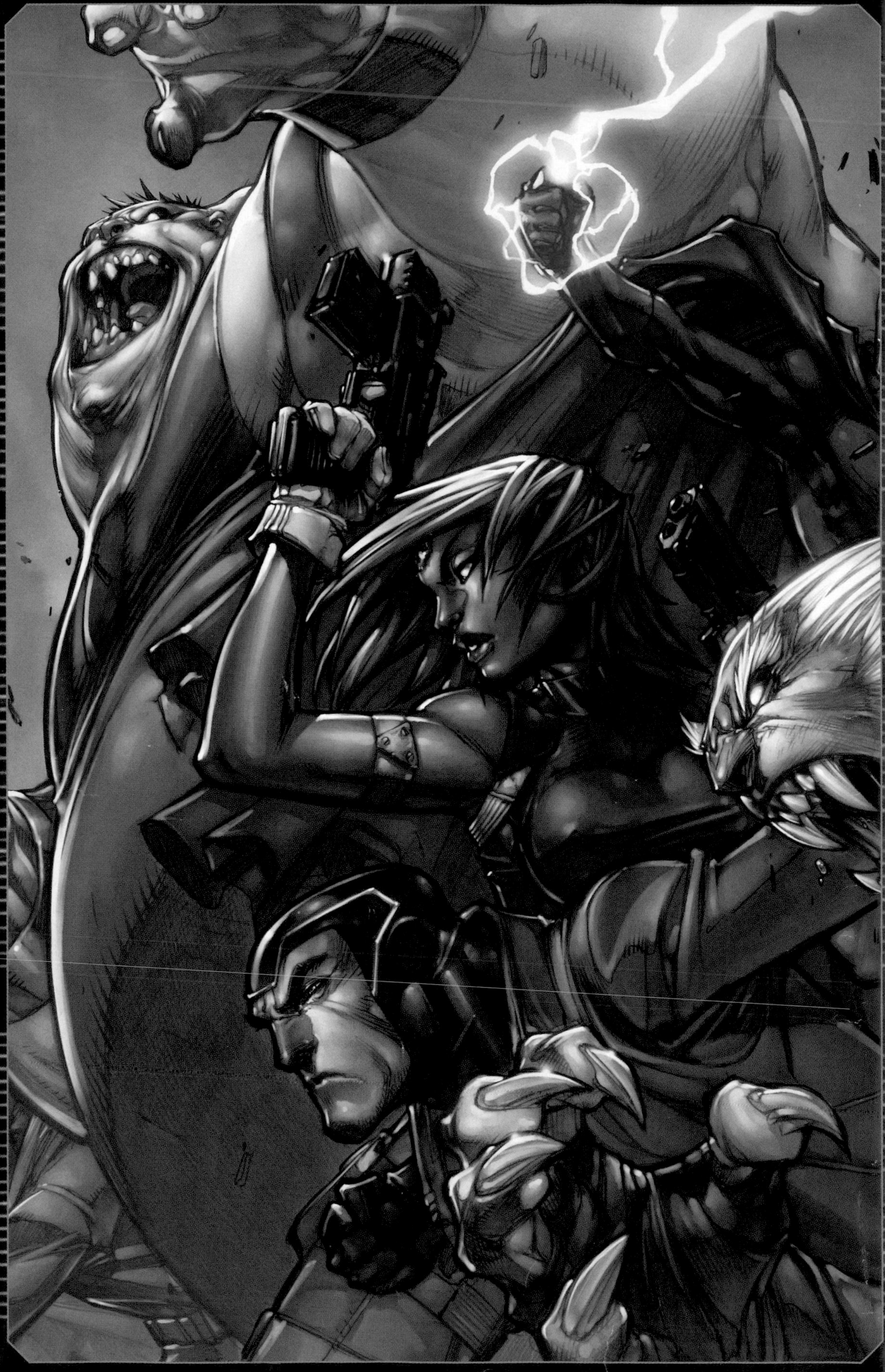

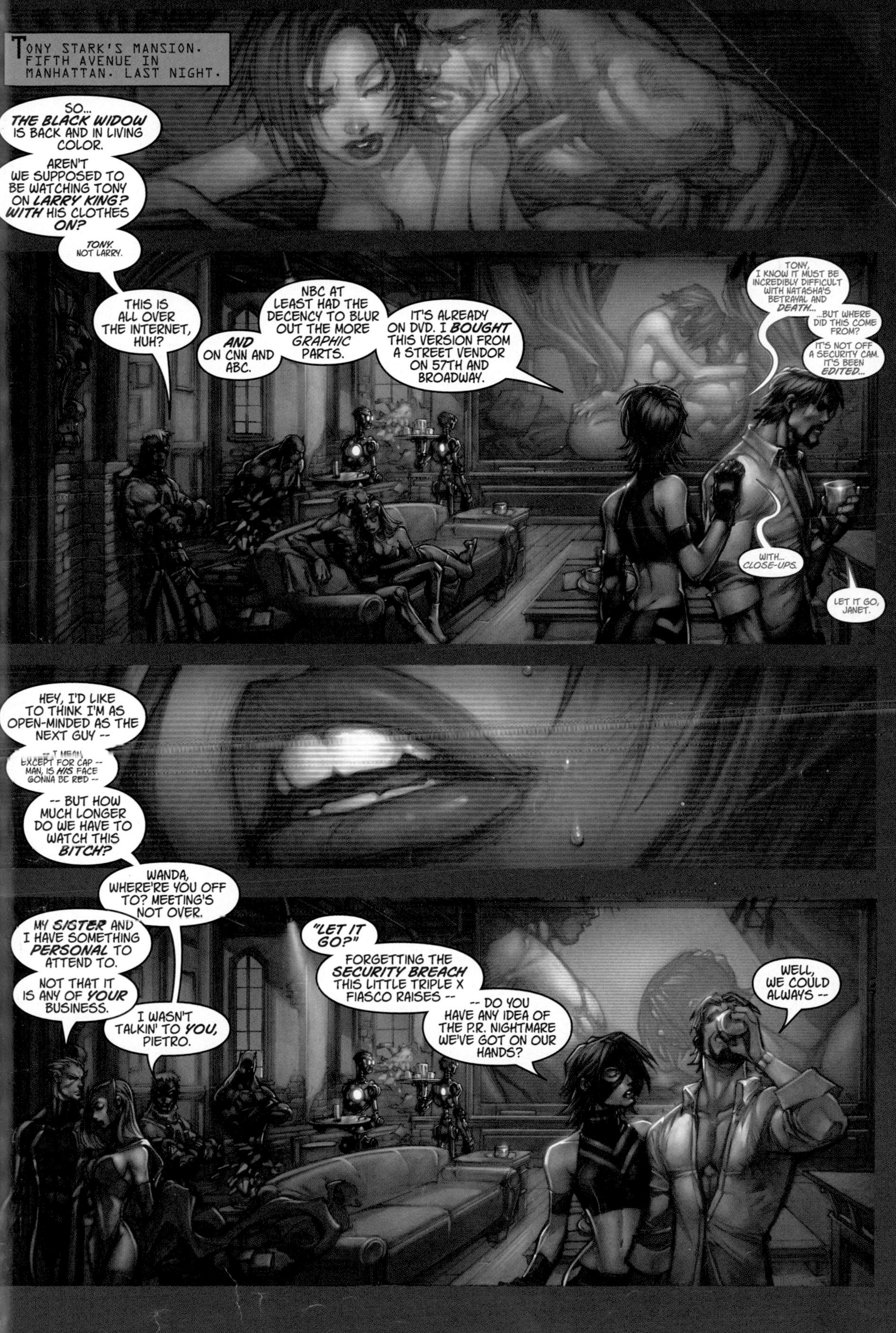
TONY STARK'S MANSION. FIFTH AVENUE IN MANHATTAN. LAST NIGHT.
SO... THE BLACK WIDOW IS BACK AND IN LIVING COLOR.
AREN'T WE SUPPOSED TO BE WATCHING TONY ON LARRY KING? WITH HIS CLOTHES ON?
TONY. NOT LARRY.
THIS IS ALL OVER THE INTERNET, HUH?
AND ON CNN AND ABC.
NBC AT LEAST HAD THE DECENCY TO BLUR OUT THE MORE GRAPHIC PARTS.
IT'S ALREADY ON DVD. I BOUGHT THIS VERSION FROM A STREET VENDOR ON 57TH AND BROADWAY.
TONY, I KNOW IT MUST BE INCREDIBLY DIFFICULT WITH NATASHA'S BETRAYAL AND DEATH...
...BUT WHERE DID THIS COME FROM?
IT'S NOT OFF A SECURITY CAM. IT'S BEEN EDITED...
WITH... CLOSE-UPS.
LET IT GO, JANET.
HEY, I'D LIKE TO THINK I'M AS OPEN-MINDED AS THE NEXT GUY --
-- I MEAN, EXCEPT FOR CAP -- MAN, IS HIS FACE GONNA BE RED --
-- BUT HOW MUCH LONGER DO WE HAVE TO WATCH THIS BITCH?
WANDA, WHERE'RE YOU OFF TO? MEETING'S NOT OVER.
MY SISTER AND I HAVE SOMETHING PERSONAL TO ATTEND TO.
NOT THAT IT IS ANY OF YOUR BUSINESS.
I WASN'T TALKIN' TO YOU, PIETRO.
"LET IT GO?"
FORGETTING THE SECURITY BREACH THIS LITTLE TRIPLE X FIASCO RAISES --
-- DO YOU HAVE ANY IDEA OF THE P.R. NIGHTMARE WE'VE GOT ON OUR HANDS?
WELL, WE COULD ALWAYS --

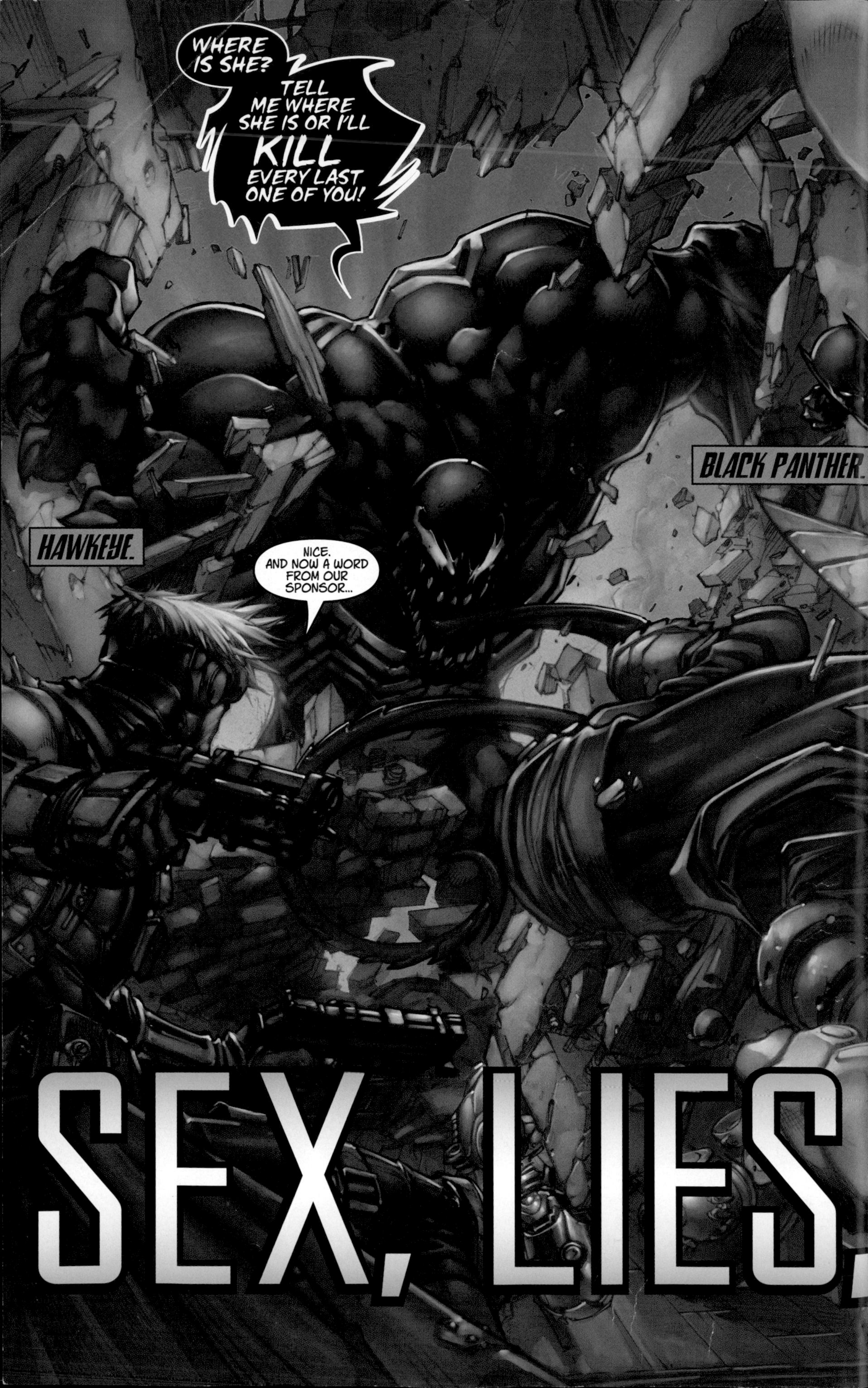
WHERE IS SHE? TELL ME WHERE SHE IS OR I'LL KILL EVERY LAST ONE OF YOU!
BLACK PANTHER.
HAWKEYE.
NICE. AND NOW A WORD FROM OUR SPONSOR...
SEX, LIES,

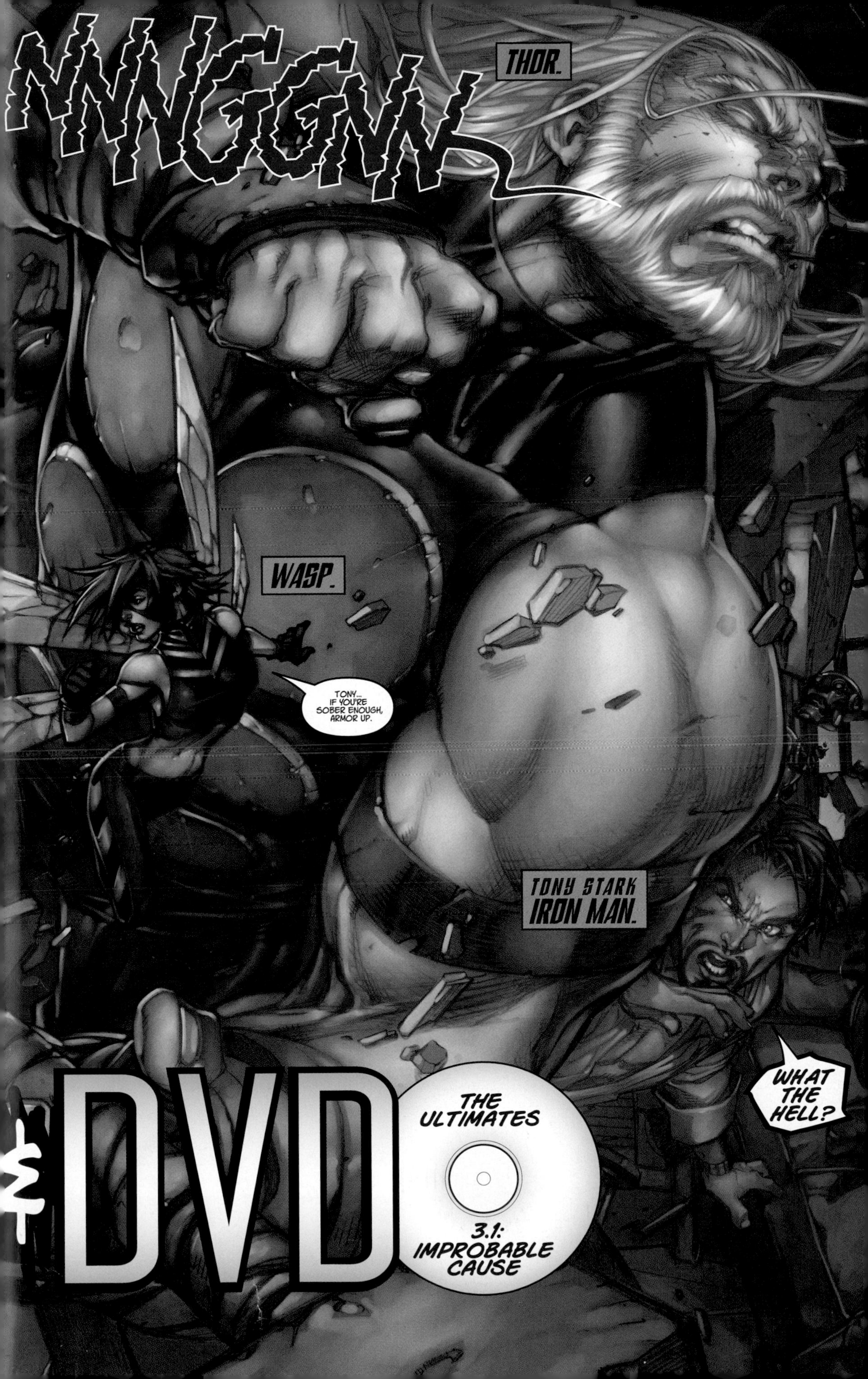
NNNGGNN
THOR.
WASP.
TONY... IF YOU'RE SOBER ENOUGH, ARMOR UP.
TONY STARK IRON MAN.
WHAT THE HELL?
DVD
THE ULTIMATES
3.1: IMPROBABLE CAUSE

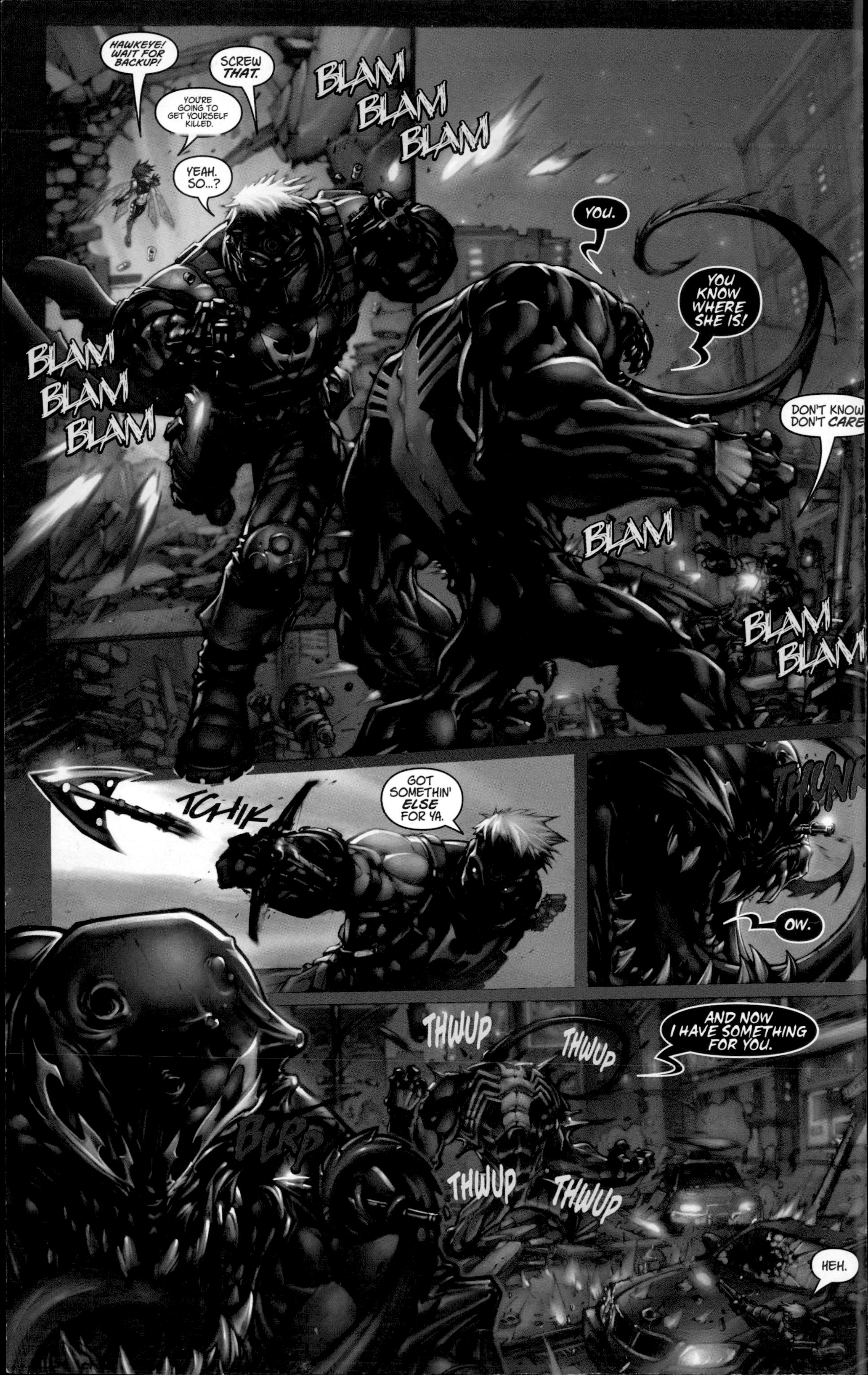
HAWKEYE! WAIT FOR BACKUP!
SCREW THAT.
YOU'RE GOING TO GET YOURSELF KILLED.
YEAH. SO...?
BLAM BLAM BLAM
BLAM BLAM BLAM
YOU.
YOU KNOW WHERE SHE IS!
DON'T KNOW DON'T CARE
BLAM
BLAM-BLAM
TCHIK
GOT SOMETHIN' ELSE FOR YA.
OW.
THWUP
THWUP
AND NOW I HAVE SOMETHING FOR YOU.
BLRP
THWUP
THWUP
HEH.

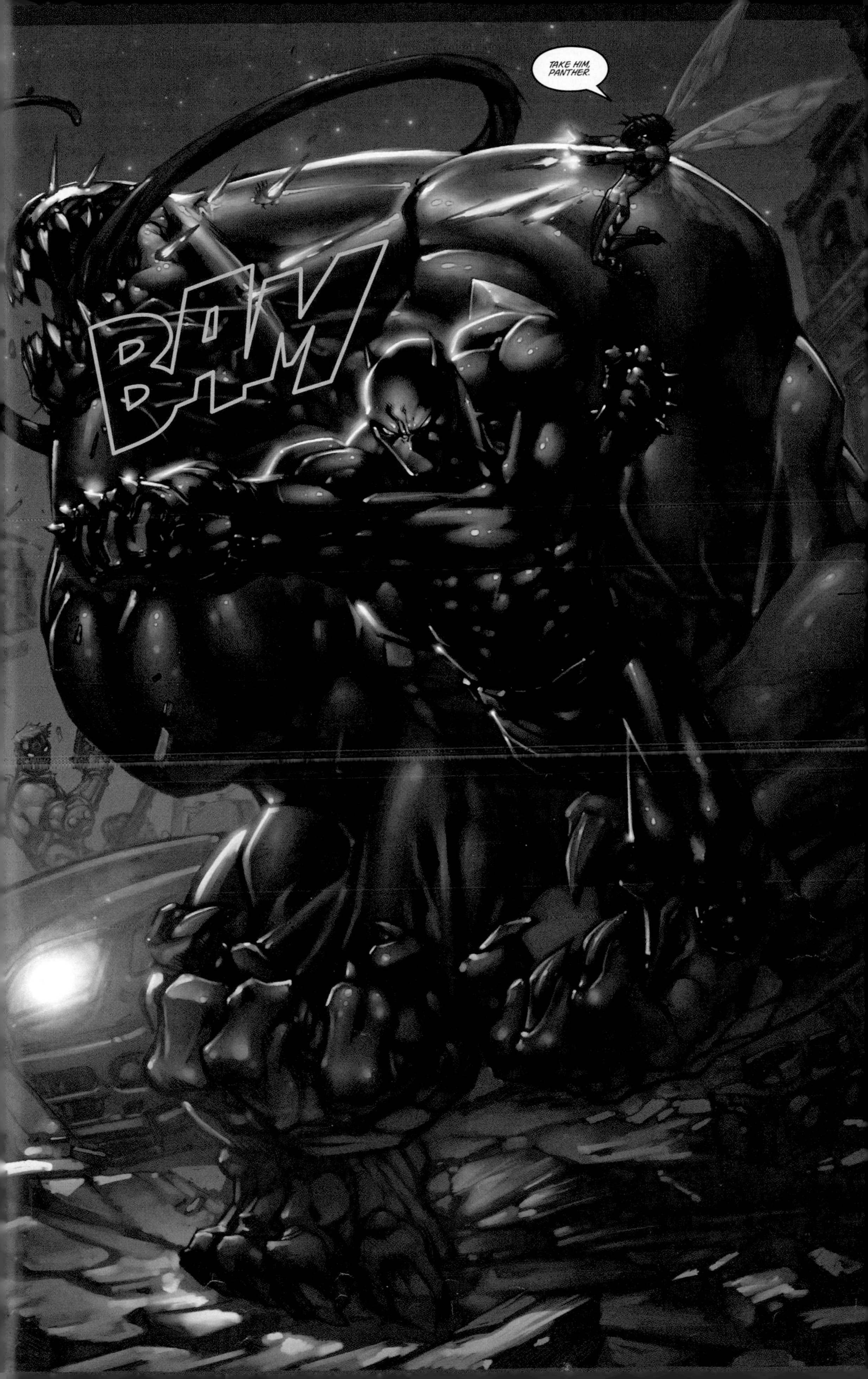
TAKE HIM, PANTHER.
BAM

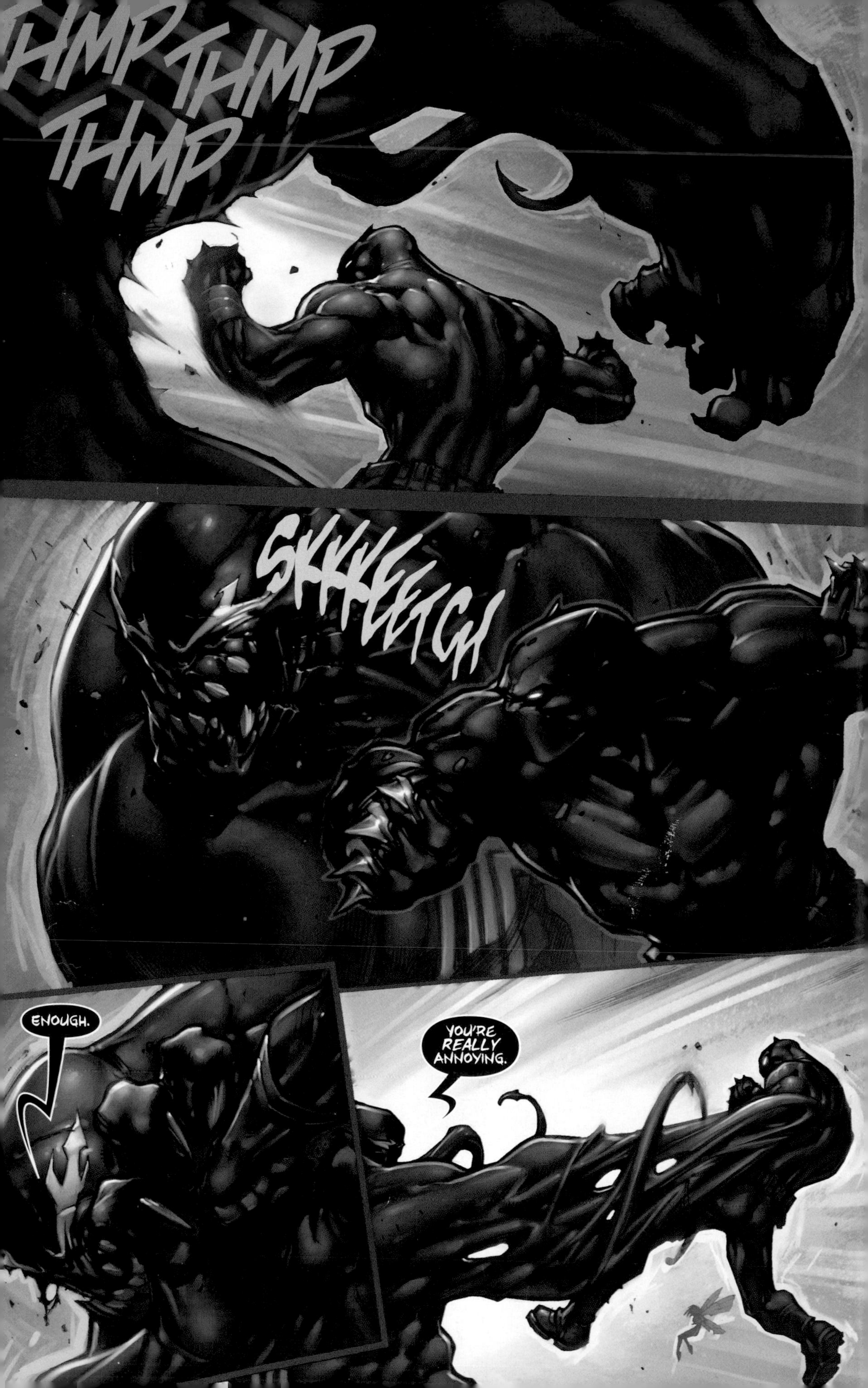
THMP THMP
THMP
SKKKEETCH
ENOUGH.
YOU'RE REALLY ANNOYING.

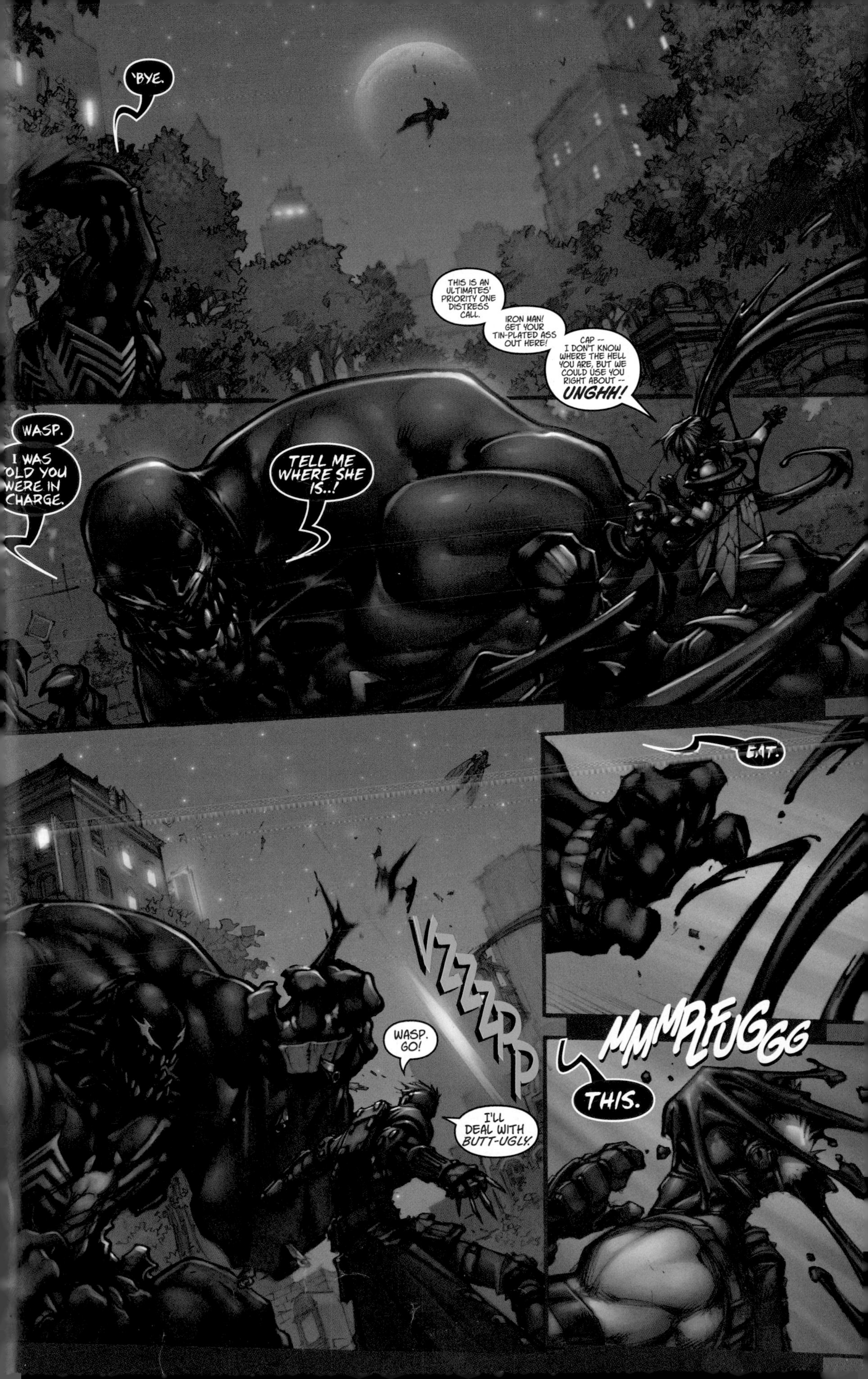
'BYE.
THIS IS AN ULTIMATES' PRIORITY ONE DISTRESS CALL.
IRON MAN! GET YOUR TIN-PLATED ASS OUT HERE!
CAP -- I DON'T KNOW WHERE THE HELL YOU ARE, BUT WE COULD USE YOU RIGHT ABOUT -- UNGHH!
WASP.
I WAS OLD YOU WERE IN CHARGE.
TELL ME WHERE SHE IS..!
VZZZZRP
WASP. GO!
I'LL DEAL WITH BUTT-UGLY.
EAT.
MMMPLFUGGG
THIS.

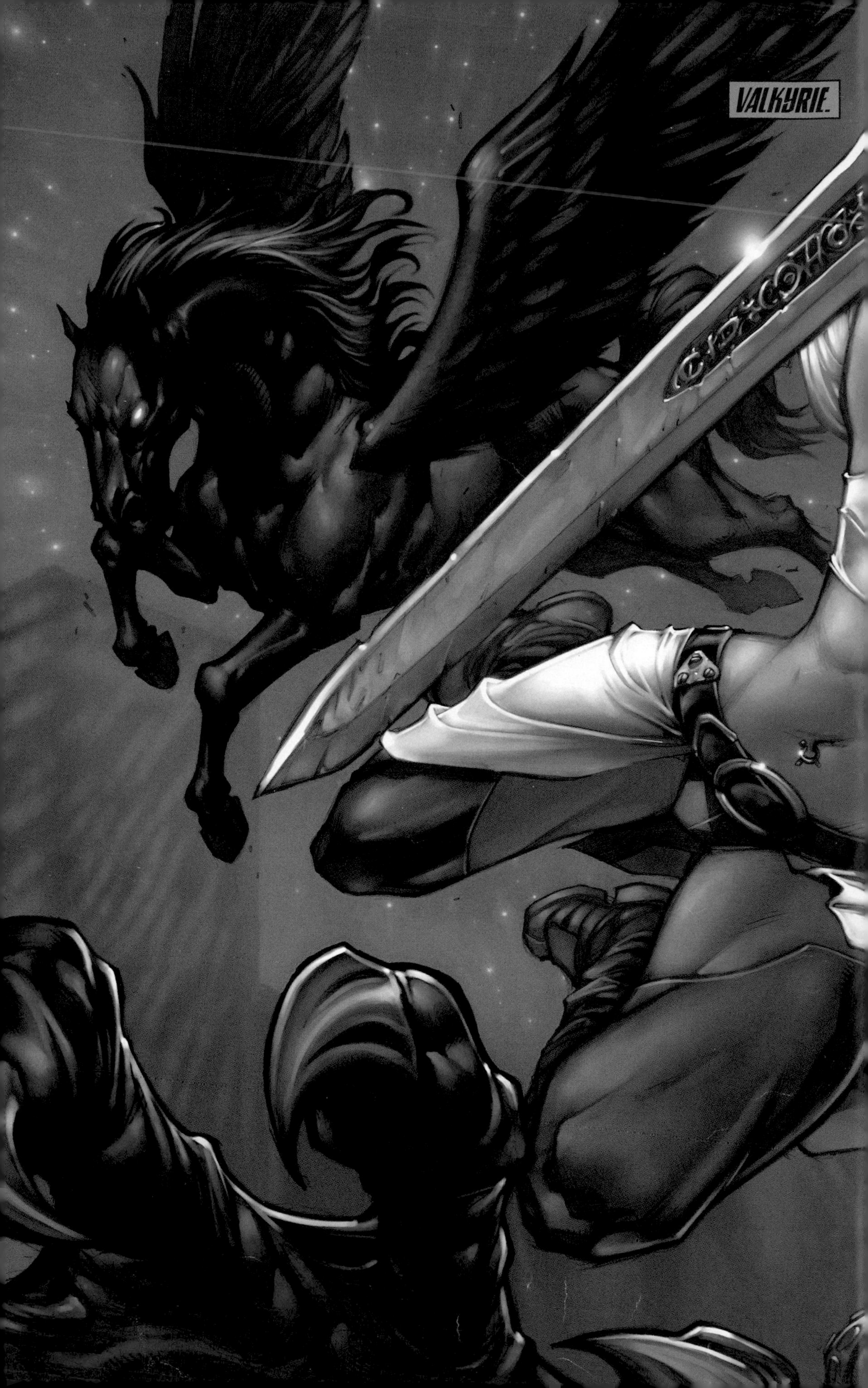
VALKYRIE.

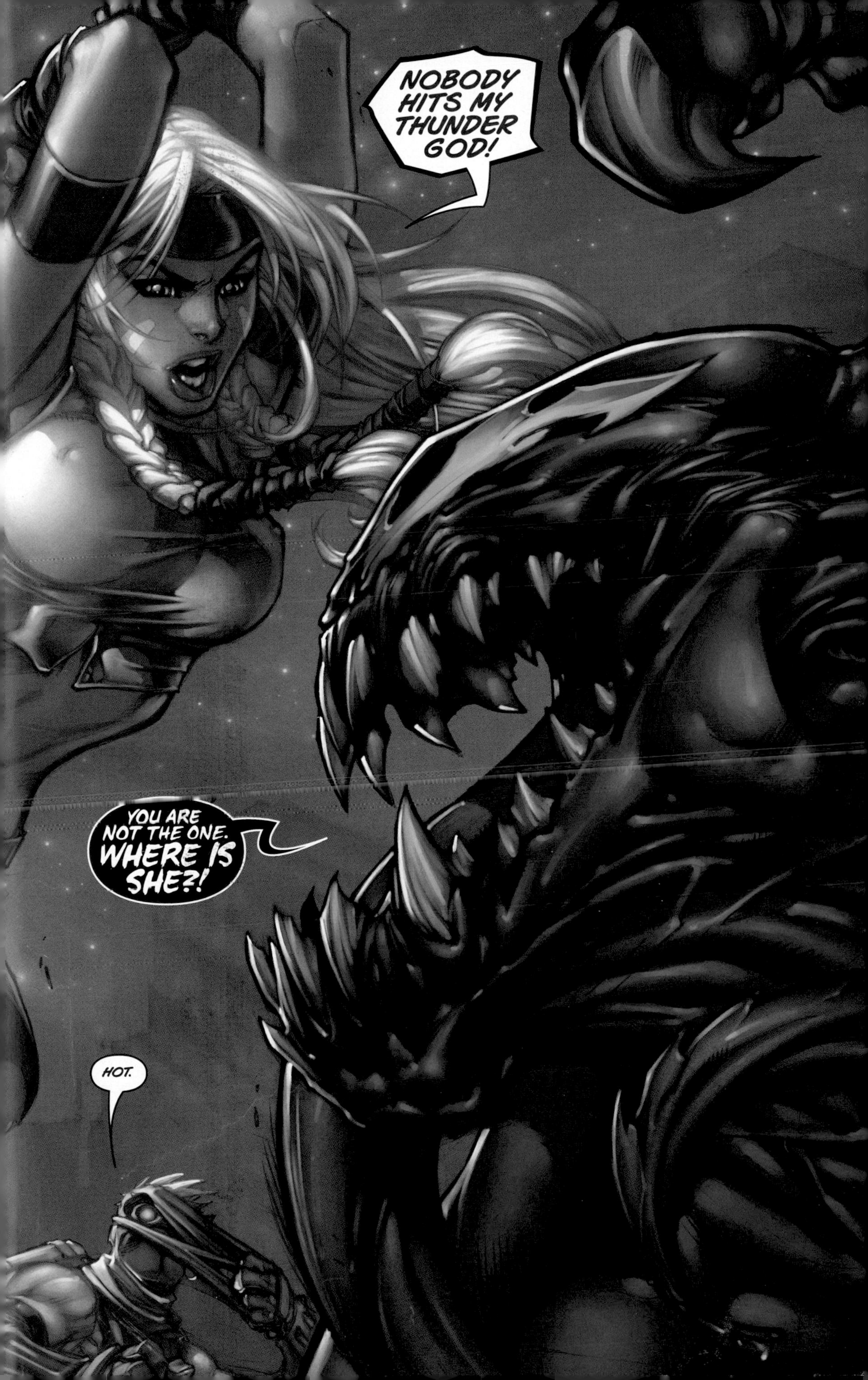
NOBODY HITS MY THUNDER GOD!
YOU ARE NOT THE ONE. WHERE IS SHE?!
HOT.

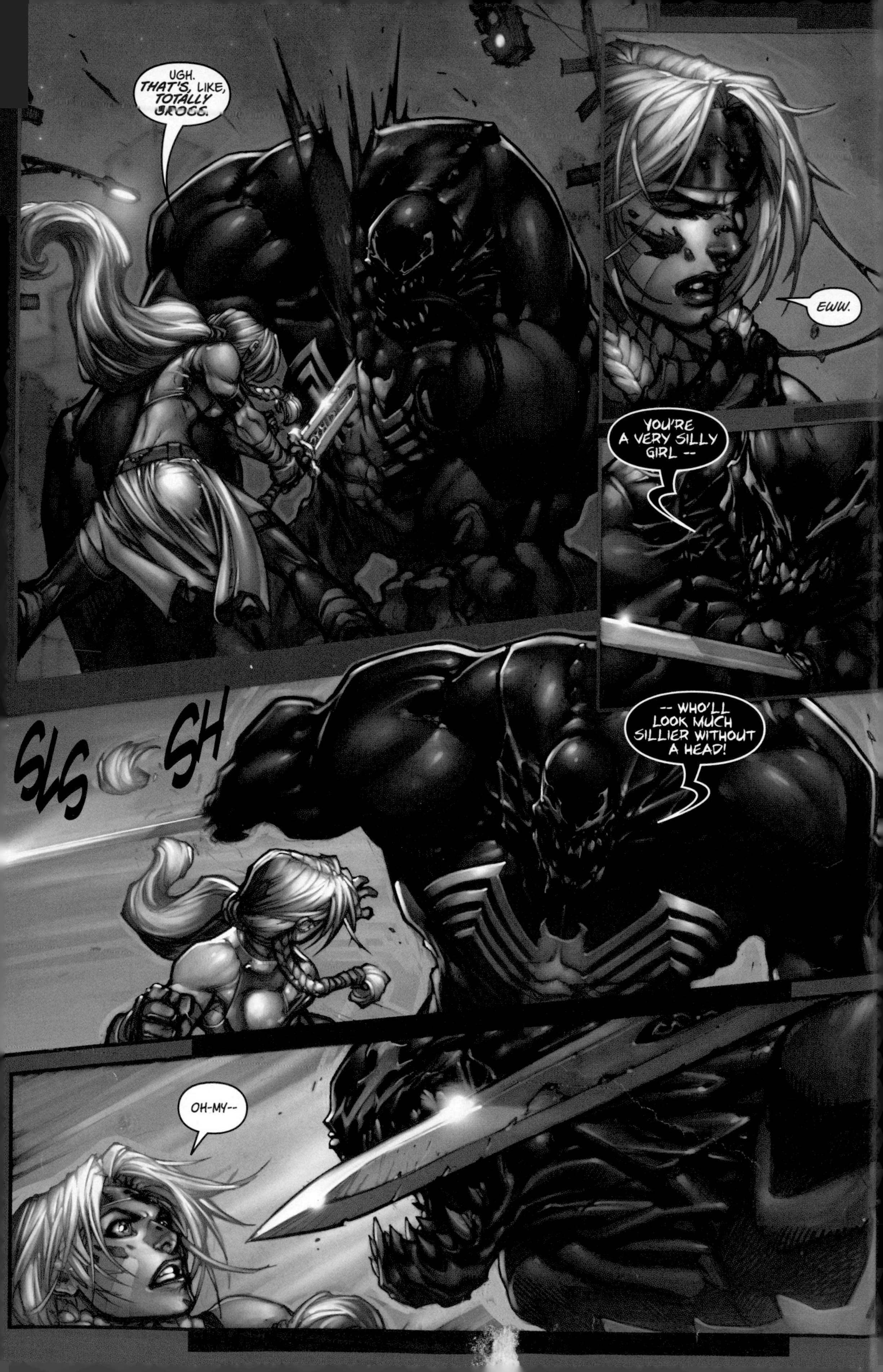
UGH. THAT'S, LIKE, TOTALLY GROSS.
EWW.
YOU'RE A VERY SILLY GIRL --
-- WHO'LL LOOK MUCH SILLIER WITHOUT A HEAD!
SLSSSH
OH-MY--

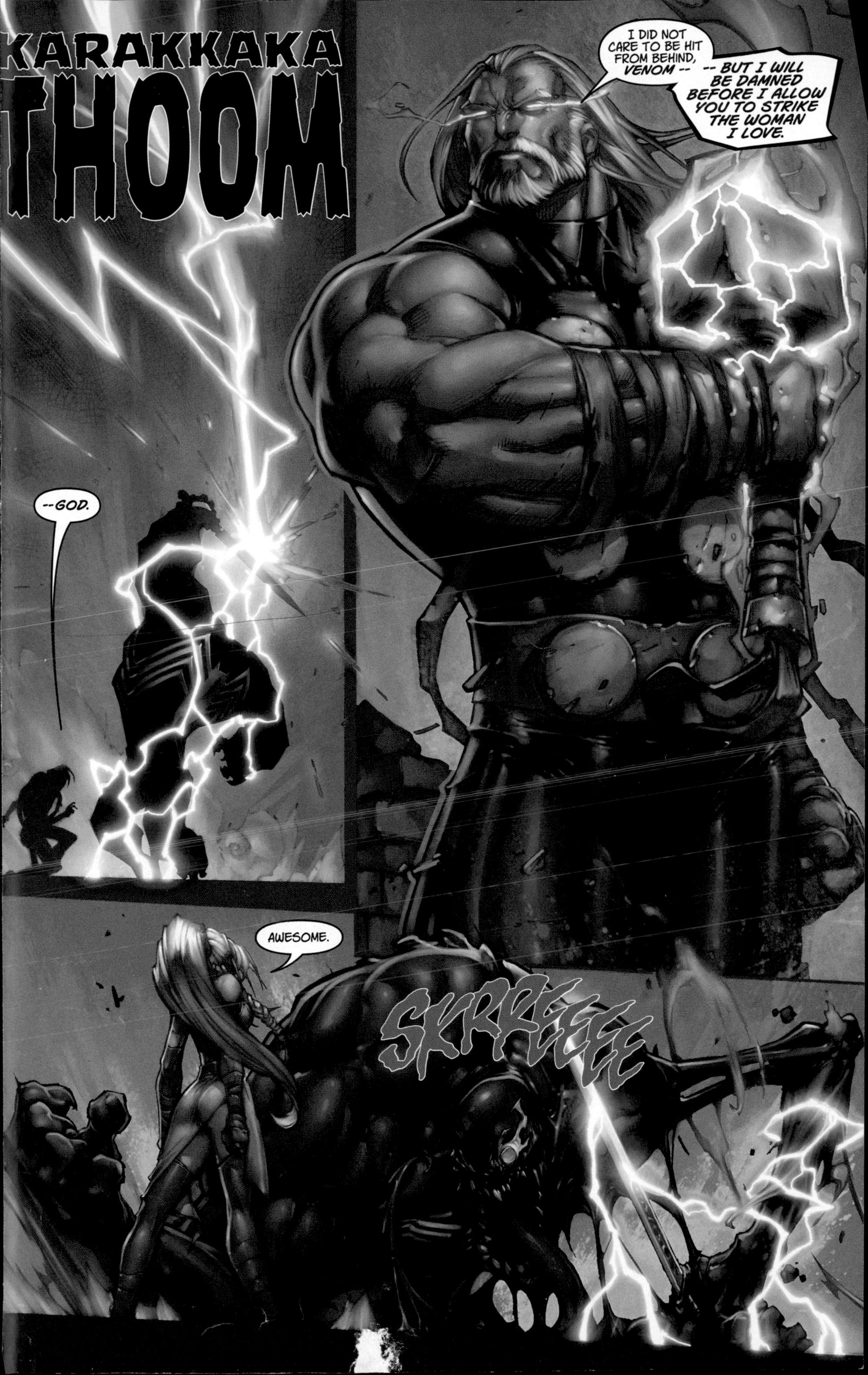
KARAKKAKA
THOOM
I DID NOT CARE TO BE HIT FROM BEHIND, VENOM --
-- BUT I WILL BE DAMNED BEFORE I ALLOW YOU TO STRIKE THE WOMAN I LOVE.
--GOD.
AWESOME.
SKRREEEE

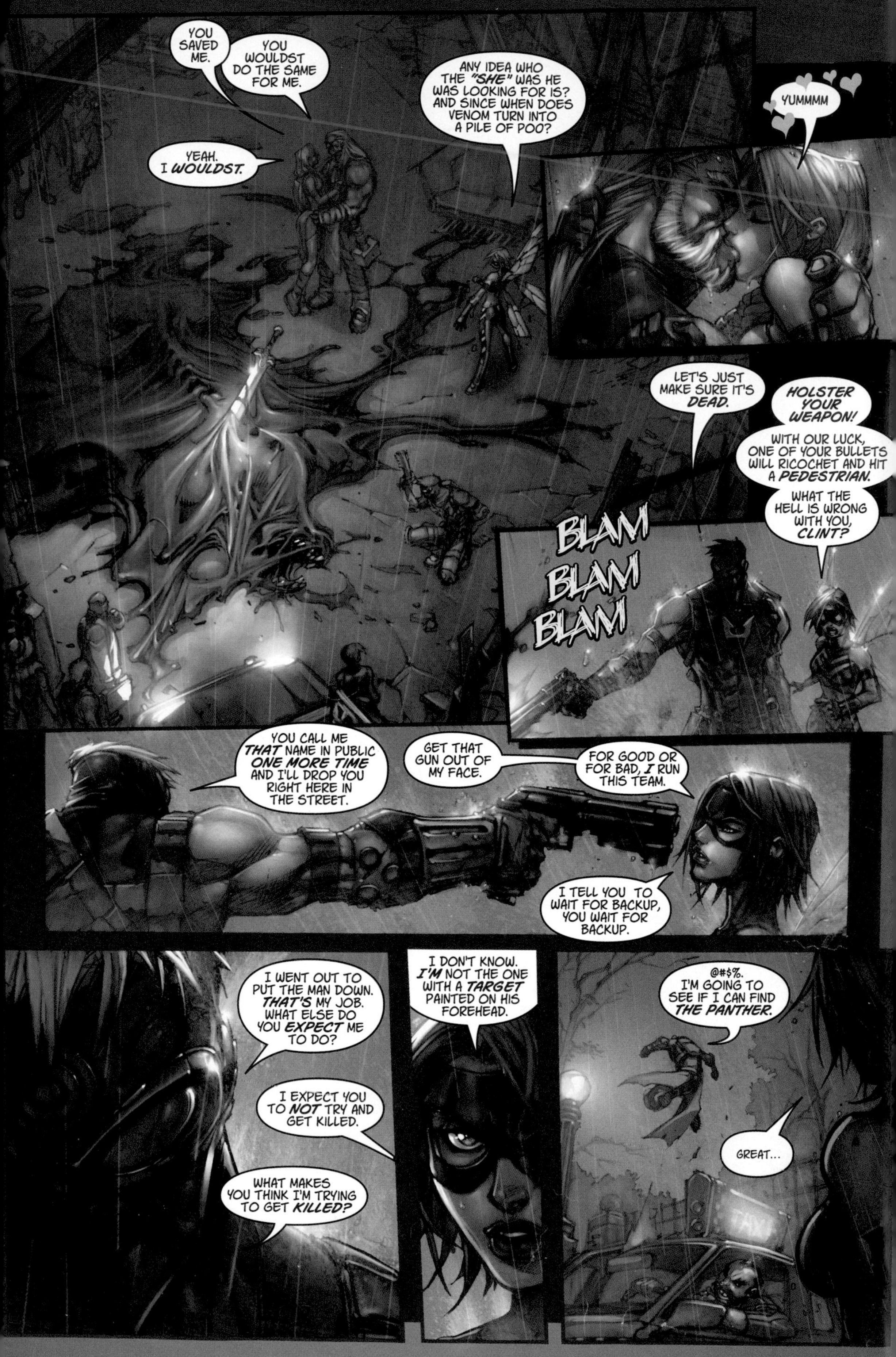
YOU SAVED ME.
YOU WOULDST DO THE SAME FOR ME.
YEAH. I WOULDST.
ANY IDEA WHO THE "SHE" WAS HE WAS LOOKING FOR IS? AND SINCE WHEN DOES VENOM TURN INTO A PILE OF POO?
YUMMMM
LET'S JUST MAKE SURE IT'S DEAD.
HOLSTER YOUR WEAPON!
WITH OUR LUCK, ONE OF YOUR BULLETS WILL RICOCHET AND HIT A PEDESTRIAN.
WHAT THE HELL IS WRONG WITH YOU, CLINT?
BLAM
BLAM
BLAM
YOU CALL ME THAT NAME IN PUBLIC ONE MORE TIME AND I'LL DROP YOU RIGHT HERE IN THE STREET.
GET THAT GUN OUT OF MY FACE.
FOR GOOD OR FOR BAD, I RUN THIS TEAM.
I TELL YOU TO WAIT FOR BACKUP, YOU WAIT FOR BACKUP.
I WENT OUT TO PUT THE MAN DOWN. THAT'S MY JOB. WHAT ELSE DO YOU EXPECT ME TO DO?
I EXPECT YOU TO NOT TRY AND GET KILLED.
WHAT MAKES YOU THINK I'M TRYING TO GET KILLED?
I DON'T KNOW. I'M NOT THE ONE WITH A TARGET PAINTED ON HIS FOREHEAD.
@#$%. I'M GOING TO SEE IF I CAN FIND THE PANTHER.
GREAT...

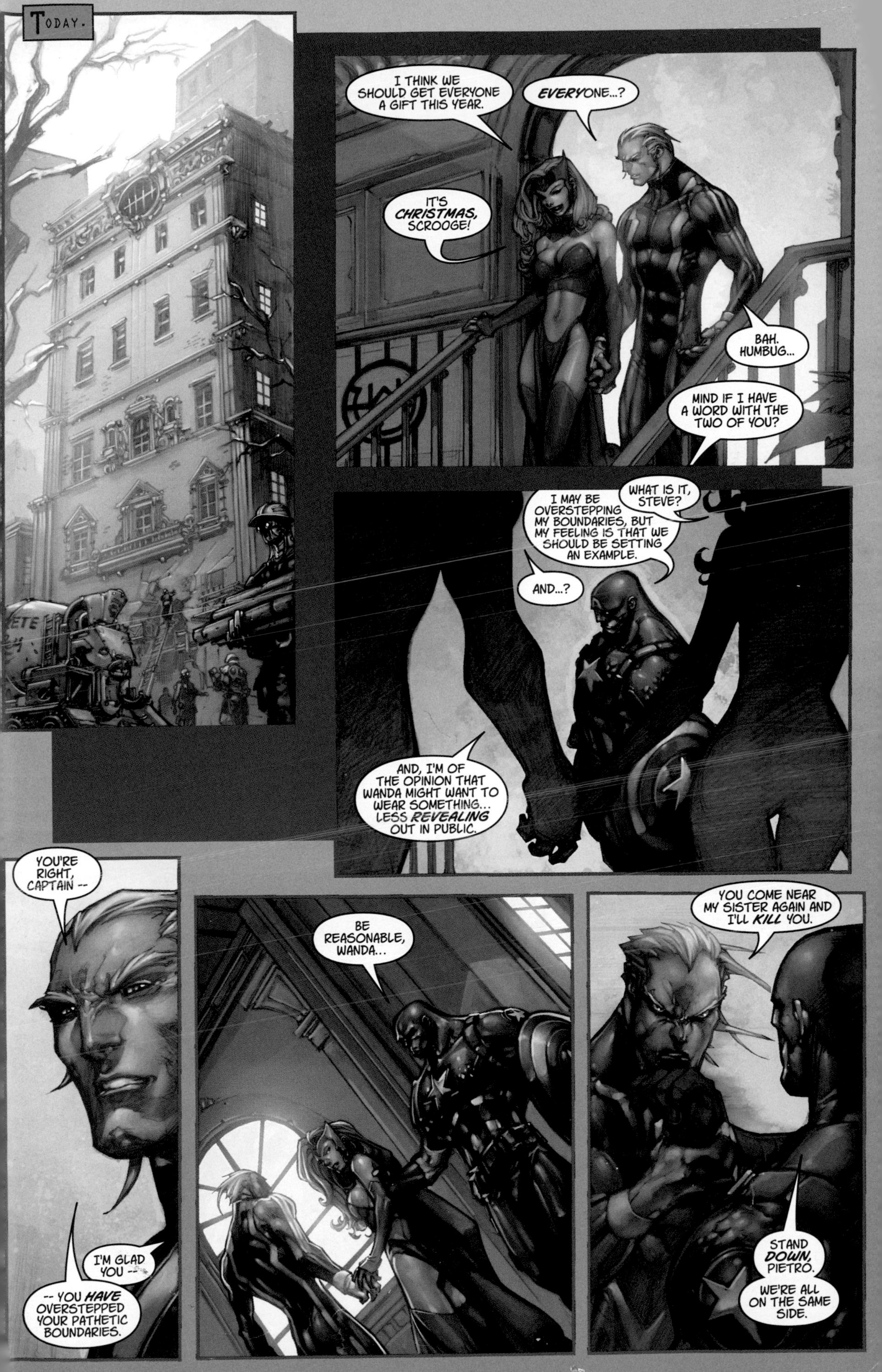
TODAY.
I THINK WE SHOULD GET EVERYONE A GIFT THIS YEAR.
EVERYONE...?
IT'S CHRISTMAS, SCROOGE!
BAH. HUMBUG...
MIND IF I HAVE A WORD WITH THE TWO OF YOU?
WHAT IS IT, STEVE?
I MAY BE OVERSTEPPING MY BOUNDARIES, BUT MY FEELING IS THAT WE SHOULD BE SETTING AN EXAMPLE.
AND...?
AND, I'M OF THE OPINION THAT WANDA MIGHT WANT TO WEAR SOMETHING... LESS REVEALING OUT IN PUBLIC.
YOU'RE RIGHT, CAPTAIN --
I'M GLAD YOU --
-- YOU HAVE OVERSTEPPED YOUR PATHETIC BOUNDARIES.
BE REASONABLE, WANDA...
YOU COME NEAR MY SISTER AGAIN AND I'LL KILL YOU.
STAND DOWN, PIETRO.
WE'RE ALL ON THE SAME SIDE.

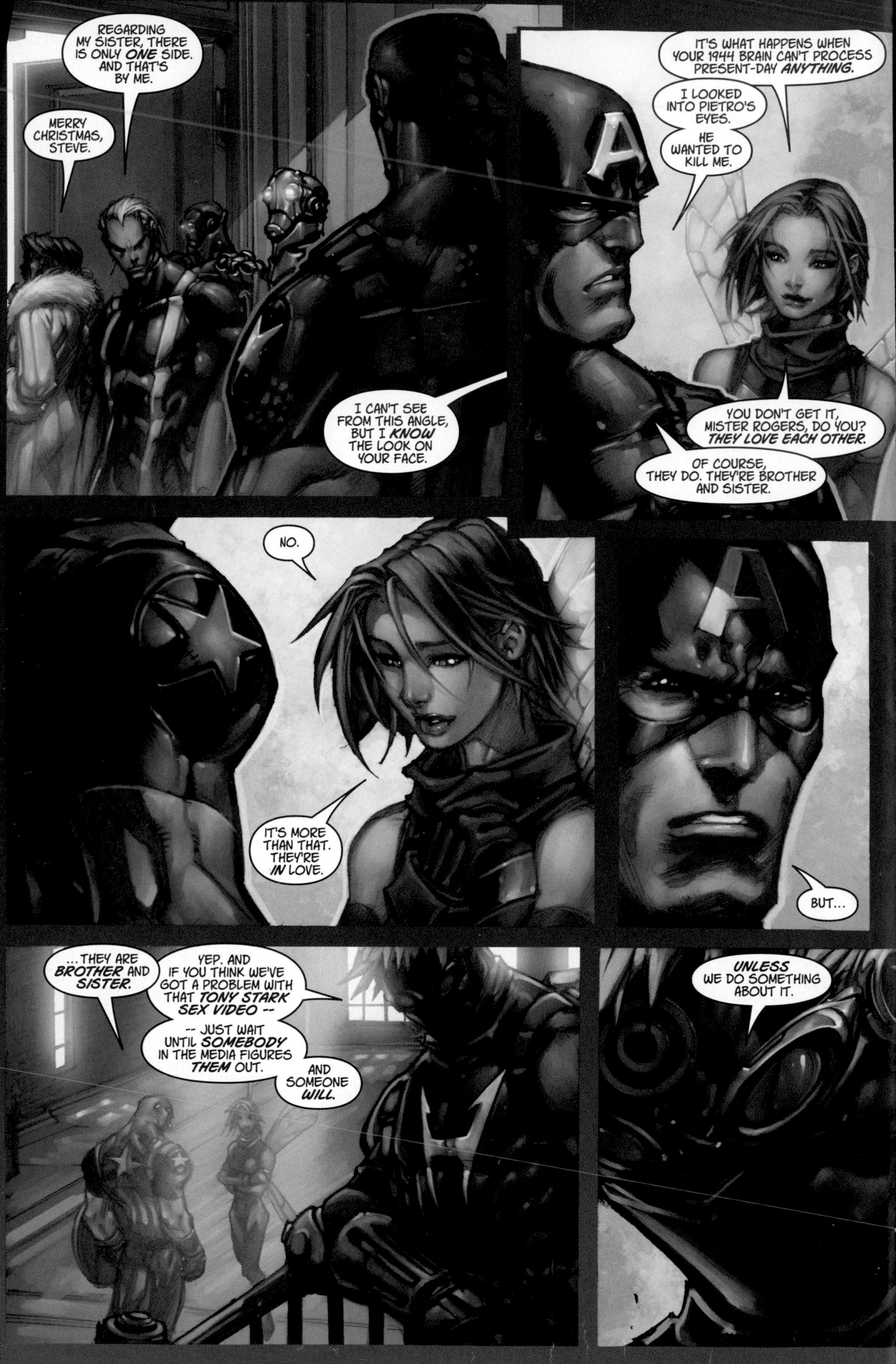
REGARDING MY SISTER, THERE IS ONLY ONE SIDE. AND THAT'S BY ME.
MERRY CHRISTMAS, STEVE.
I CAN'T SEE FROM THIS ANGLE, BUT I KNOW THE LOOK ON YOUR FACE.
IT'S WHAT HAPPENS WHEN YOUR 1944 BRAIN CAN'T PROCESS PRESENT-DAY ANYTHING.
I LOOKED INTO PIETRO'S EYES.
HE WANTED TO KILL ME.
YOU DON'T GET IT, MISTER ROGERS, DO YOU? THEY LOVE EACH OTHER.
OF COURSE, THEY DO. THEY'RE BROTHER AND SISTER.
NO.
IT'S MORE THAN THAT. THEY'RE IN LOVE.
BUT...
...THEY ARE BROTHER AND SISTER.
YEP. AND IF YOU THINK WE'VE GOT A PROBLEM WITH THAT TONY STARK SEX VIDEO --
-- JUST WAIT UNTIL SOMEBODY IN THE MEDIA FIGURES THEM OUT.
AND SOMEONE WILL.
UNLESS WE DO SOMETHING ABOUT IT.

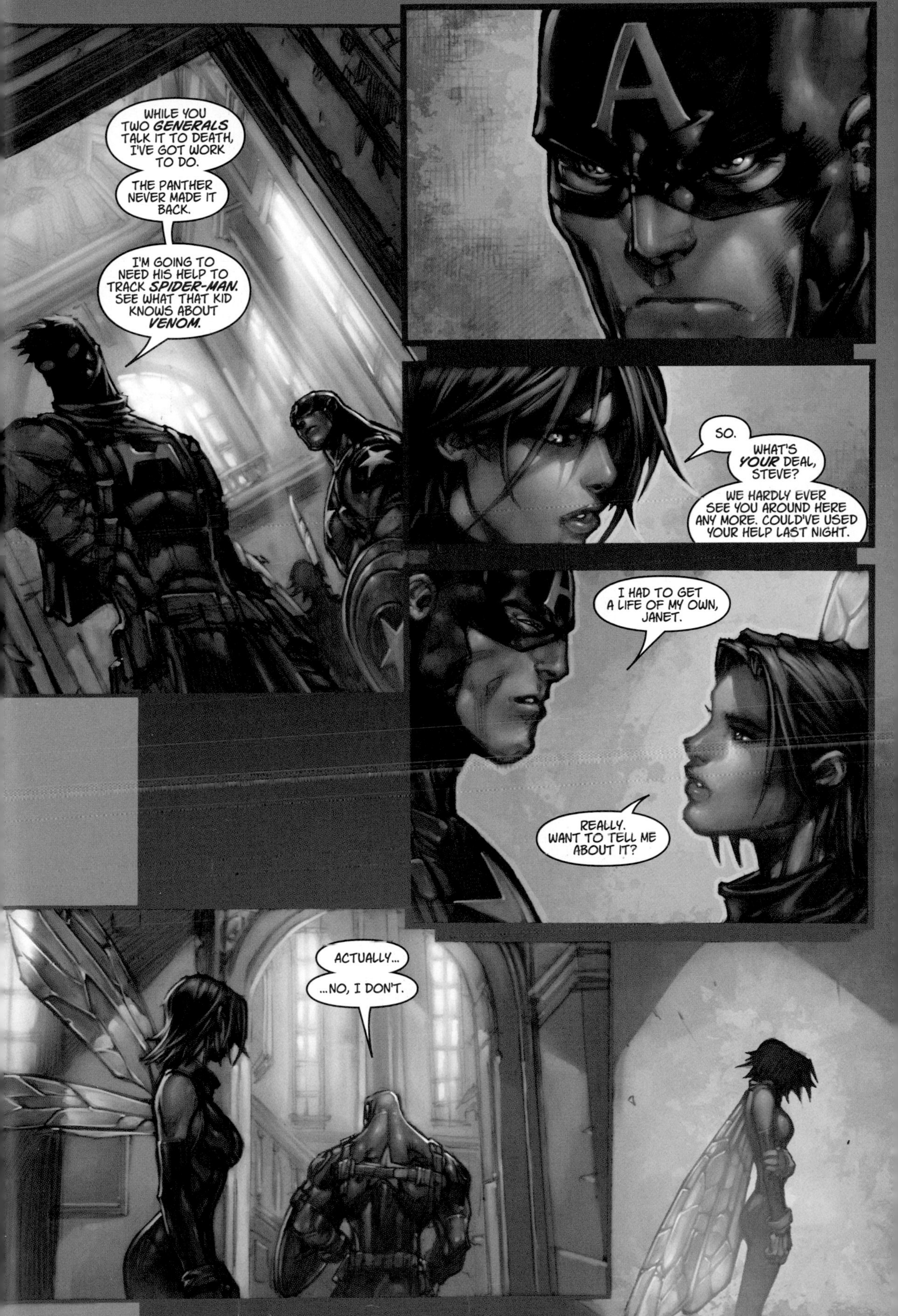
WHILE YOU TWO GENERALS TALK IT TO DEATH, I'VE GOT WORK TO DO.
THE PANTHER NEVER MADE IT BACK.
I'M GOING TO NEED HIS HELP TO TRACK SPIDER-MAN. SEE WHAT THAT KID KNOWS ABOUT VENOM.
SO.
WHAT'S YOUR DEAL, STEVE?
WE HARDLY EVER SEE YOU AROUND HERE ANY MORE. COULD'VE USED YOUR HELP LAST NIGHT.
I HAD TO GET A LIFE OF MY OWN, JANET.
REALLY. WANT TO TELL ME ABOUT IT?
ACTUALLY...
...NO, I DON'T.

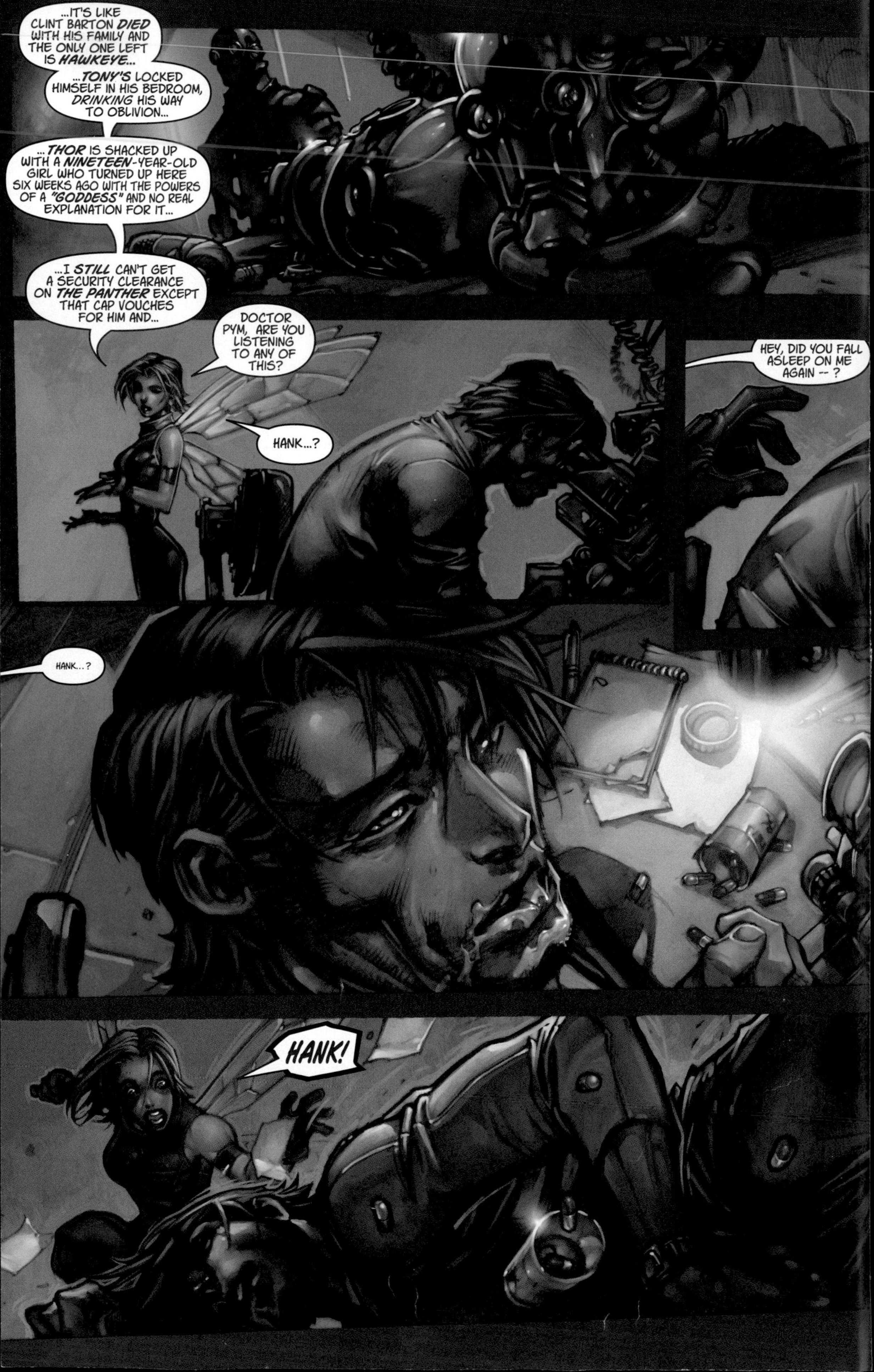
...IT'S LIKE CLINT BARTON DIED WITH HIS FAMILY AND THE ONLY ONE LEFT IS HAWKEYE...
...TONY'S LOCKED HIMSELF IN HIS BEDROOM, DRINKING HIS WAY TO OBLIVION...
...THOR IS SHACKED UP WITH A NINETEEN-YEAR-OLD GIRL WHO TURNED UP HERE SIX WEEKS AGO WITH THE POWERS OF A "GODDESS" AND NO REAL EXPLANATION FOR IT...
...I STILL CAN'T GET A SECURITY CLEARANCE ON THE PANTHER EXCEPT THAT CAP VOUCHES FOR HIM AND...
DOCTOR PYM, ARE YOU LISTENING TO ANY OF THIS?
HANK...?
HEY, DID YOU FALL ASLEEP ON ME AGAIN -- ?
HANK...?
HANK!

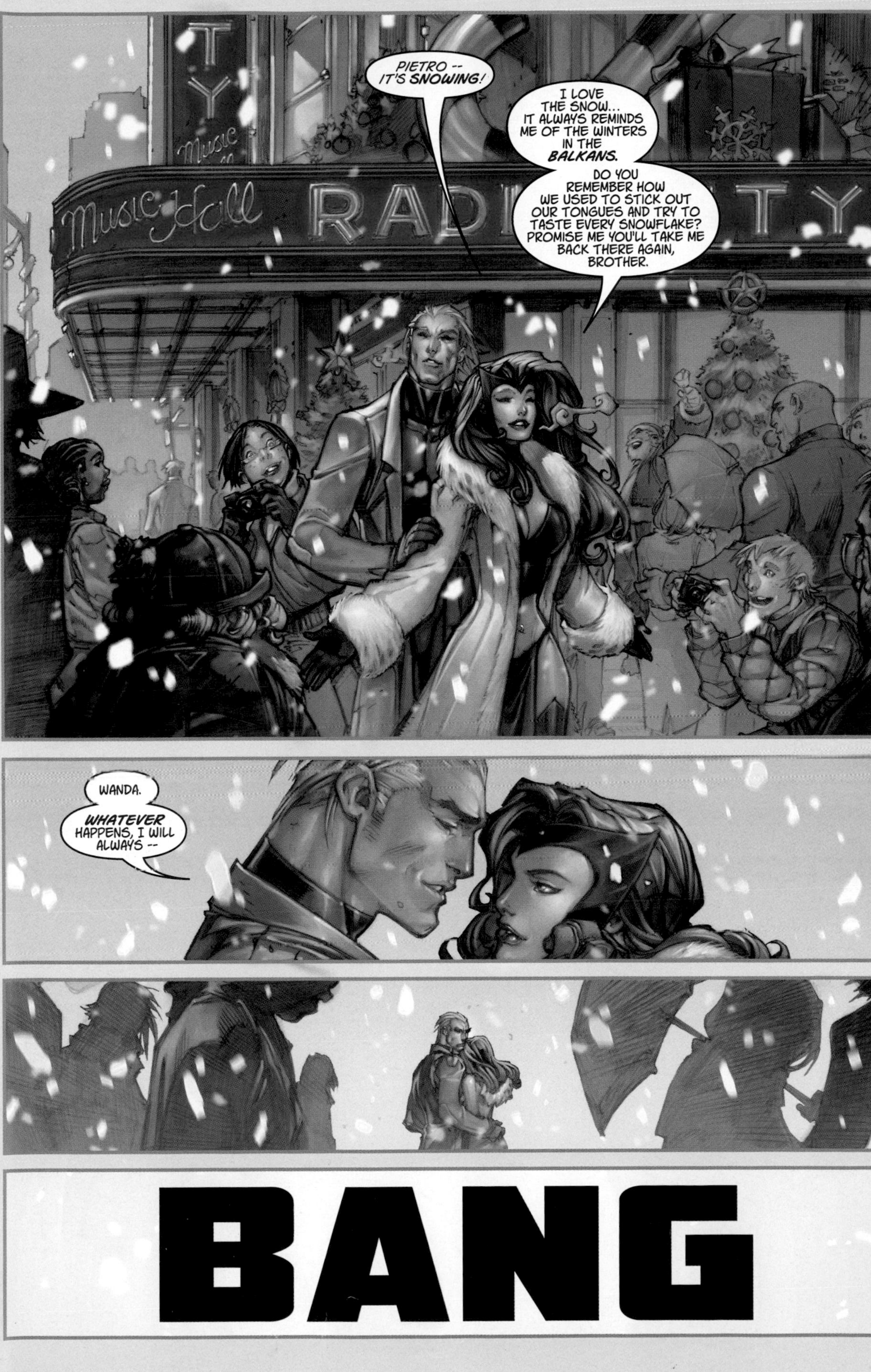

PIETRO -- IT'S SNOWING!
I LOVE THE SNOW... IT ALWAYS REMINDS ME OF THE WINTERS IN THE BALKANS.
DO YOU REMEMBER HOW WE USED TO STICK OUT OUR TONGUES AND TRY TO TASTE EVERY SNOWFLAKE? PROMISE ME YOU'LL TAKE ME BACK THERE AGAIN, BROTHER.
WANDA.
WHATEVER HAPPENS, I WILL ALWAYS --
BANG

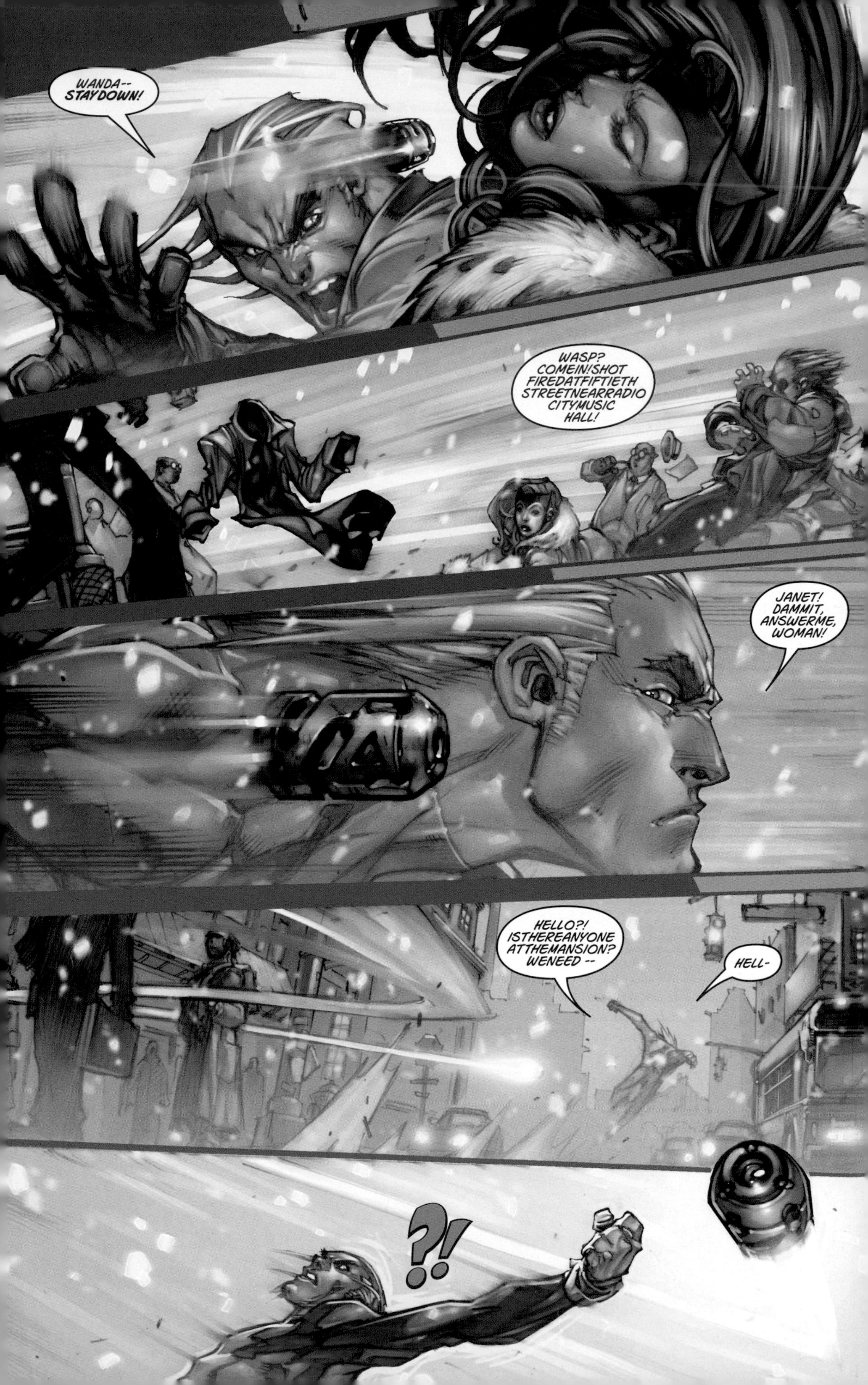
WANDA-- STAYDOWN!
WASP? COMEIN!SHOT FIREDATFIFTIETH STREETNEARRADIO CITYMUSIC HALL!
JANET! DAMMIT, ANSWERME, WOMAN!
HELLO?! ISTHEREANYONE ATTHEMANSION? WENEED --
HELL-
?!

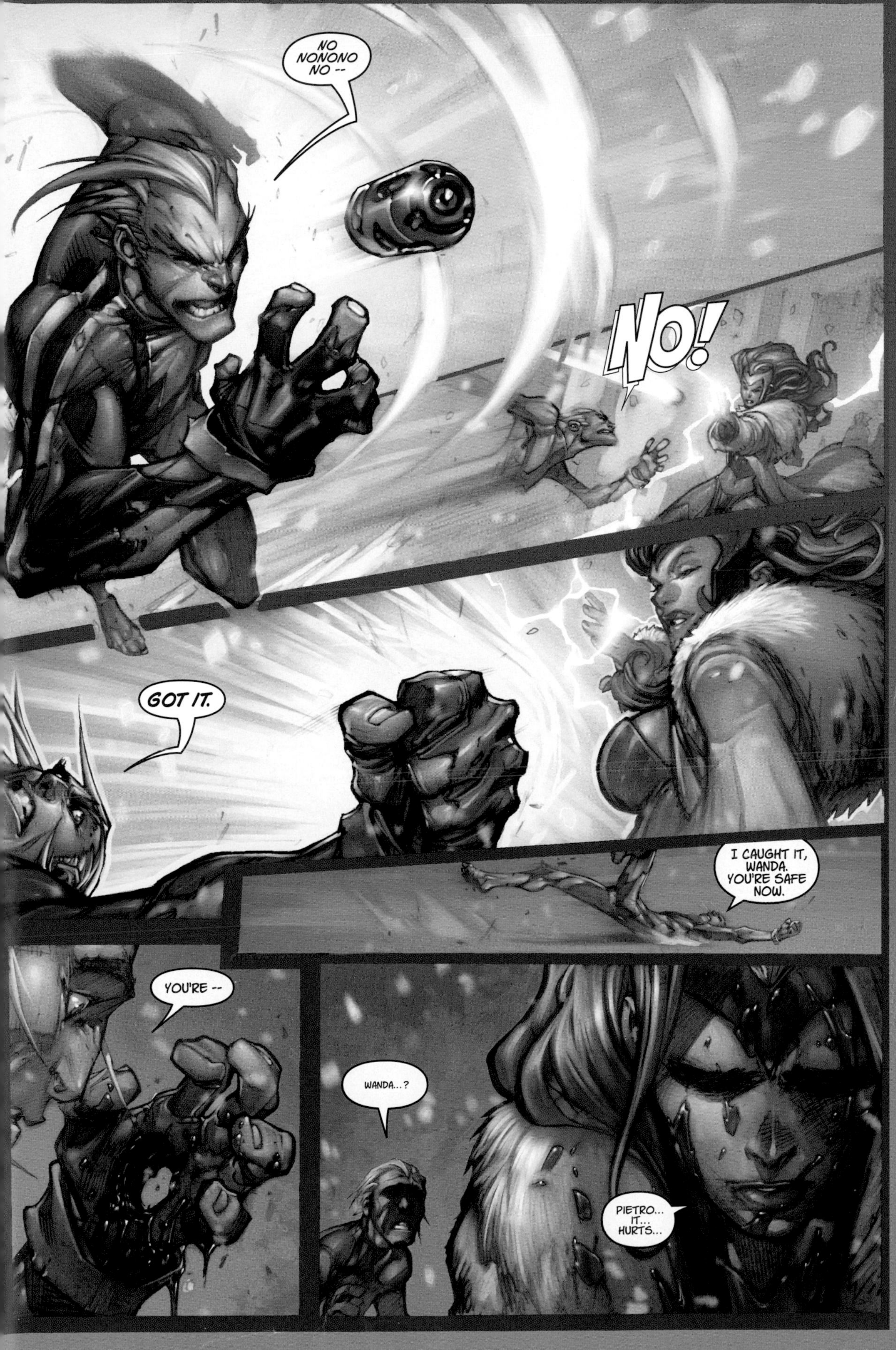
NO NONONO NO --
NO!
GOT IT.
I CAUGHT IT, WANDA. YOU'RE SAFE NOW.
YOU'RE --
WANDA...?
PIETRO... IT... HURTS...

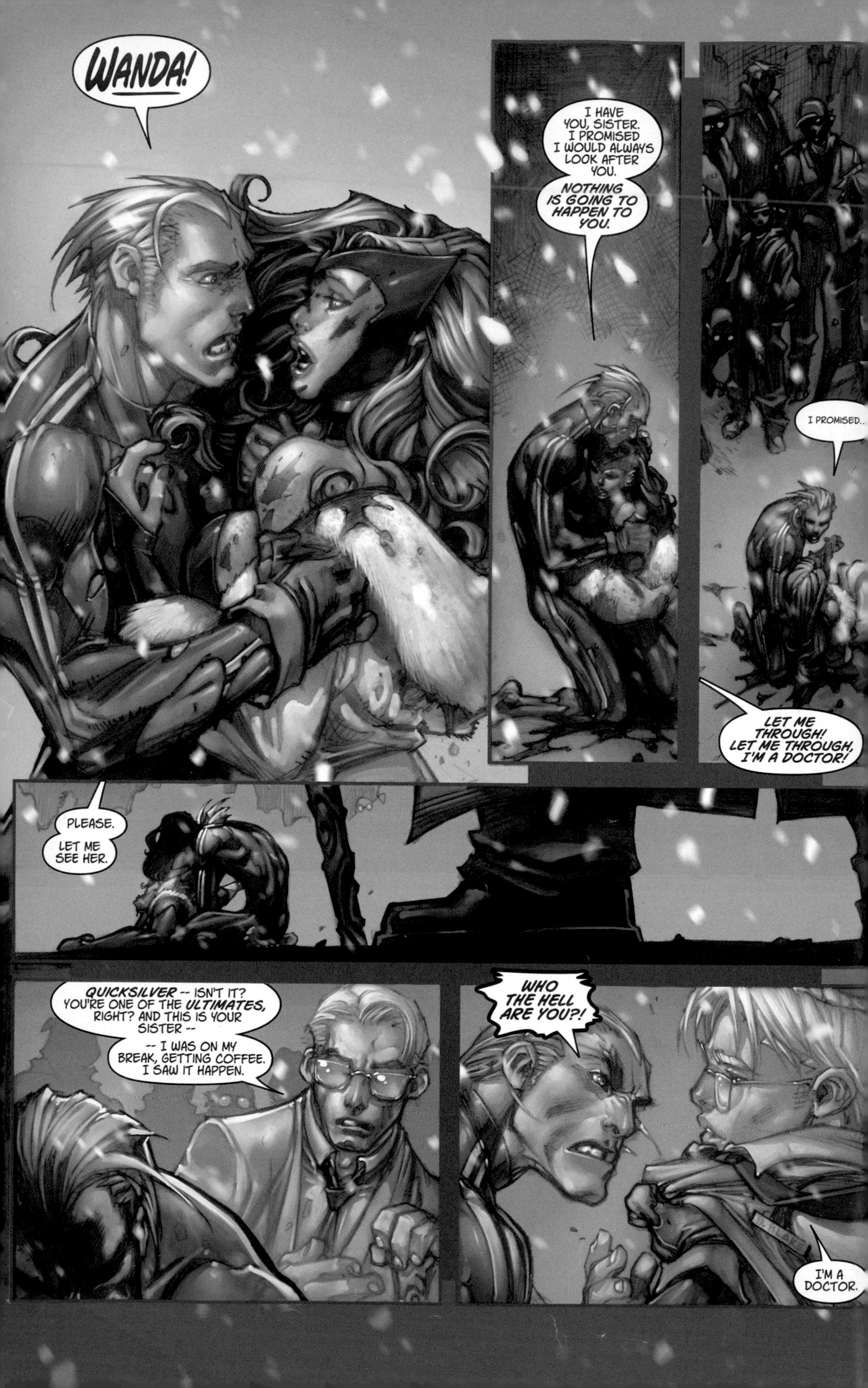
WANDA!
I HAVE YOU, SISTER. I PROMISED I WOULD ALWAYS LOOK AFTER YOU.
NOTHING IS GOING TO HAPPEN TO YOU.
I PROMISED...
LET ME THROUGH! LET ME THROUGH, I'M A DOCTOR!
PLEASE.
LET ME SEE HER.
QUICKSILVER -- ISN'T IT? YOU'RE ONE OF THE ULTIMATES, RIGHT? AND THIS IS YOUR SISTER --
-- I WAS ON MY BREAK, GETTING COFFEE. I SAW IT HAPPEN.
WHO THE HELL ARE YOU?!
I'M A DOCTOR.

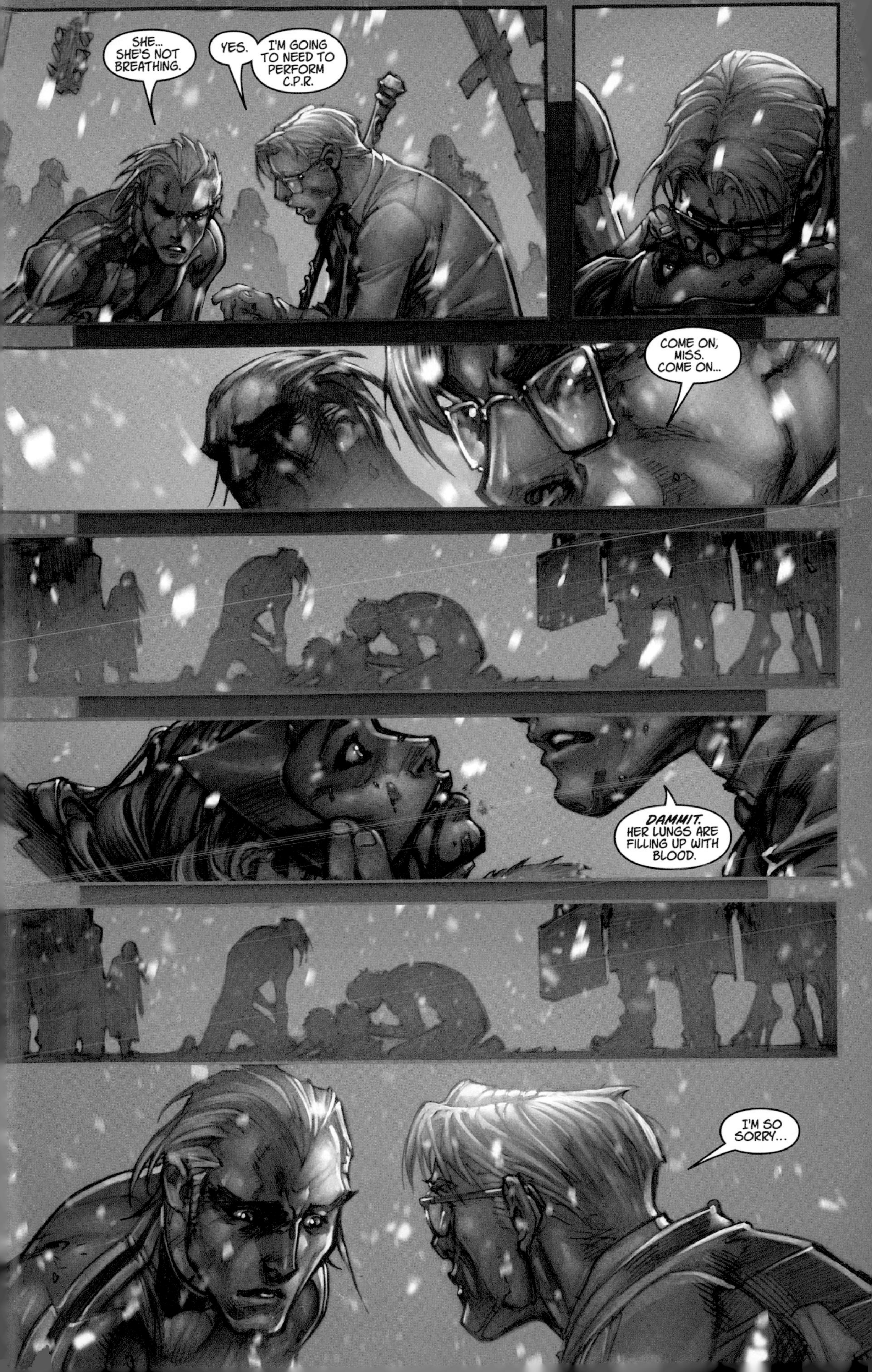
SHE... SHE'S NOT BREATHING.
YES.
I'M GOING TO NEED TO PERFORM C.P.R.
COME ON, MISS. COME ON...
DAMMIT. HER LUNGS ARE FILLING UP WITH BLOOD.
I'M SO SORRY...

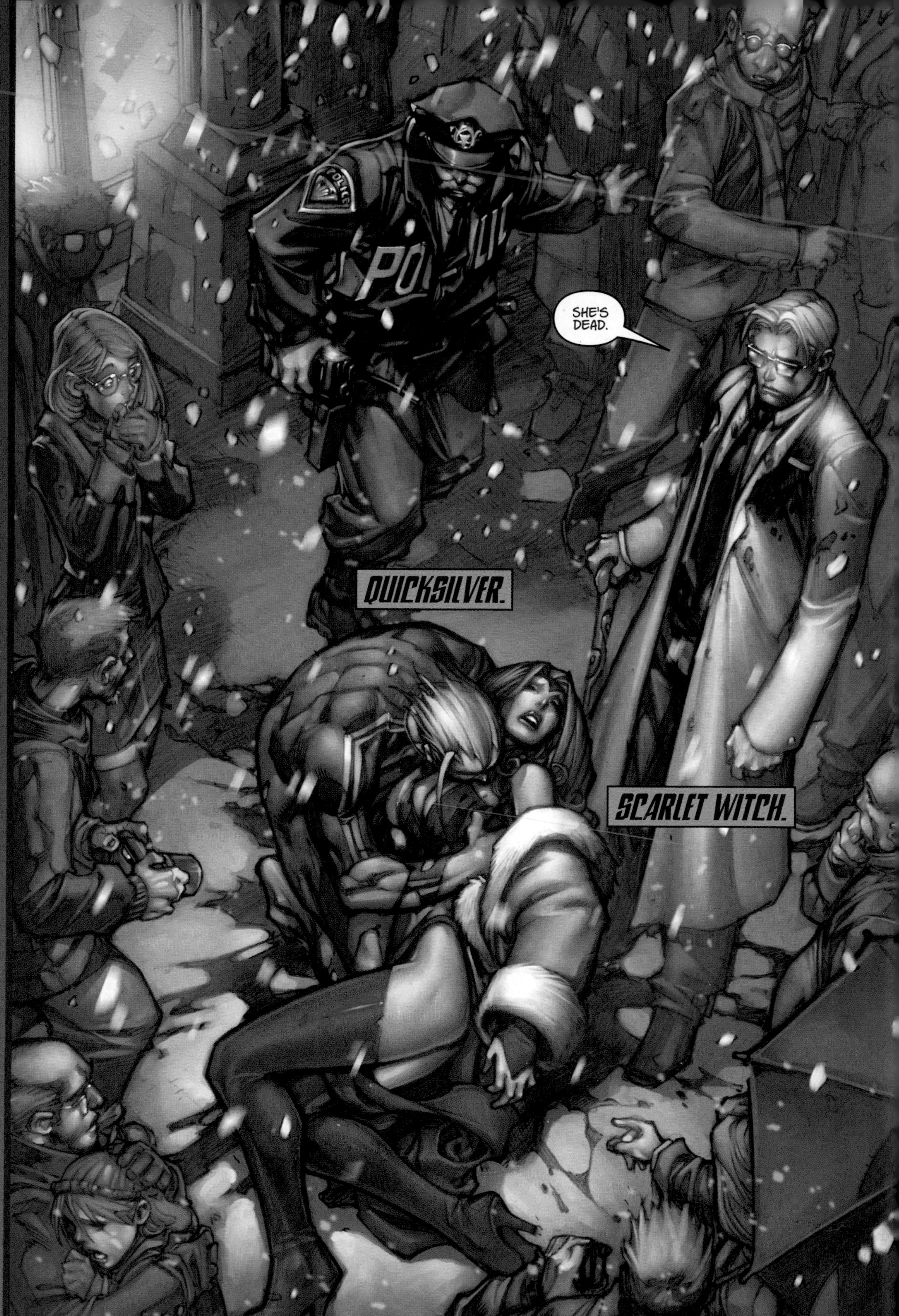
SHE'S DEAD.
QUICKSILVER.
SCARLET WITCH.

TWO

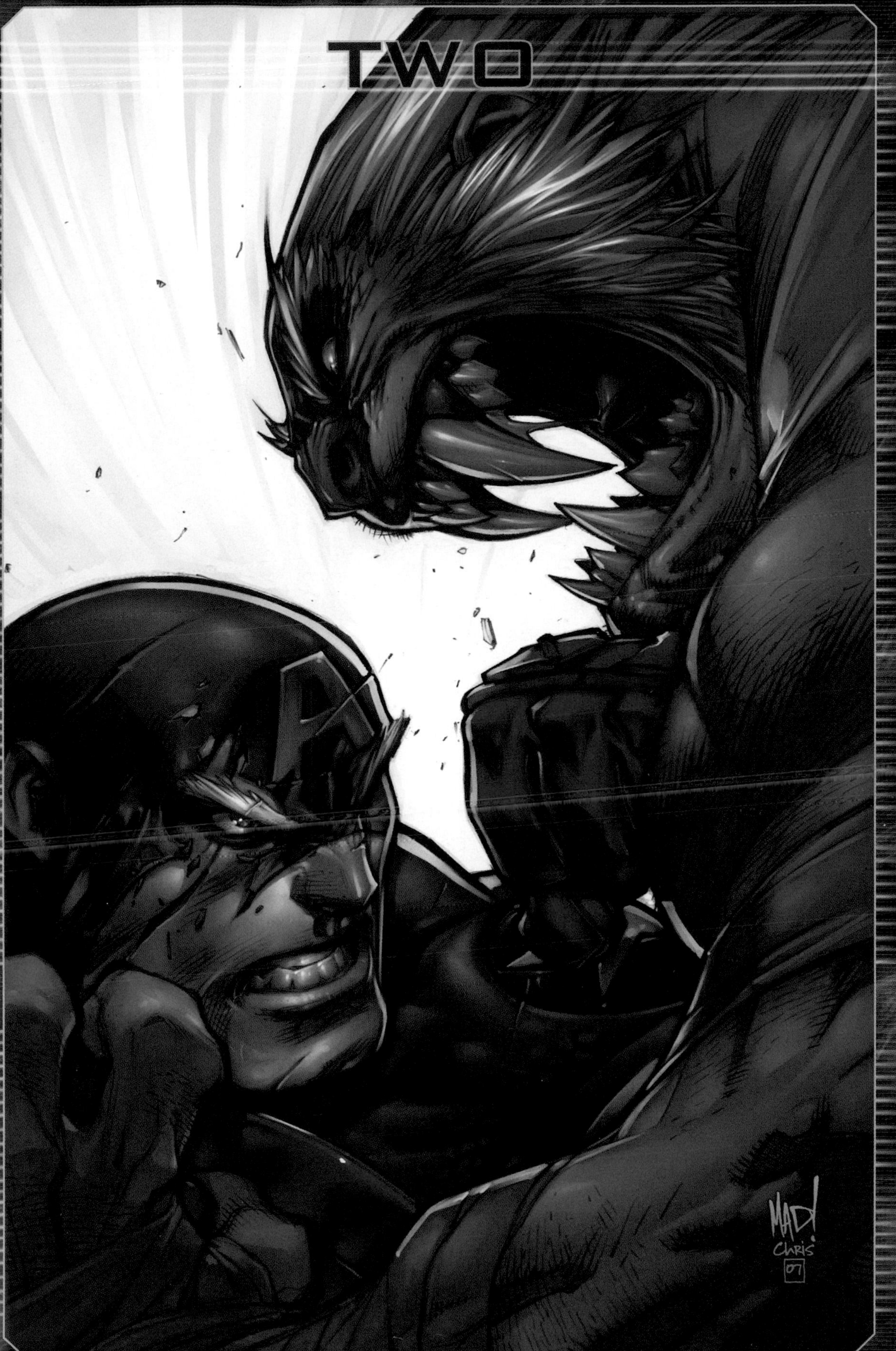
MAD!
Chris
07

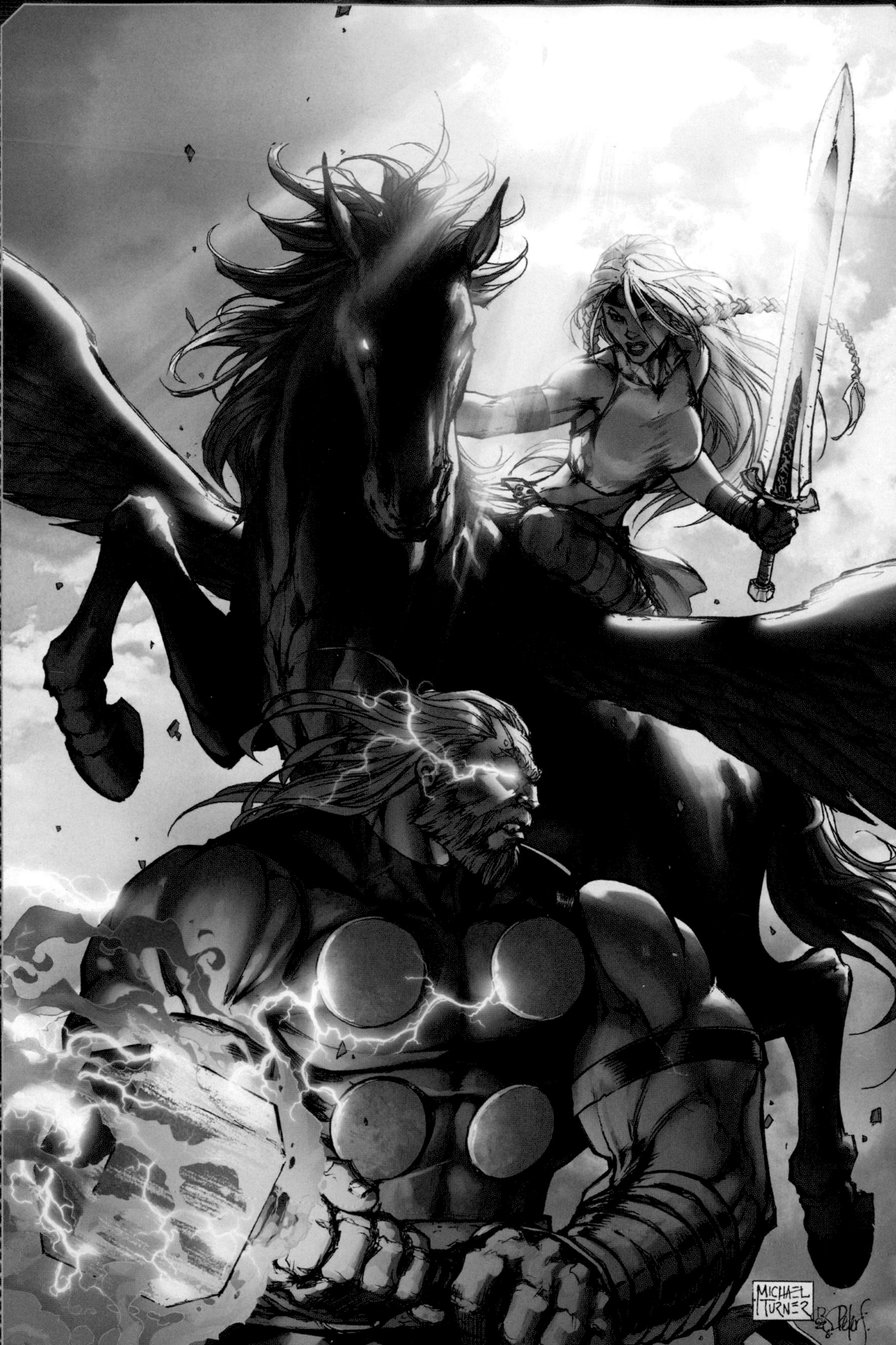
MICHAEL TURNER

ISSUE #2 VARIANT COVER BY MICHAEL TURNER

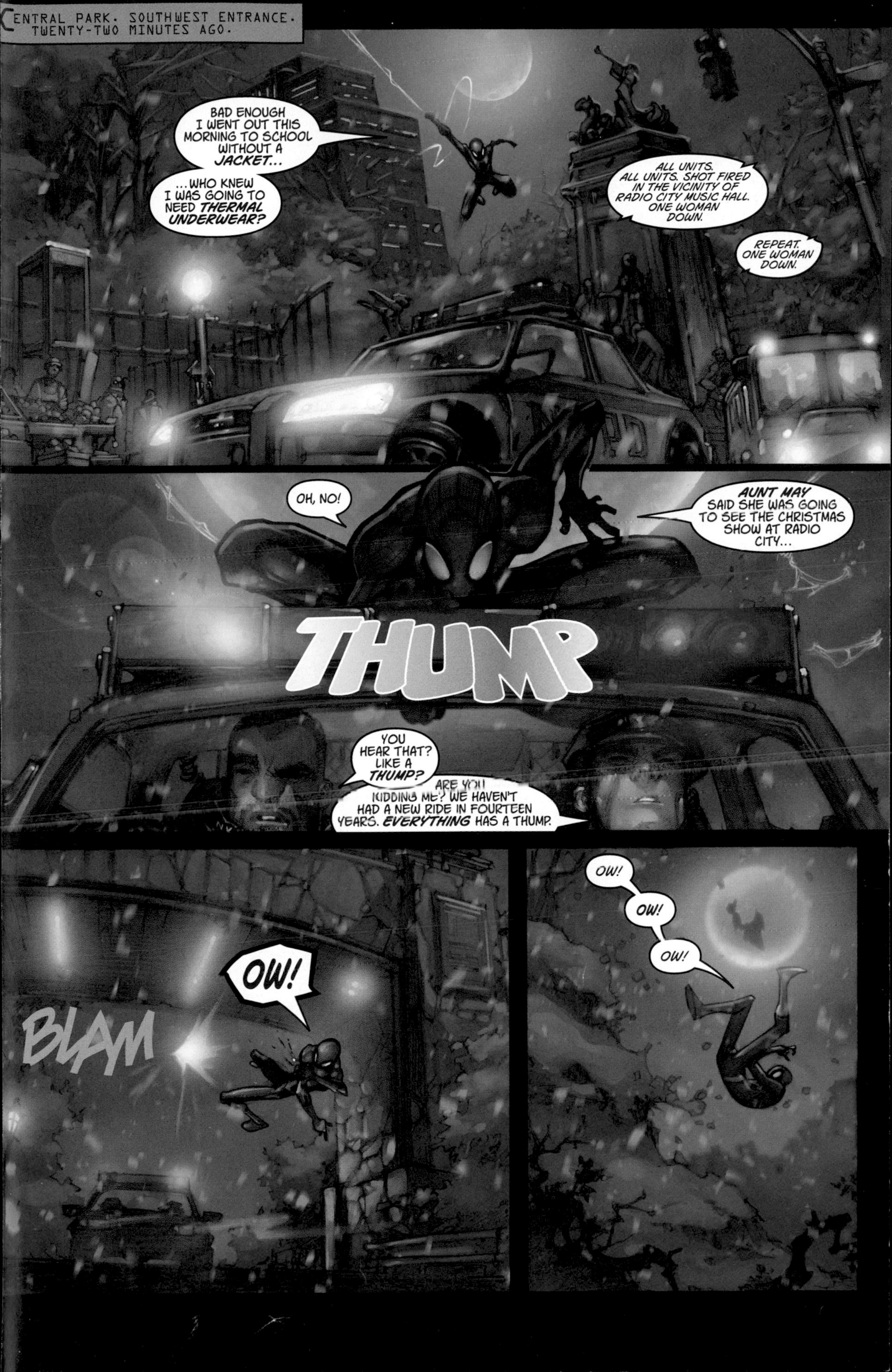
CENTRAL PARK. SOUTHWEST ENTRANCE.
TWENTY-TWO MINUTES AGO.
BAD ENOUGH I WENT OUT THIS MORNING TO SCHOOL WITHOUT A JACKET...
...WHO KNEW I WAS GOING TO NEED THERMAL UNDERWEAR?
ALL UNITS. ALL UNITS. SHOT FIRED IN THE VICINITY OF RADIO CITY MUSIC HALL. ONE WOMAN DOWN.
REPEAT. ONE WOMAN DOWN.
OH, NO!
AUNT MAY SAID SHE WAS GOING TO SEE THE CHRISTMAS SHOW AT RADIO CITY...
THUMP
YOU HEAR THAT? LIKE A THUMP?
ARE YOU KIDDING ME? WE HAVEN'T HAD A NEW RIDE IN FOURTEEN YEARS. EVERYTHING HAS A THUMP.
BLAM
OW!
OW!
OW!
OW!

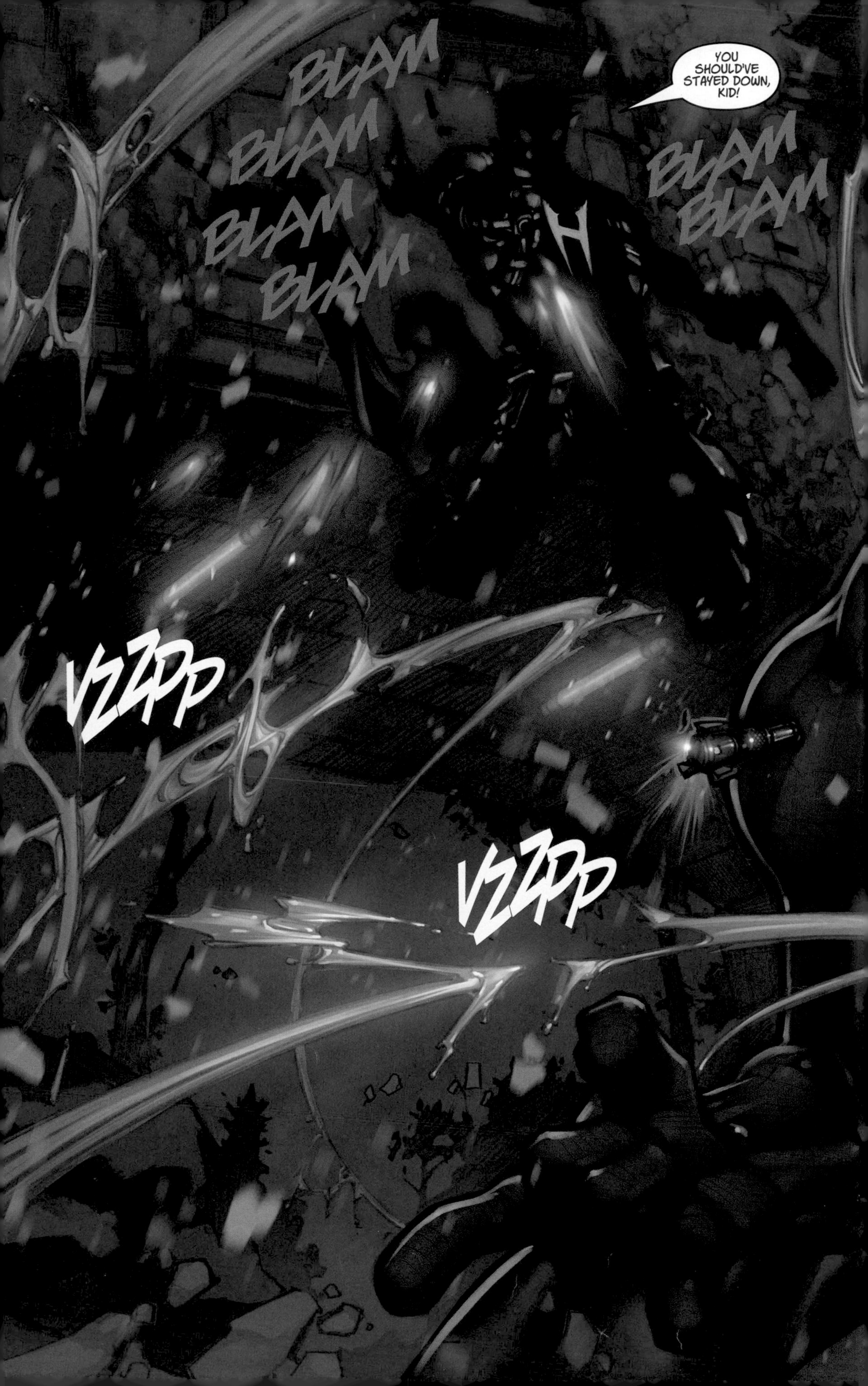
BLAM
BLAM
BLAM
BLAM
YOU SHOULD'VE STAYED DOWN, KID!
BLAM
BLAM
VZZPP
VZZPP

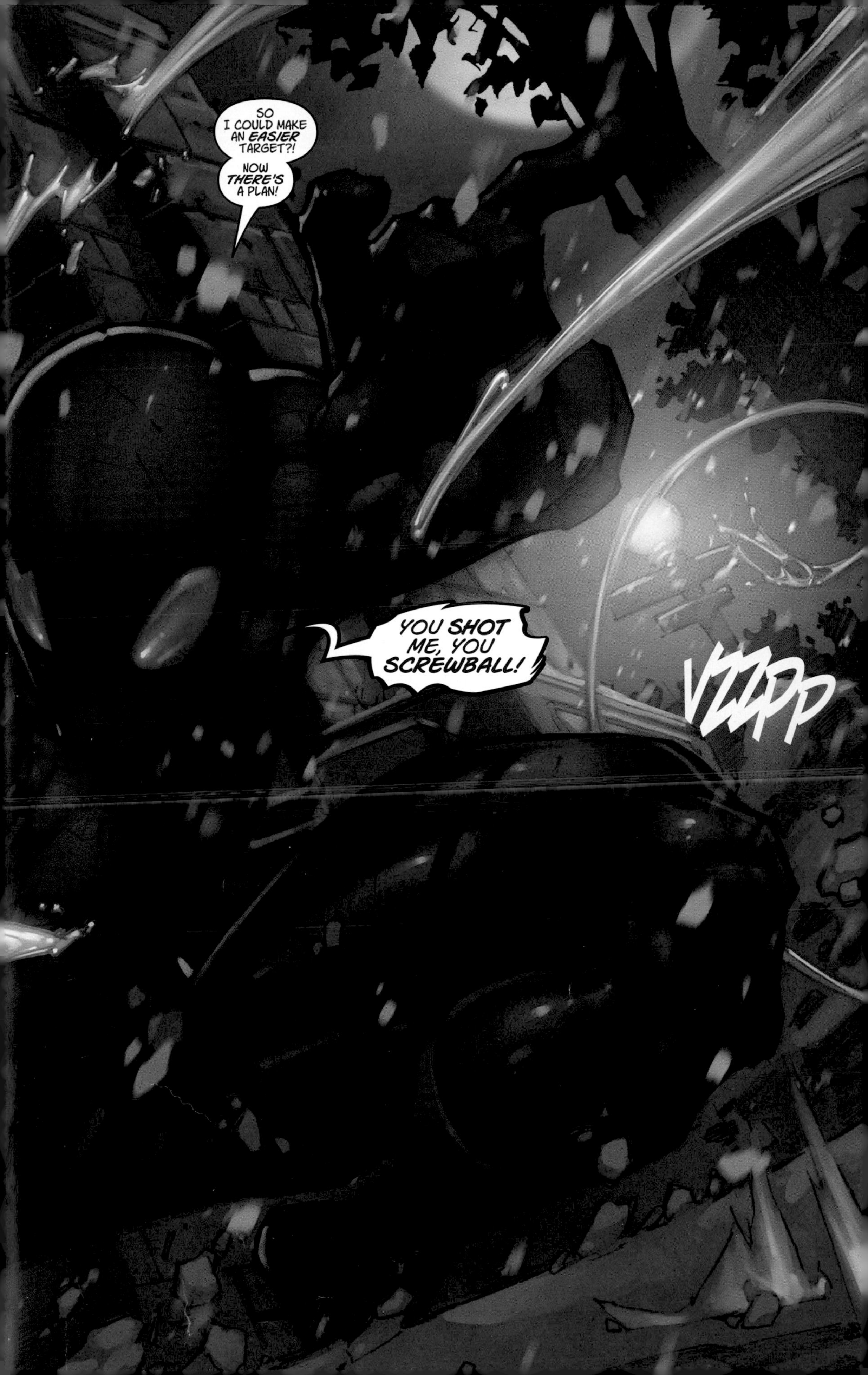
SO I COULD MAKE AN EASIER TARGET?!
NOW THERE'S A PLAN!
YOU SHOT ME, YOU SCREWBALL!
VZZPP

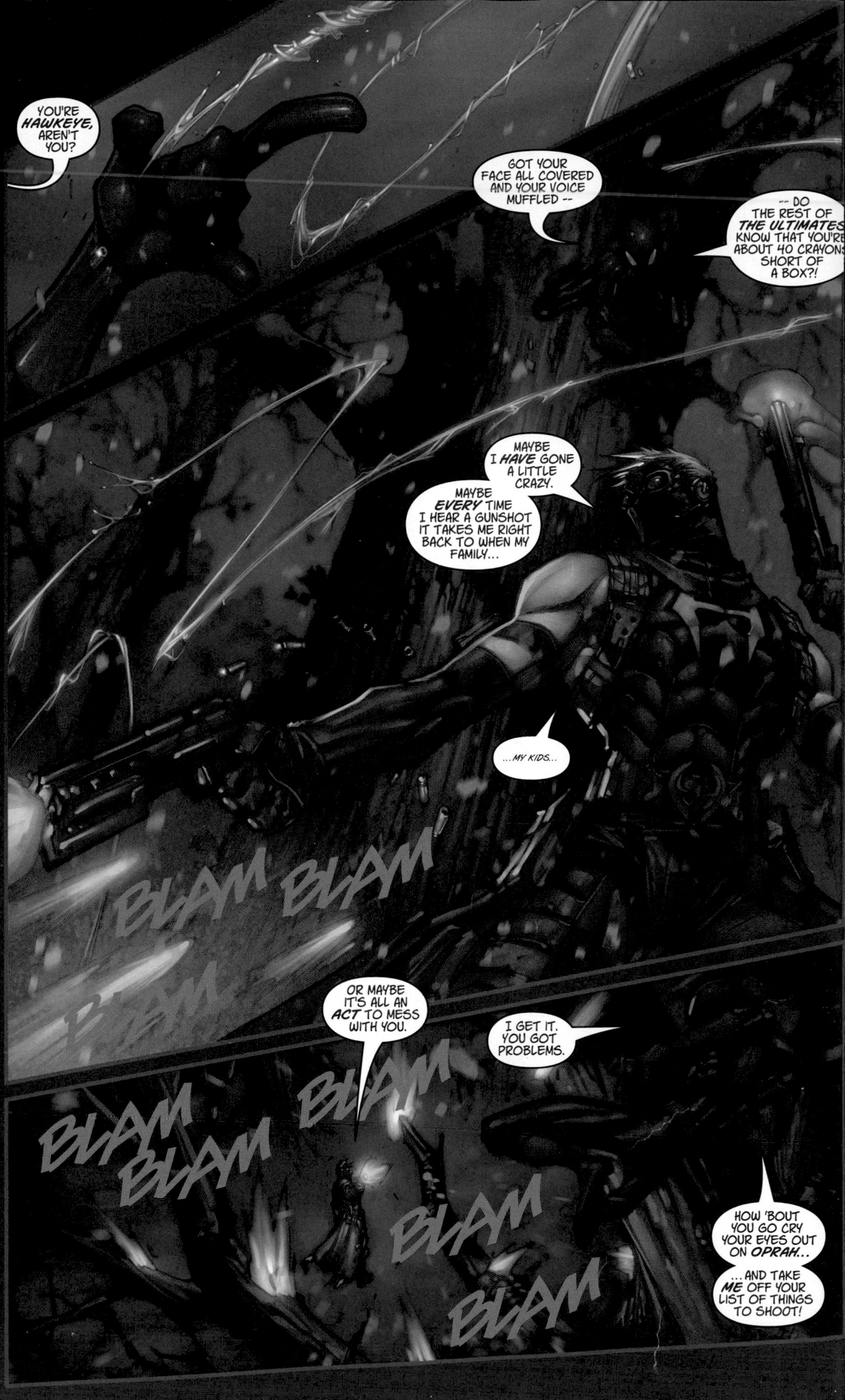
YOU'RE HAWKEYE, AREN'T YOU?
GOT YOUR FACE ALL COVERED AND YOUR VOICE MUFFLED --
-- DO THE REST OF THE ULTIMATES KNOW THAT YOU'RE ABOUT 40 CRAYONS SHORT OF A BOX?!
MAYBE I HAVE GONE A LITTLE CRAZY.
MAYBE EVERY TIME I HEAR A GUNSHOT IT TAKES ME RIGHT BACK TO WHEN MY FAMILY...
...MY KIDS...
BLAM BLAM
OR MAYBE IT'S ALL AN ACT TO MESS WITH YOU.
I GET IT. YOU GOT PROBLEMS.
BLAM BLAM BLAM
BLAM
BLAM
HOW 'BOUT YOU GO CRY YOUR EYES OUT ON OPRAH...
...AND TAKE ME OFF YOUR LIST OF THINGS TO SHOOT!

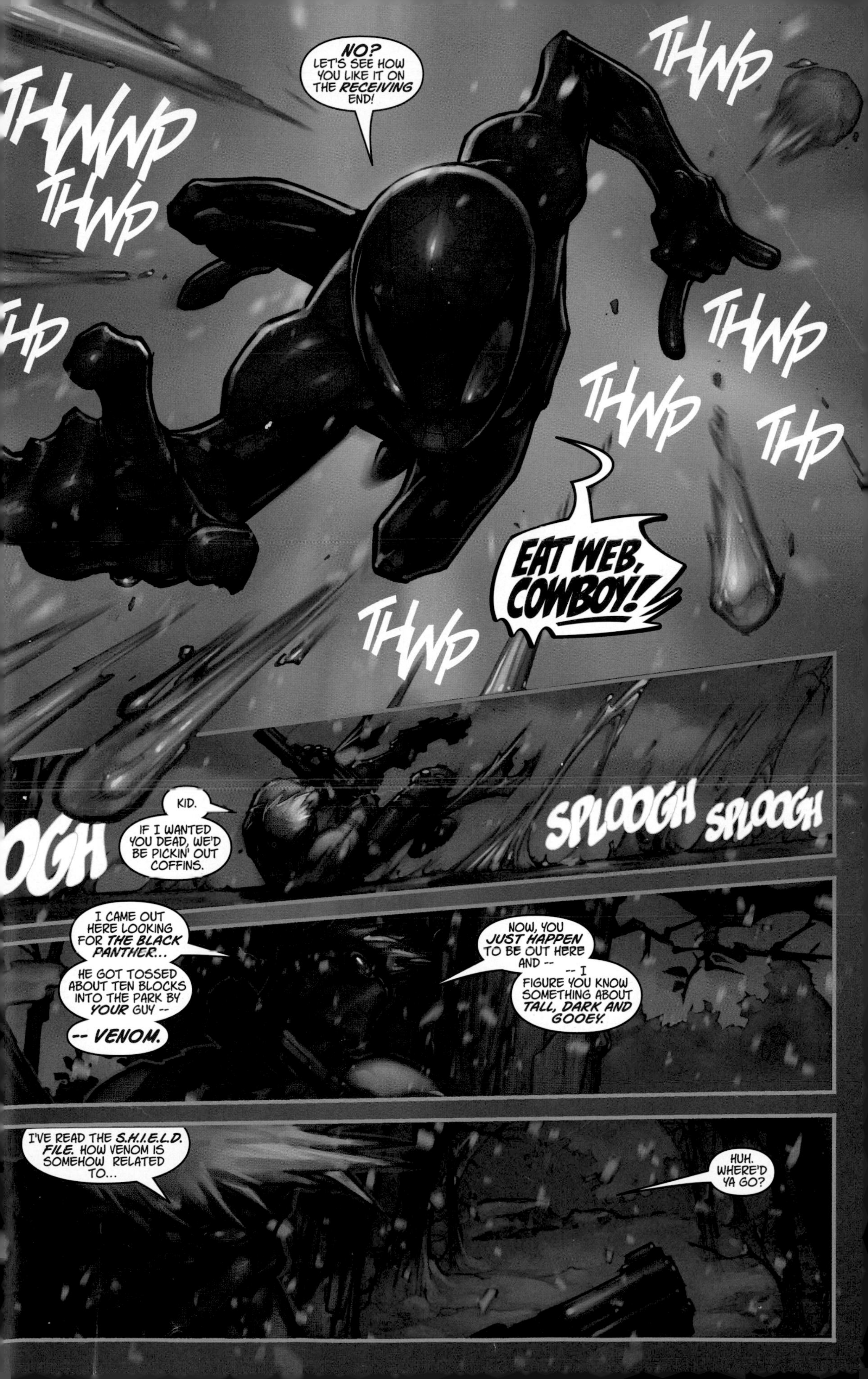

NO? LET'S SEE HOW YOU LIKE IT ON THE RECEIVING END!
THWNP THWNP
THWNP
THWP
THWNP
THWNP
THWP
EAT WEB, COWBOY!
THWNP
KID.
IF I WANTED YOU DEAD, WE'D BE PICKIN' OUT COFFINS.
SPLOOGH SPLOOGH
I CAME OUT HERE LOOKING FOR THE BLACK PANTHER...
HE GOT TOSSED ABOUT TEN BLOCKS INTO THE PARK BY YOUR GUY --
-- VENOM.
NOW, YOU JUST HAPPEN TO BE OUT HERE AND --
-- I FIGURE YOU KNOW SOMETHING ABOUT TALL, DARK AND GOOEY.
I'VE READ THE S.H.I.E.L.D. FILE. HOW VENOM IS SOMEHOW RELATED TO...
HUH. WHERE'D YA GO?

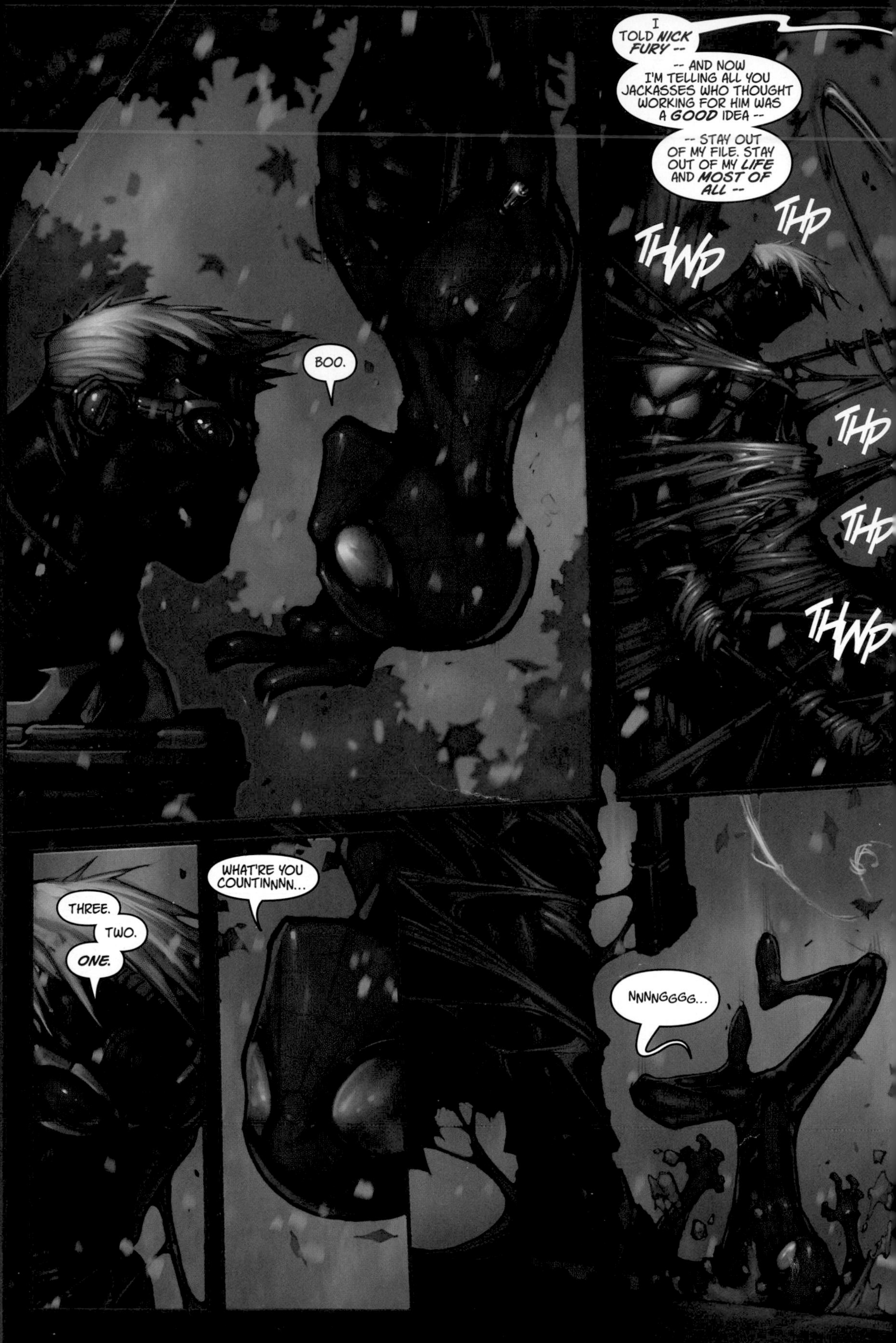
I TOLD NICK FURY --
-- AND NOW I'M TELLING ALL YOU JACKASSES WHO THOUGHT WORKING FOR HIM WAS A GOOD IDEA --
-- STAY OUT OF MY FILE. STAY OUT OF MY LIFE AND MOST OF ALL --
BOO.
THP
THWP
THP
THP
THWP
THREE.
TWO.
ONE.
WHAT'RE YOU COUNTINNNN...
NNNNGGGG...

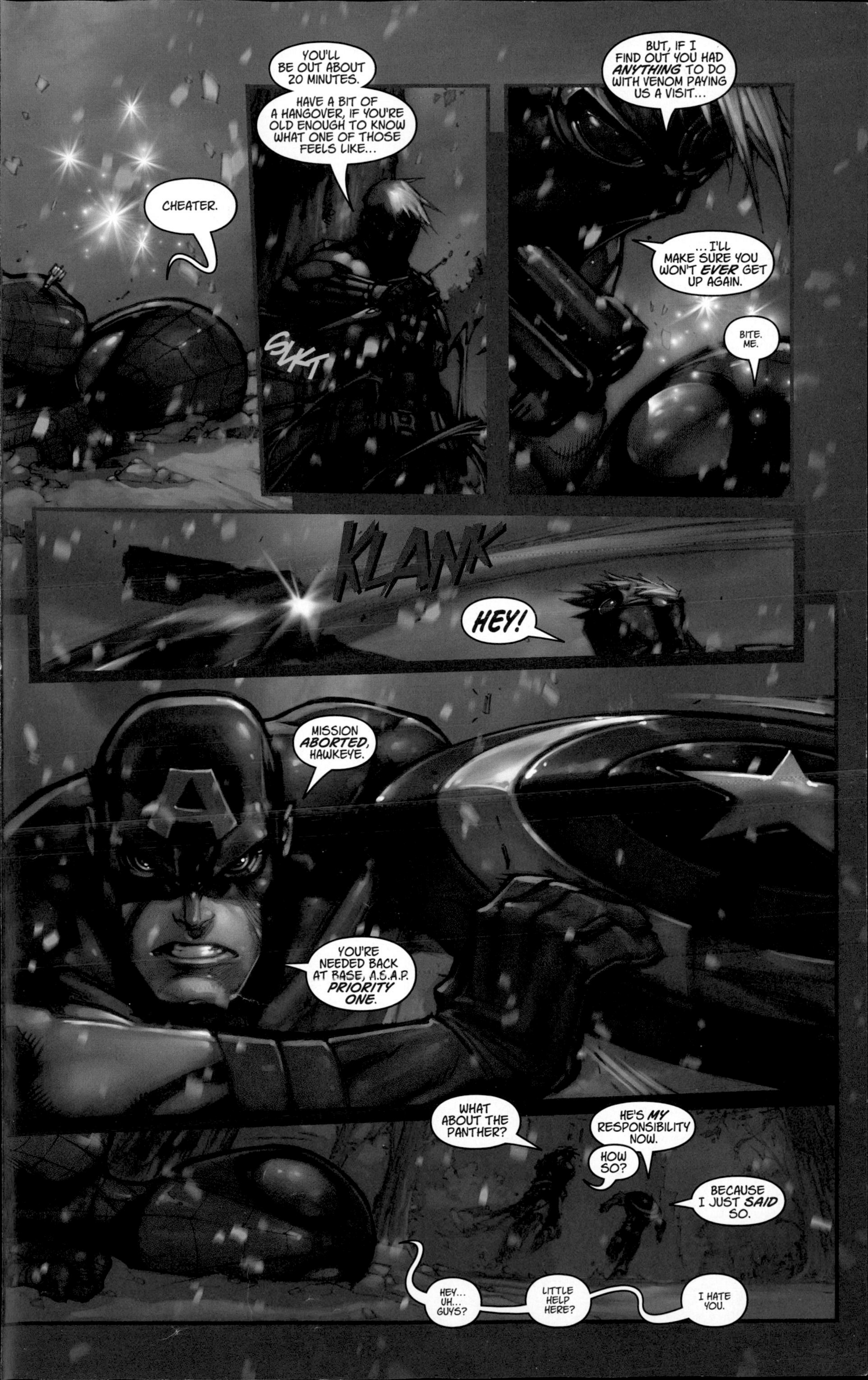
CHEATER.
YOU'LL BE OUT ABOUT 20 MINUTES.
HAVE A BIT OF A HANGOVER, IF YOU'RE OLD ENOUGH TO KNOW WHAT ONE OF THOSE FEELS LIKE...
SNKT
BUT, IF I FIND OUT YOU HAD ANYTHING TO DO WITH VENOM PAYING US A VISIT...
...I'LL MAKE SURE YOU WON'T EVER GET UP AGAIN.
BITE. ME.
KLANK
HEY!
MISSION ABORTED, HAWKEYE.
YOU'RE NEEDED BACK AT BASE, A.S.A.P. PRIORITY ONE.
WHAT ABOUT THE PANTHER?
HE'S MY RESPONSIBILITY NOW.
HOW SO?
BECAUSE I JUST SAID SO.
HEY... UH... GUYS?
LITTLE HELP HERE?
I HATE YOU.

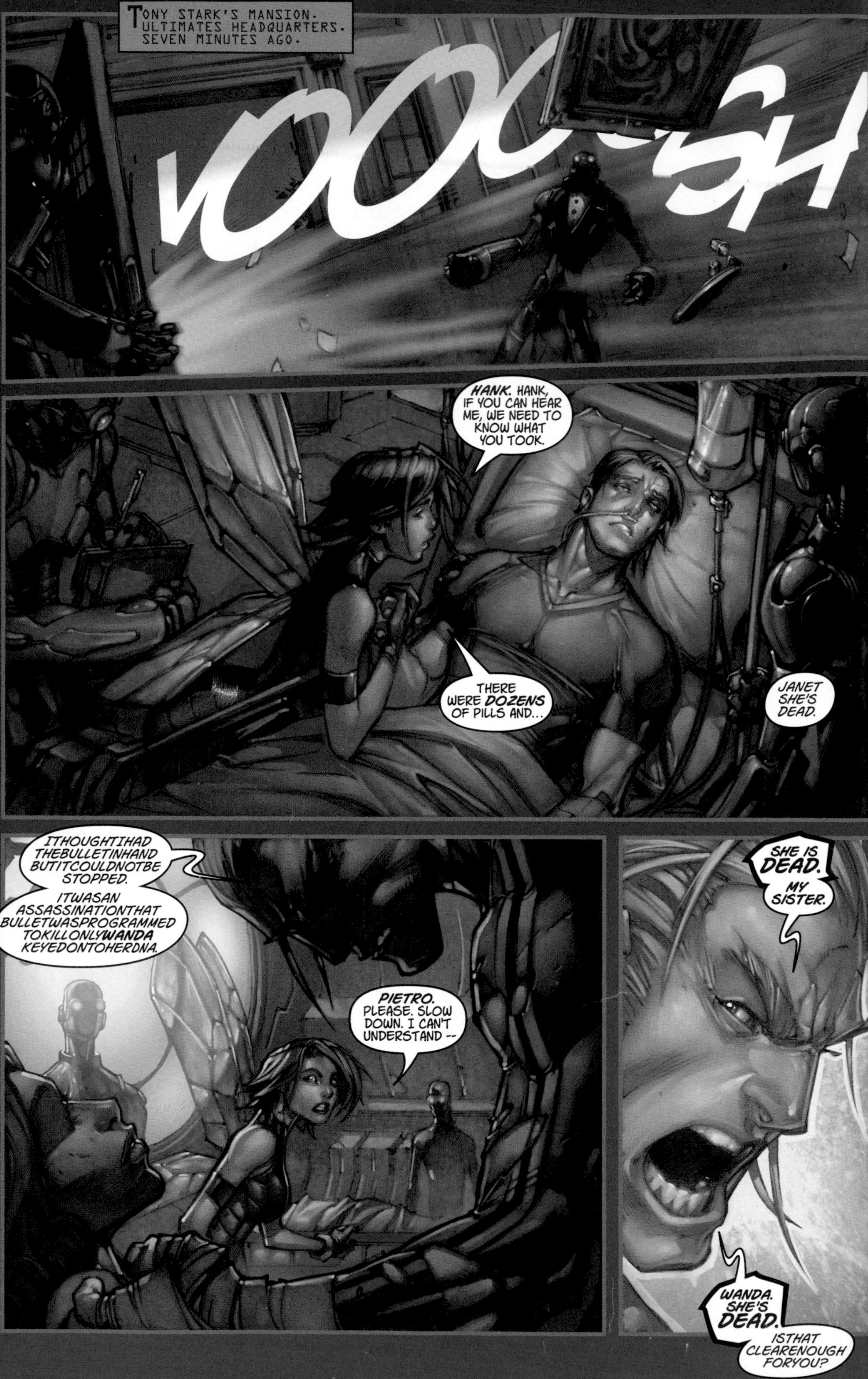
TONY STARK'S MANSION. ULTIMATES HEADQUARTERS. SEVEN MINUTES AGO.
VOOOSH
HANK. HANK, IF YOU CAN HEAR ME, WE NEED TO KNOW WHAT YOU TOOK.
THERE WERE DOZENS OF PILLS AND...
JANET SHE'S DEAD.
ITHOUGHTIHAD THEBULLETINHAND BUTITCOULDNOTBE STOPPED.
ITWASAN ASSASSINATIONTHAT BULLETWASPROGRAMMED TOKILLONLYWANDA KEYEDONTOHERDNA.
PIETRO. PLEASE. SLOW DOWN. I CAN'T UNDERSTAND --
SHE IS DEAD. MY SISTER.
WANDA. SHE'S DEAD.
ISTHAT CLEARENOUGH FORYOU?

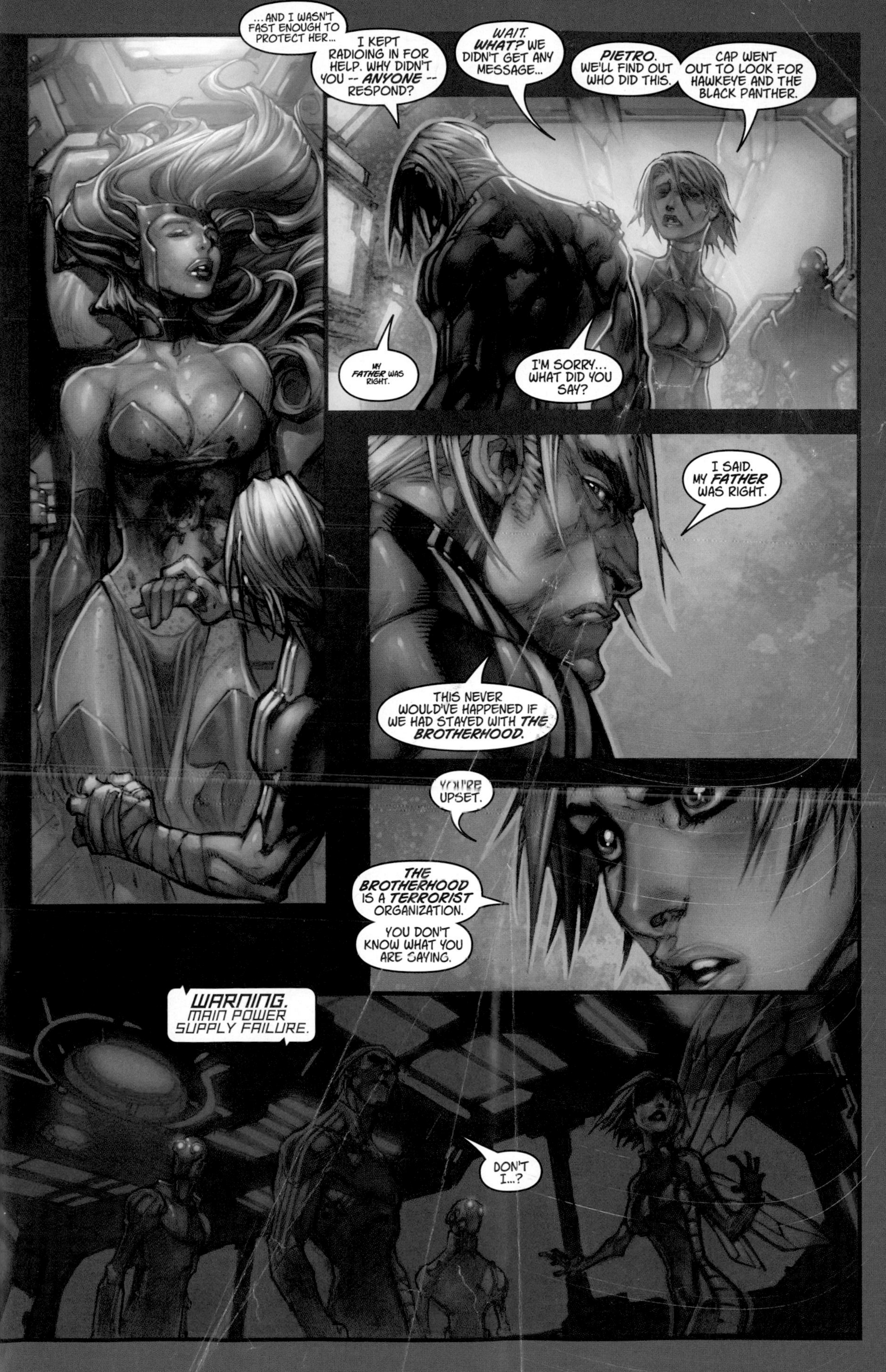
...AND I WASN'T FAST ENOUGH TO PROTECT HER...
I KEPT RADIOING IN FOR HELP. WHY DIDN'T YOU -- ANYONE -- RESPOND?
WAIT. WHAT? WE DIDN'T GET ANY MESSAGE...
PIETRO. WE'LL FIND OUT WHO DID THIS.
CAP WENT OUT TO LOOK FOR HAWKEYE AND THE BLACK PANTHER.
MY FATHER WAS RIGHT.
I'M SORRY... WHAT DID YOU SAY?
I SAID. MY FATHER WAS RIGHT.
THIS NEVER WOULD'VE HAPPENED IF WE HAD STAYED WITH THE BROTHERHOOD.
YOU'RE UPSET.
THE BROTHERHOOD IS A TERRORIST ORGANIZATION.
YOU DON'T KNOW WHAT YOU ARE SAYING.
WARNING. MAIN POWER SUPPLY FAILURE.
DON'T I...?

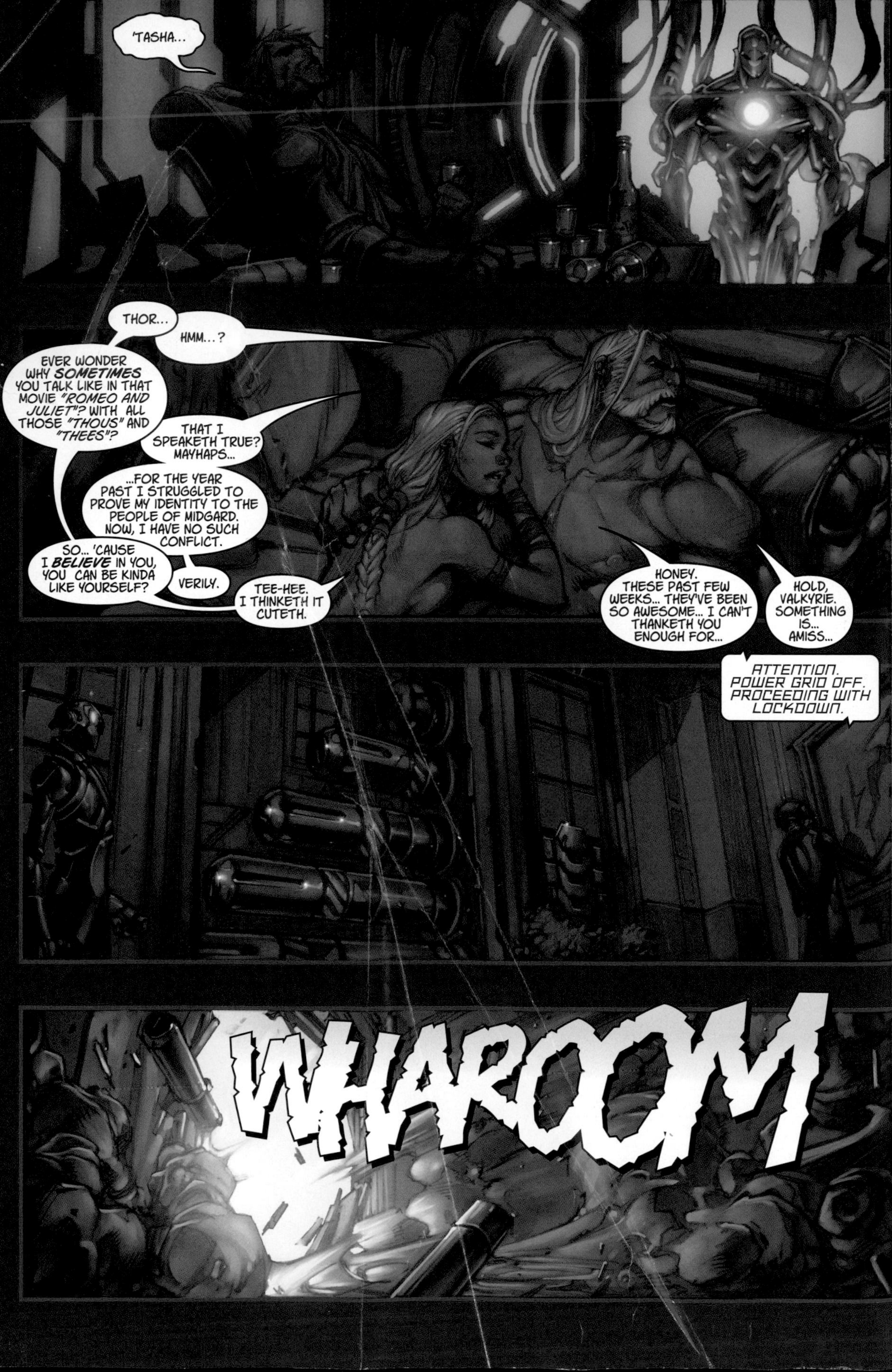
'TASHA...
THOR...
HMM...?
EVER WONDER WHY SOMETIMES YOU TALK LIKE IN THAT MOVIE "ROMEO AND JULIET"? WITH ALL THOSE "THOUS" AND "THEES"?
THAT I SPEAKETH TRUE? MAYHAPS...
...FOR THE YEAR PAST I STRUGGLED TO PROVE MY IDENTITY TO THE PEOPLE OF MIDGARD. NOW, I HAVE NO SUCH CONFLICT.
SO... 'CAUSE I BELIEVE IN YOU, YOU CAN BE KINDA LIKE YOURSELF?
VERILY.
TEE-HEE. I THINKETH IT CUTETH.
HONEY. THESE PAST FEW WEEKS... THEY'VE BEEN SO AWESOME... I CAN'T THANKETH YOU ENOUGH FOR...
HOLD, VALKYRIE. SOMETHING IS... AMISS...
ATTENTION. POWER GRID OFF. PROCEEDING WITH LOCKDOWN.
WHAROOM

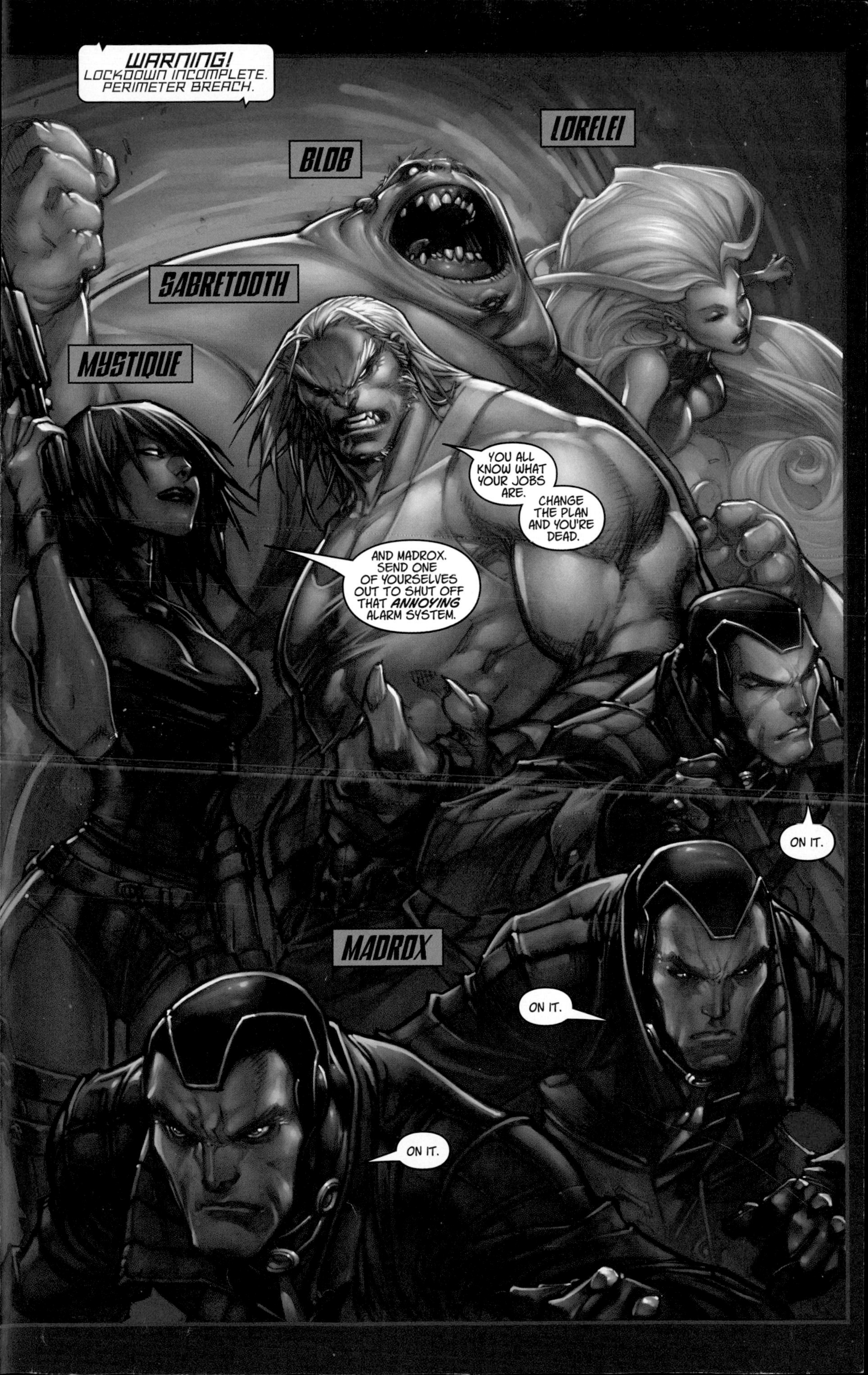
WARNING!
LOCKDOWN INCOMPLETE.
PERIMETER BREACH.
BLOB
LORELEI
SABRETOOTH
MYSTIQUE
YOU ALL KNOW WHAT YOUR JOBS ARE.
CHANGE THE PLAN AND YOU'RE DEAD.
AND MADROX. SEND ONE OF YOURSELVES OUT TO SHUT OFF THAT ANNOYING ALARM SYSTEM.
ON IT.
MADROX
ON IT.
ON IT.

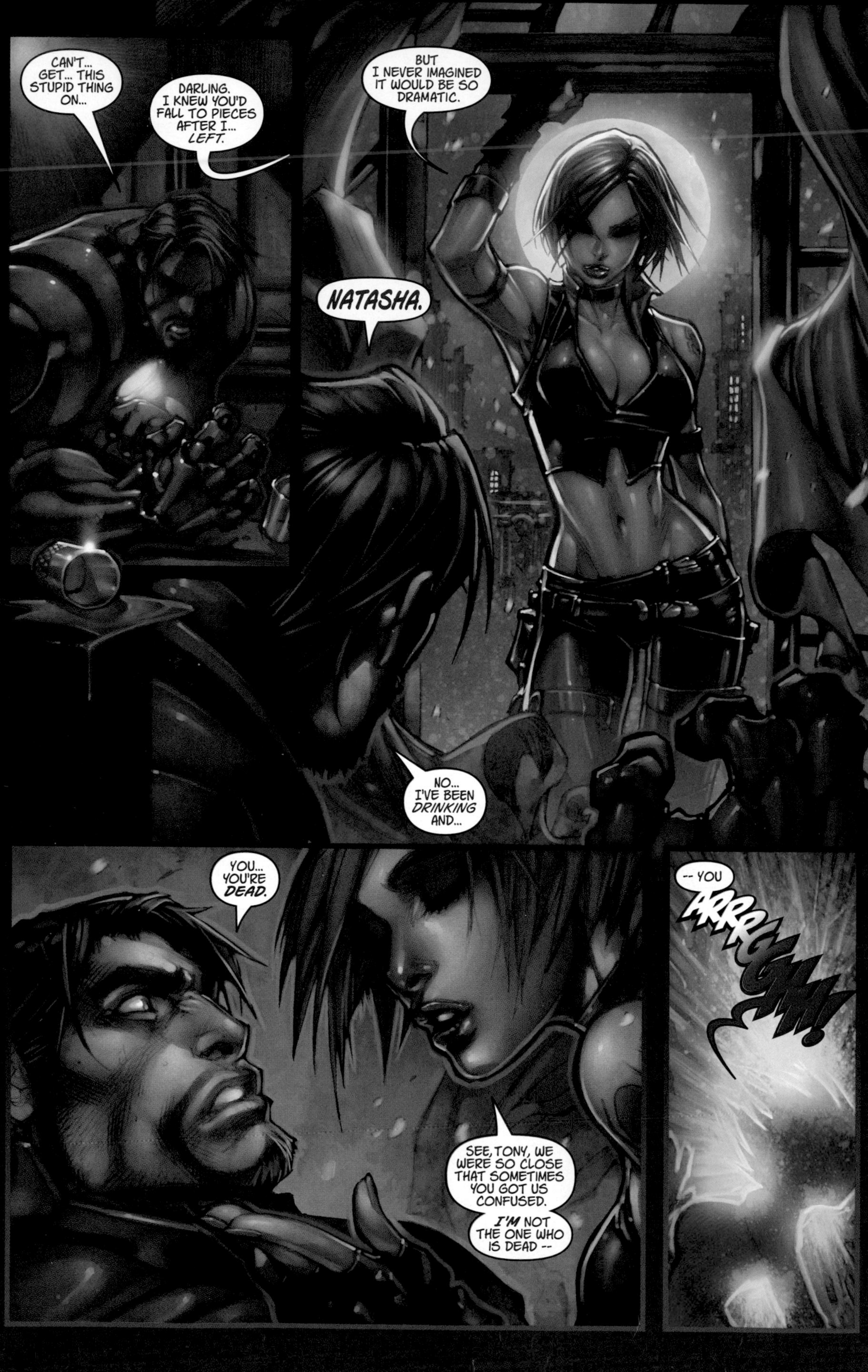
CAN'T... GET... THIS STUPID THING ON...
DARLING. I KNEW YOU'D FALL TO PIECES AFTER I... *LEFT.*
BUT I NEVER IMAGINED IT WOULD BE SO DRAMATIC.
NATASHA.
NO... I'VE BEEN *DRINKING* AND...
YOU... YOU'RE *DEAD.*
SEE, TONY, WE WERE SO CLOSE THAT SOMETIMES YOU GOT US CONFUSED.
I'M NOT THE ONE WHO IS DEAD --
-- YOU
ARRRGHH!

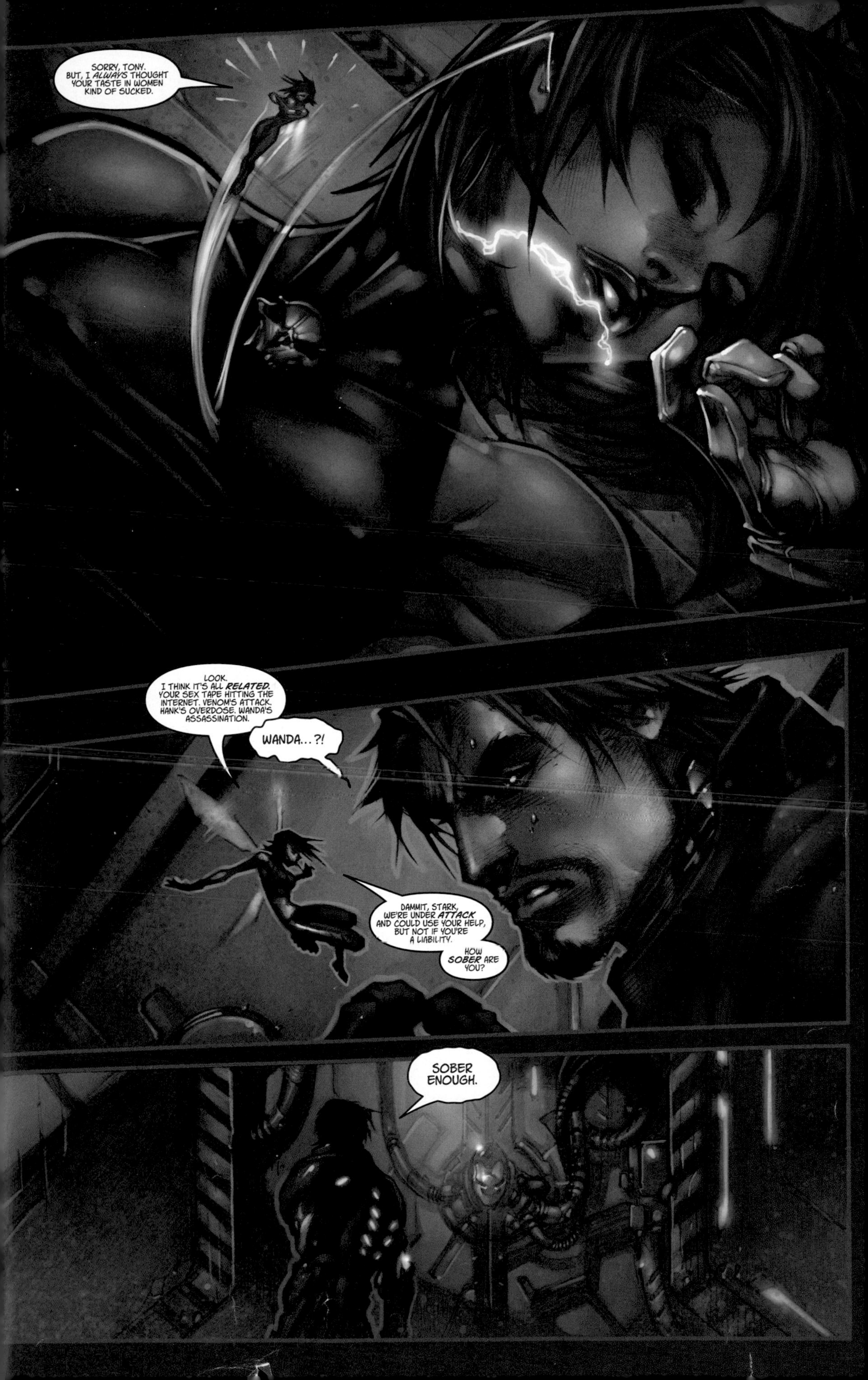
SORRY, TONY. BUT, I *ALWAYS* THOUGHT YOUR TASTE IN WOMEN KIND OF SUCKED.
LOOK. I THINK IT'S ALL *RELATED*. YOUR SEX TAPE HITTING THE INTERNET. VENOM'S ATTACK. HANK'S OVERDOSE. WANDA'S ASSASSINATION.
WANDA...?!
DAMMIT, STARK, WE'RE UNDER *ATTACK* AND COULD USE YOUR HELP, BUT NOT IF YOU'RE A LIABILITY.
HOW *SOBER* ARE YOU?
SOBER ENOUGH.

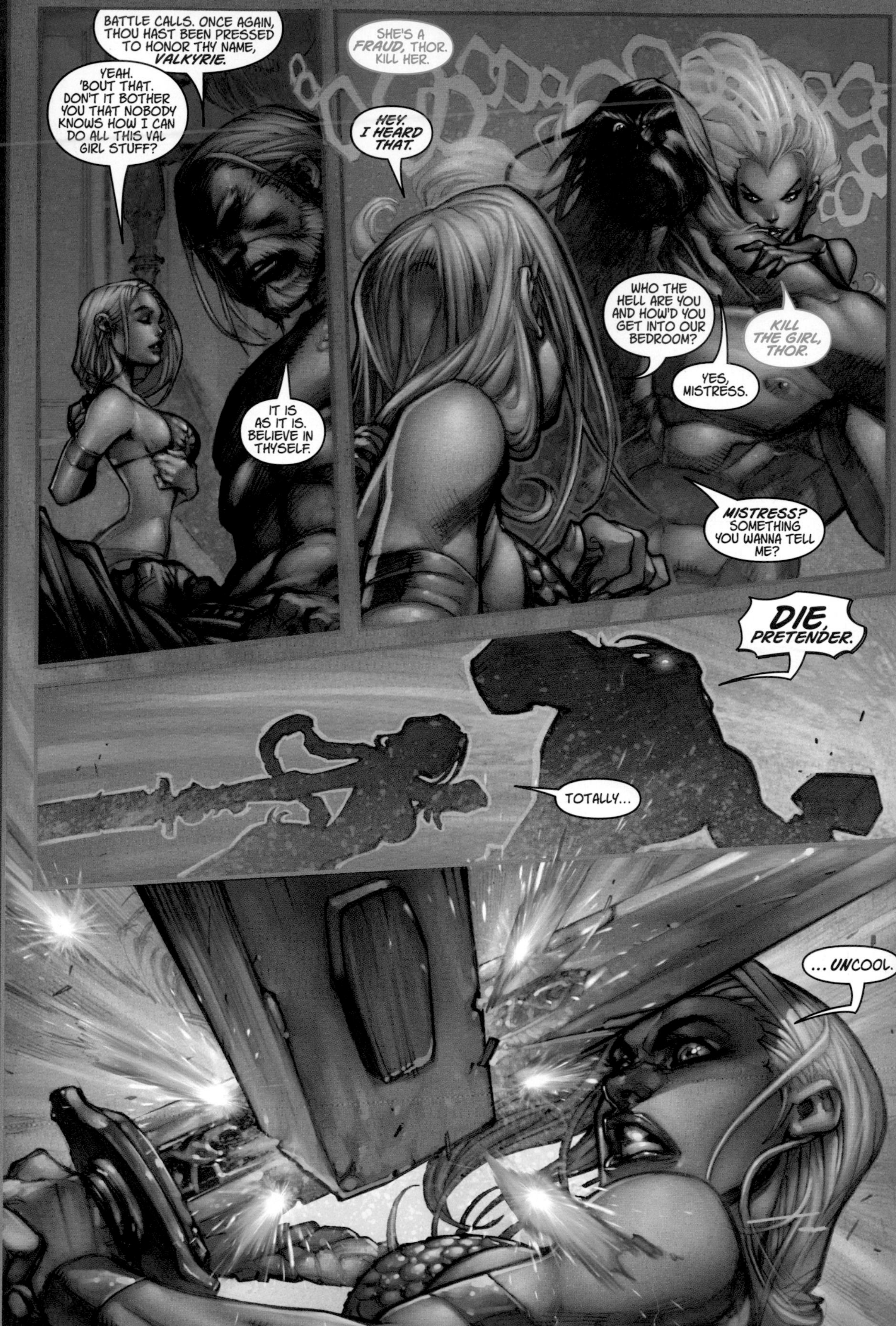
BATTLE CALLS. ONCE AGAIN, THOU HAST BEEN PRESSED TO HONOR THY NAME, VALKYRIE.
YEAH. 'BOUT THAT. DON'T IT BOTHER YOU THAT NOBODY KNOWS HOW I CAN DO ALL THIS VAL GIRL STUFF?
IT IS AS IT IS. BELIEVE IN THYSELF.
SHE'S A FRAUD, THOR. KILL HER.
HEY. I HEARD THAT.
WHO THE HELL ARE YOU AND HOW'D YOU GET INTO OUR BEDROOM?
KILL THE GIRL, THOR.
YES, MISTRESS.
MISTRESS? SOMETHING YOU WANNA TELL ME?
DIE, PRETENDER.
TOTALLY...
...UNCOOL.

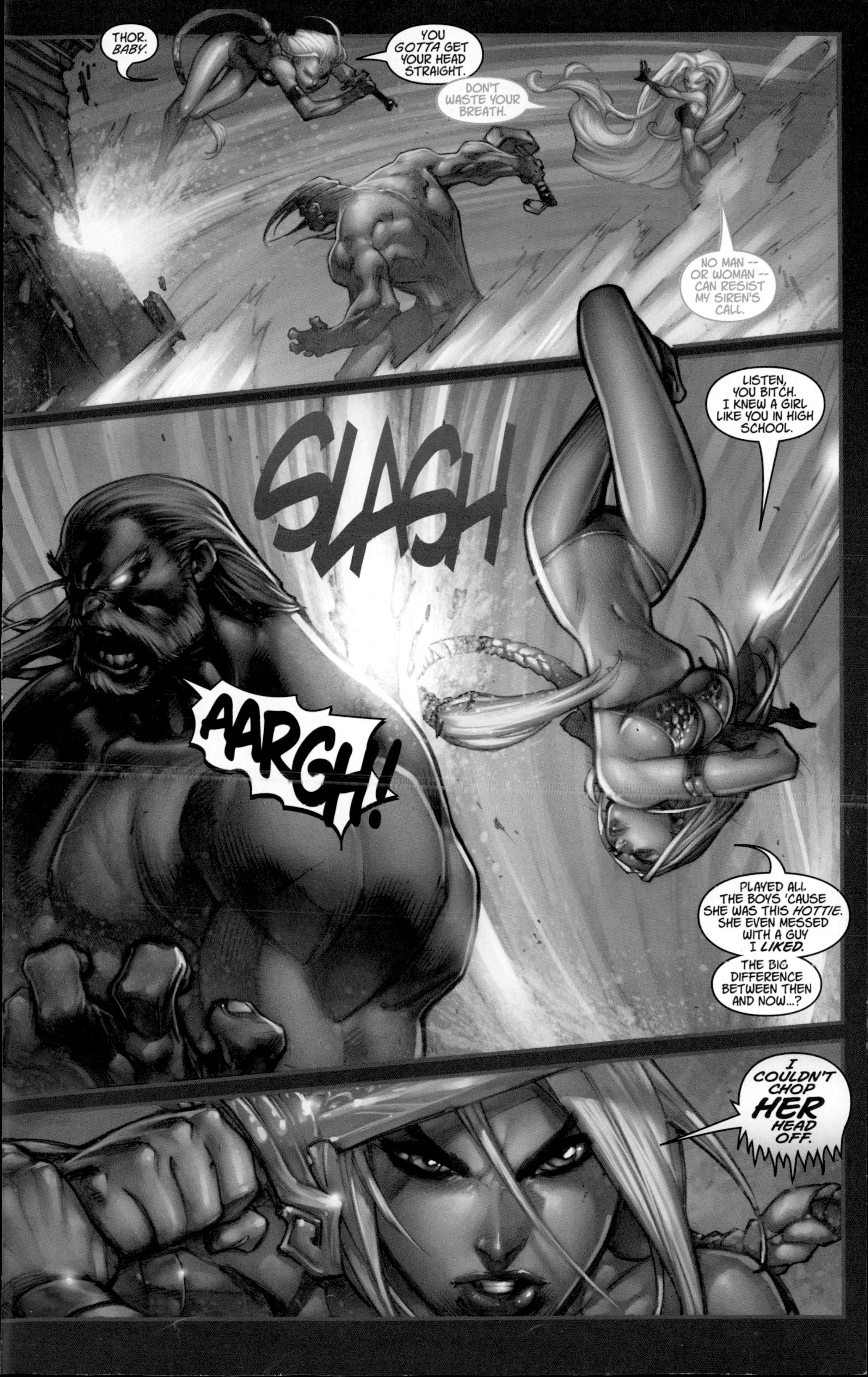

THOR. BABY.
YOU GOTTA GET YOUR HEAD STRAIGHT.
DON'T WASTE YOUR BREATH.
NO MAN -- OR WOMAN -- CAN RESIST MY SIREN'S CALL.
LISTEN, YOU BITCH. I KNEW A GIRL LIKE YOU IN HIGH SCHOOL.
SLASH
AARGH!
PLAYED ALL THE BOYS 'CAUSE SHE WAS THIS HOTTIE. SHE EVEN MESSED WITH A GUY I LIKED.
THE BIG DIFFERENCE BETWEEN THEN AND NOW...?
I COULDN'T CHOP HER HEAD OFF.

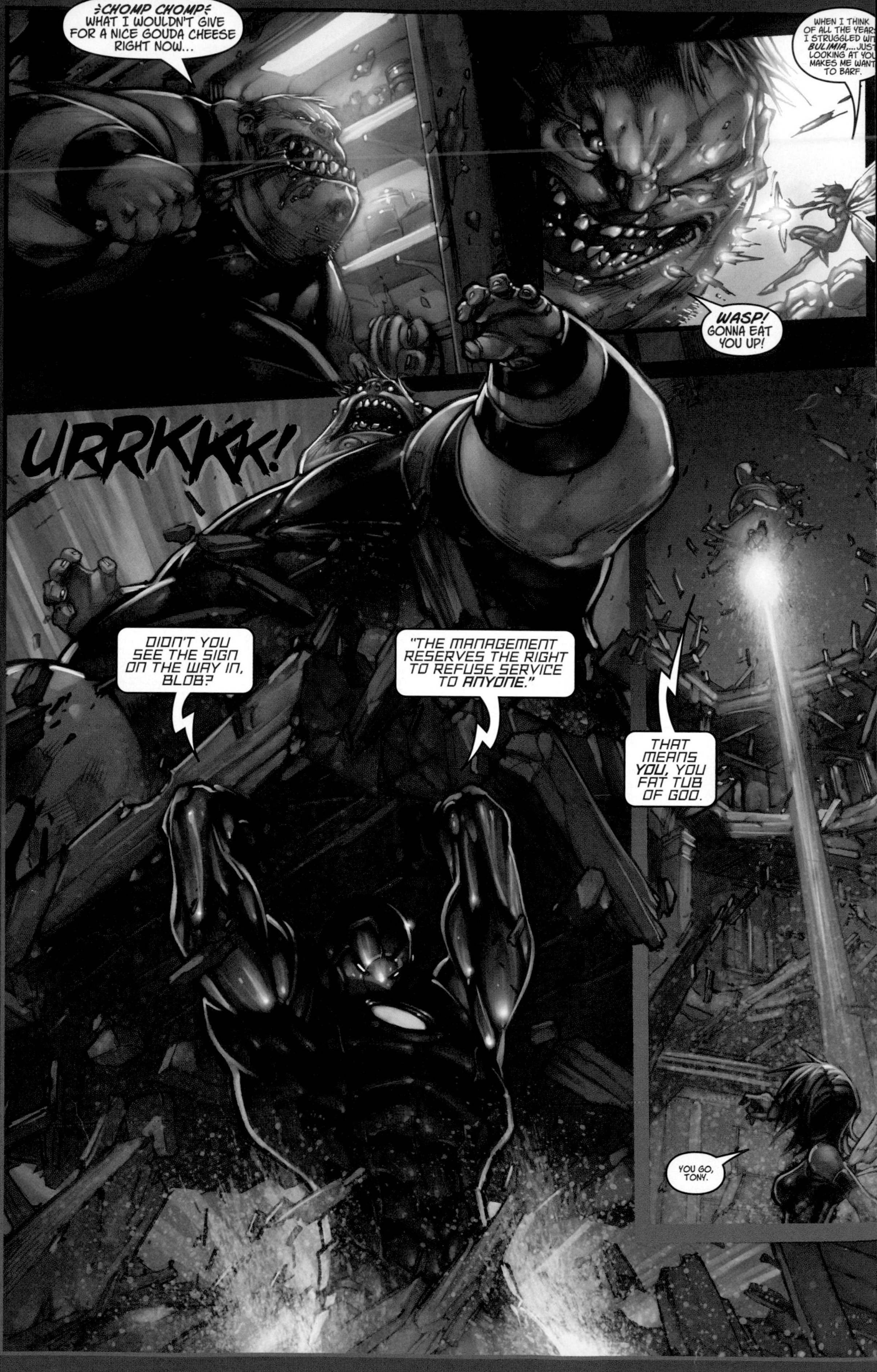

CHOMP CHOMP WHAT I WOULDN'T GIVE FOR A NICE GOUDA CHEESE RIGHT NOW...
WHEN I THINK OF ALL THE YEARS I STRUGGLED WITH BULIMIA,...JUST LOOKING AT YOU MAKES ME WANT TO BARF.
WASP! GONNA EAT YOU UP!
URRKKK!
DIDN'T YOU SEE THE SIGN ON THE WAY IN, BLOB?
"THE MANAGEMENT RESERVES THE RIGHT TO REFUSE SERVICE TO ANYONE."
THAT MEANS YOU, YOU FAT TUB OF GOO.
YOU GO, TONY.

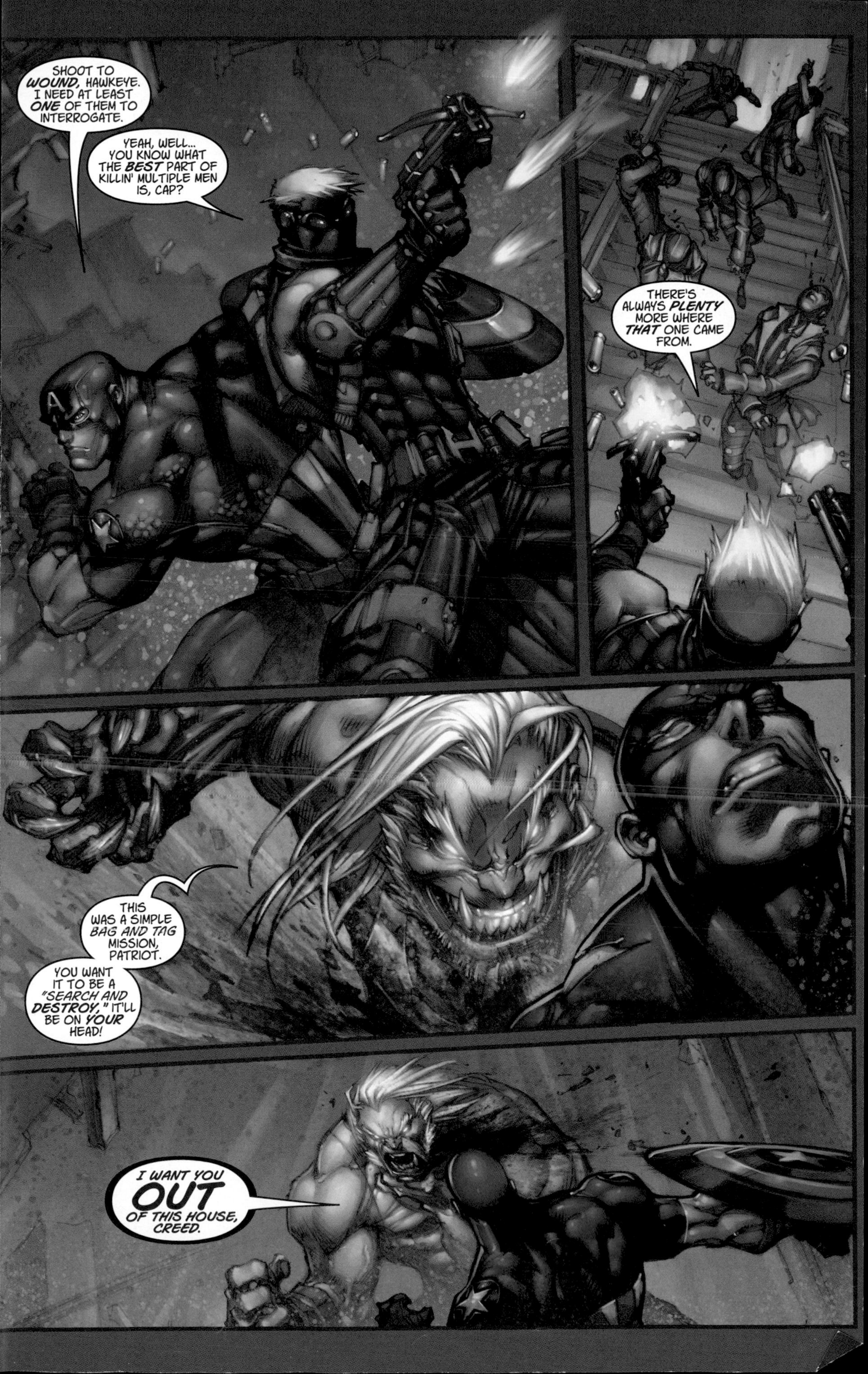
SHOOT TO WOUND, HAWKEYE. I NEED AT LEAST ONE OF THEM TO INTERROGATE.
YEAH, WELL... YOU KNOW WHAT THE BEST PART OF KILLIN' MULTIPLE MEN IS, CAP?
THERE'S ALWAYS PLENTY MORE WHERE THAT ONE CAME FROM.
THIS WAS A SIMPLE BAG AND TAG MISSION, PATRIOT.
YOU WANT IT TO BE A "SEARCH AND DESTROY," IT'LL BE ON YOUR HEAD!
I WANT YOU OUT OF THIS HOUSE, CREED.

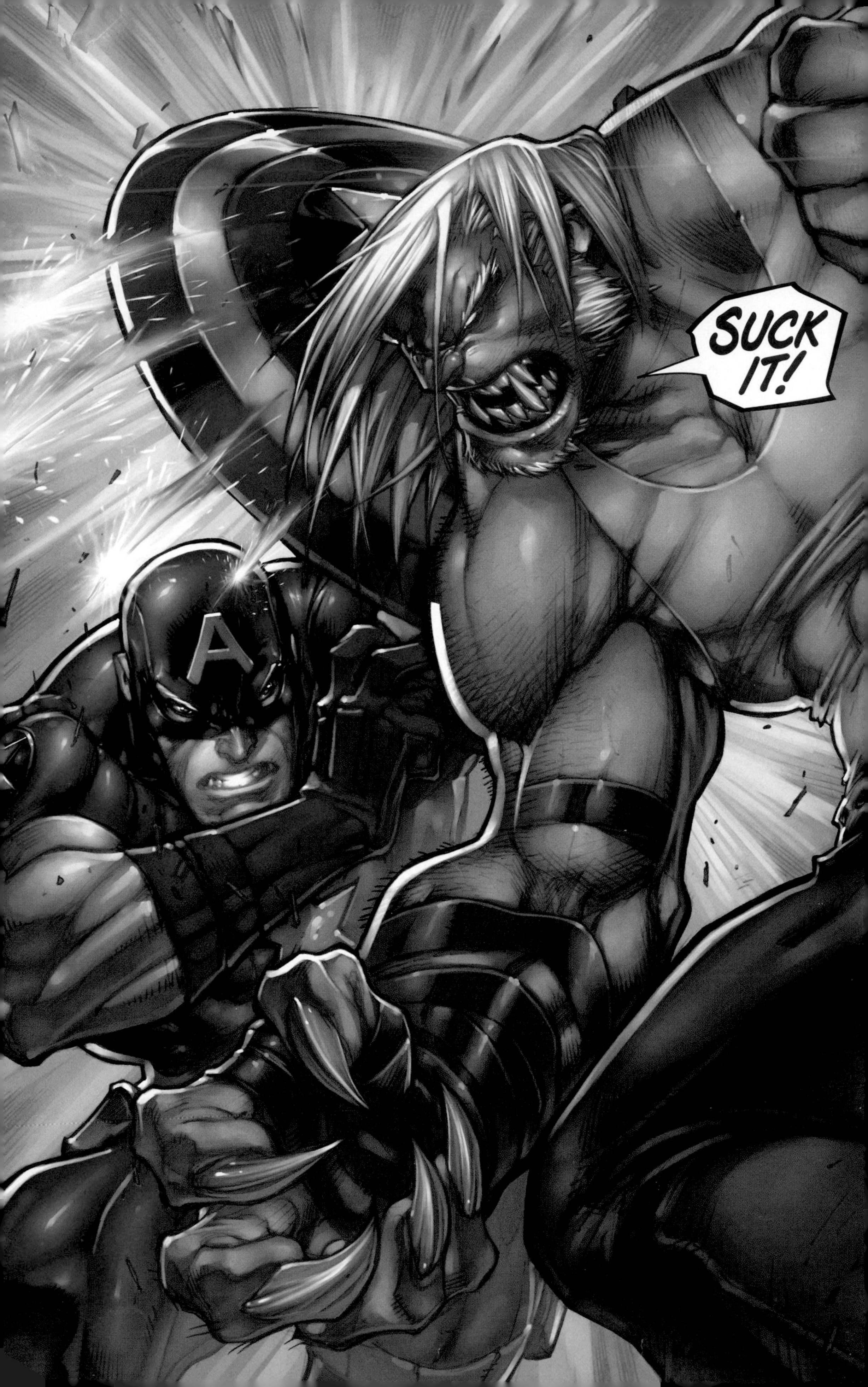
SUCK IT!

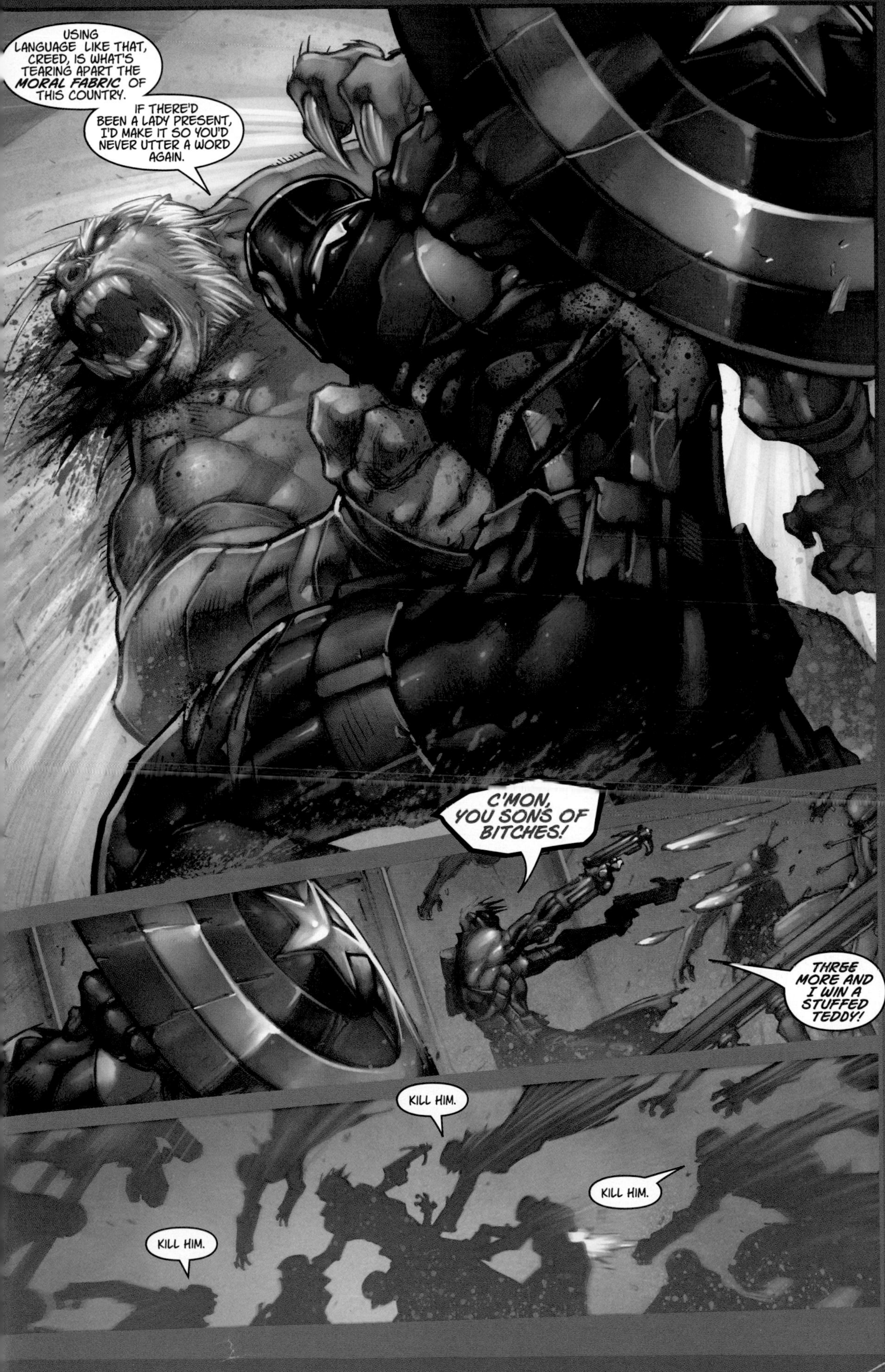
USING LANGUAGE LIKE THAT, CREED, IS WHAT'S TEARING APART THE MORAL FABRIC OF THIS COUNTRY.
IF THERE'D BEEN A LADY PRESENT, I'D MAKE IT SO YOU'D NEVER UTTER A WORD AGAIN.
C'MON, YOU SONS OF BITCHES!
THREE MORE AND I WIN A STUFFED TEDDY!
KILL HIM.
KILL HIM.
KILL HIM.

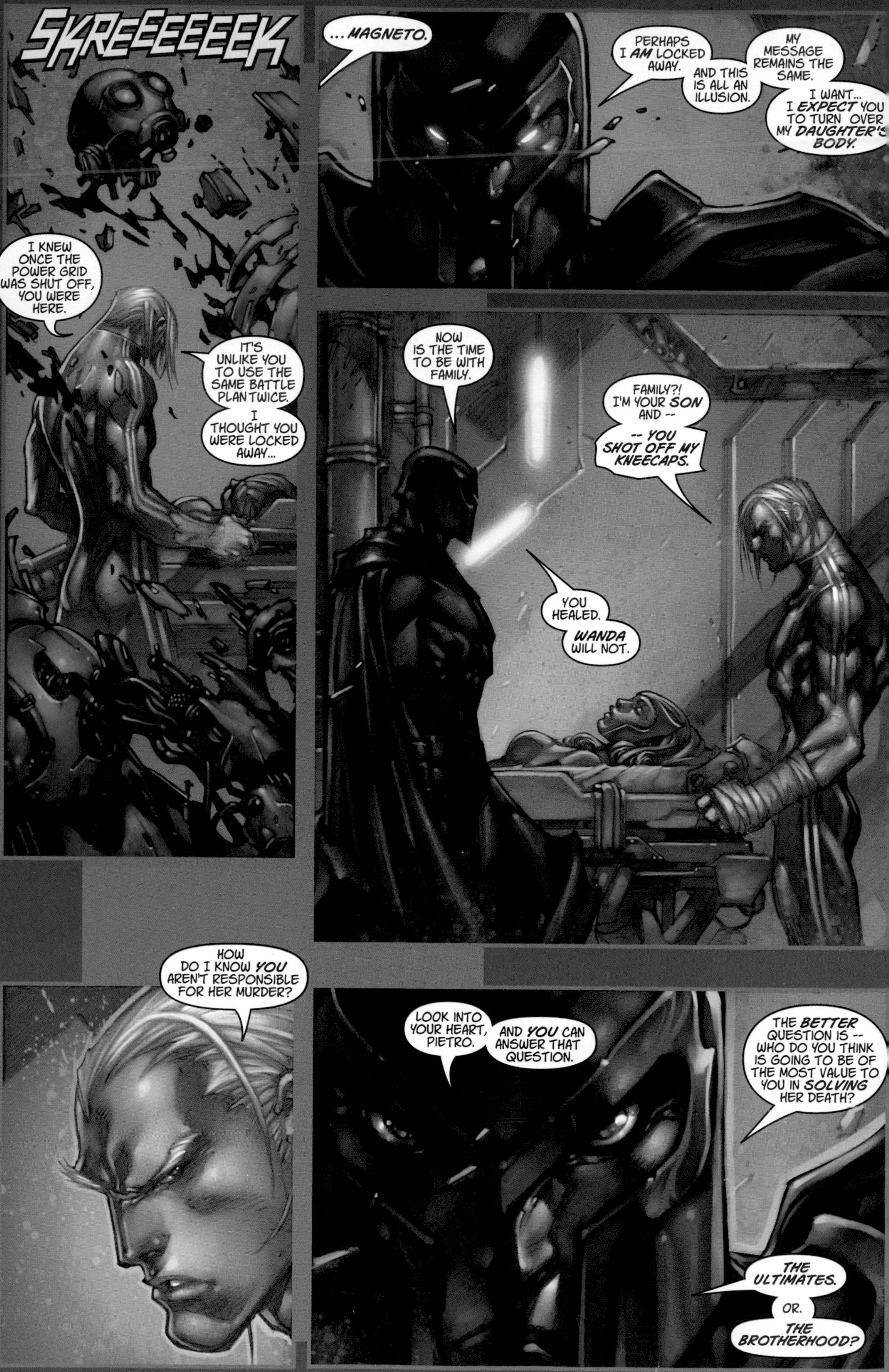
SKREEEEEEK
I KNEW ONCE THE POWER GRID WAS SHUT OFF, YOU WERE HERE.
IT'S UNLIKE YOU TO USE THE SAME BATTLE PLAN TWICE.
I THOUGHT YOU WERE LOCKED AWAY...
... MAGNETO.
PERHAPS I AM LOCKED AWAY.
AND THIS IS ALL AN ILLUSION.
MY MESSAGE REMAINS THE SAME.
I WANT... I EXPECT YOU TO TURN OVER MY DAUGHTER'S BODY.
NOW IS THE TIME TO BE WITH FAMILY.
FAMILY?! I'M YOUR SON AND --
-- YOU SHOT OFF MY KNEECAPS.
YOU HEALED.
WANDA WILL NOT.
HOW DO I KNOW YOU AREN'T RESPONSIBLE FOR HER MURDER?
LOOK INTO YOUR HEART, PIETRO.
AND YOU CAN ANSWER THAT QUESTION.
THE BETTER QUESTION IS -- WHO DO YOU THINK IS GOING TO BE OF THE MOST VALUE TO YOU IN SOLVING HER DEATH?
THE ULTIMATES.
OR.
THE BROTHERHOOD?

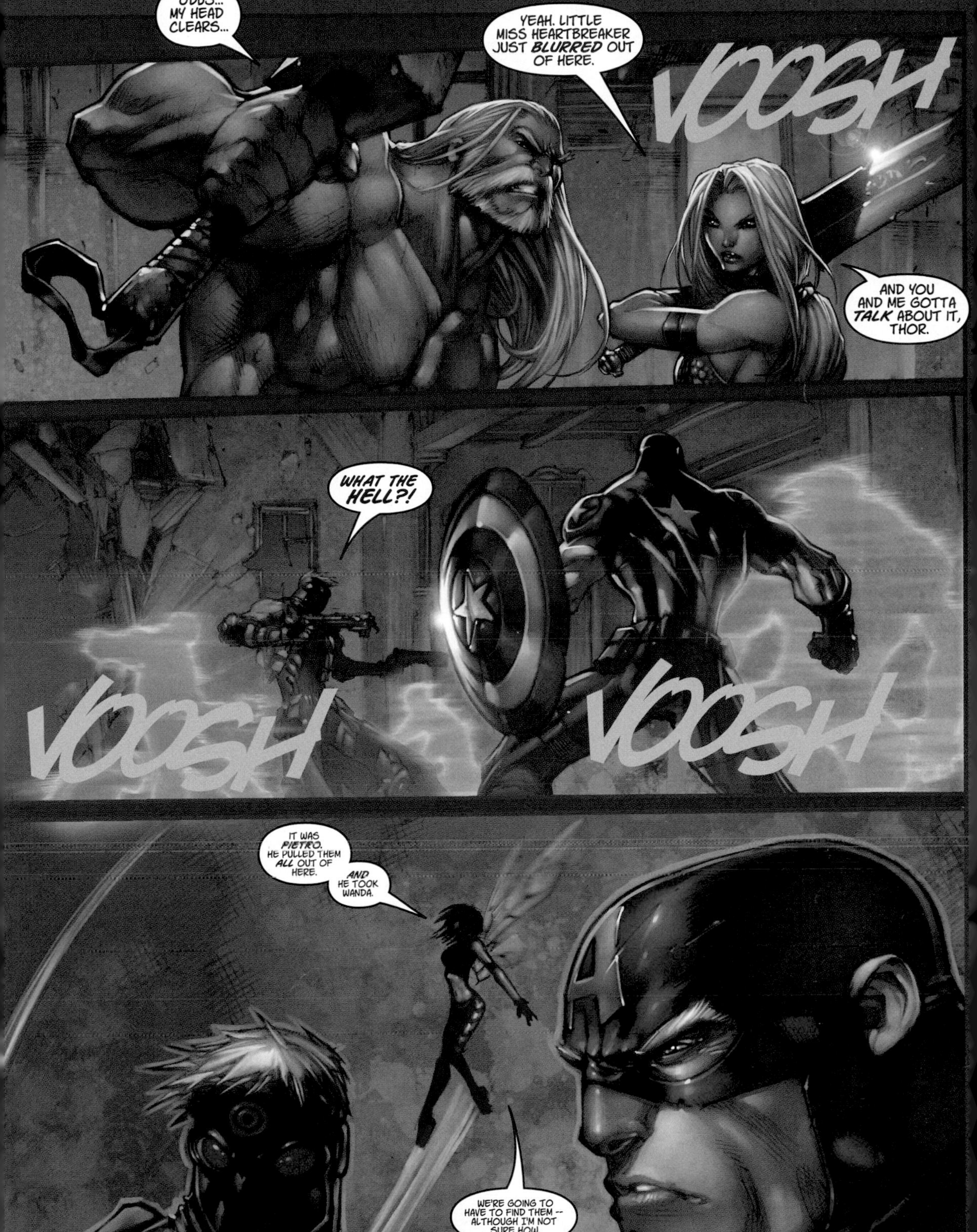
ODDS... MY HEAD CLEARS...
YEAH. LITTLE MISS HEARTBREAKER JUST BLURRED OUT OF HERE.
VOOSH
AND YOU AND ME GOTTA TALK ABOUT IT, THOR.
WHAT THE HELL?!
VOOSH
VOOSH
IT WAS PIETRO. HE PULLED THEM ALL OUT OF HERE.
AND HE TOOK WANDA.
WE'RE GOING TO HAVE TO FIND THEM -- ALTHOUGH I'M NOT SURE HOW.
I KNOW YOU THINK YOU'VE GOT A MURDER TO SOLVE. BUT, BELIEVE ME --

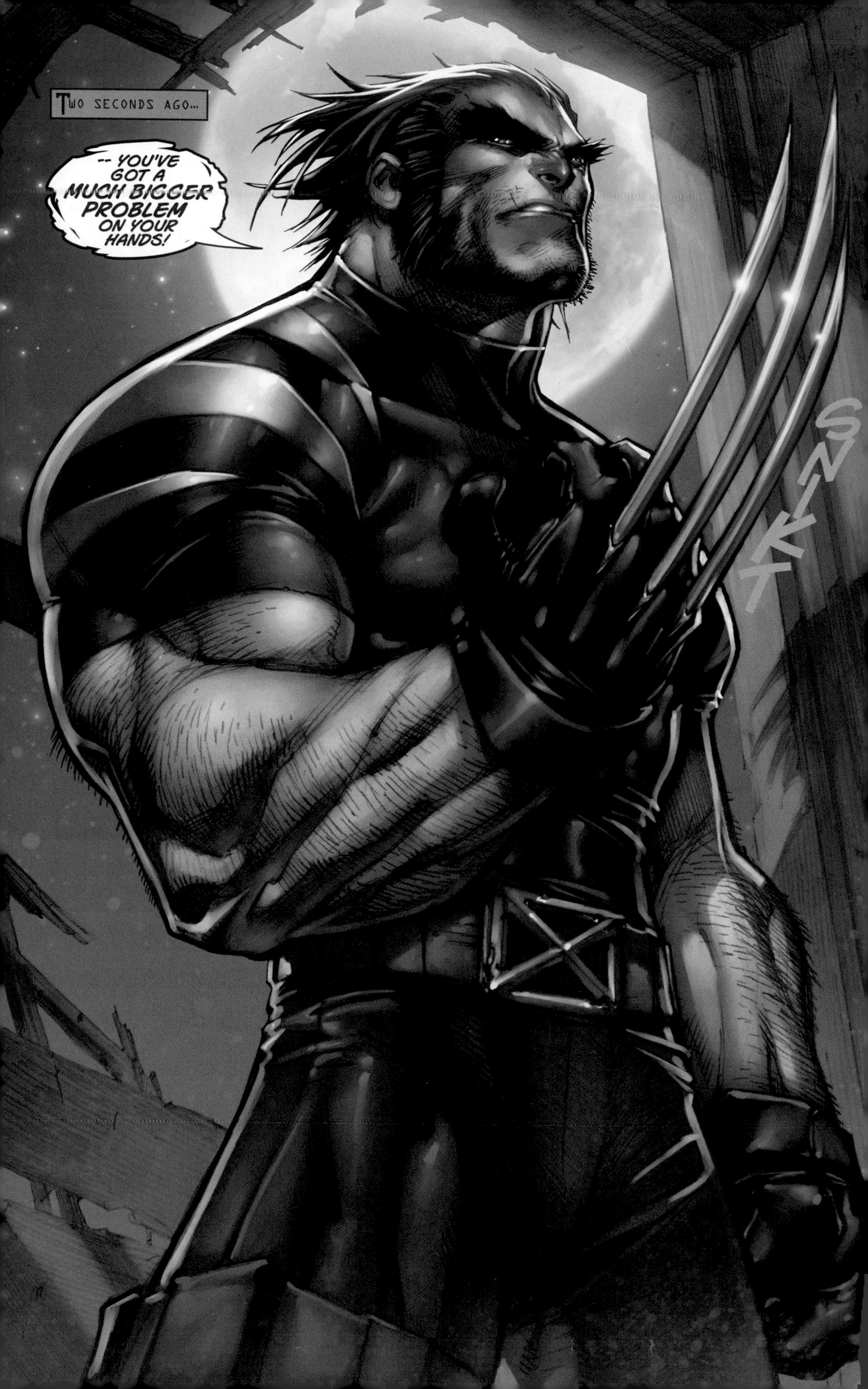
Two seconds ago...
-- YOU'VE GOT A MUCH BIGGER PROBLEM ON YOUR HANDS!
SNIKT

THREE

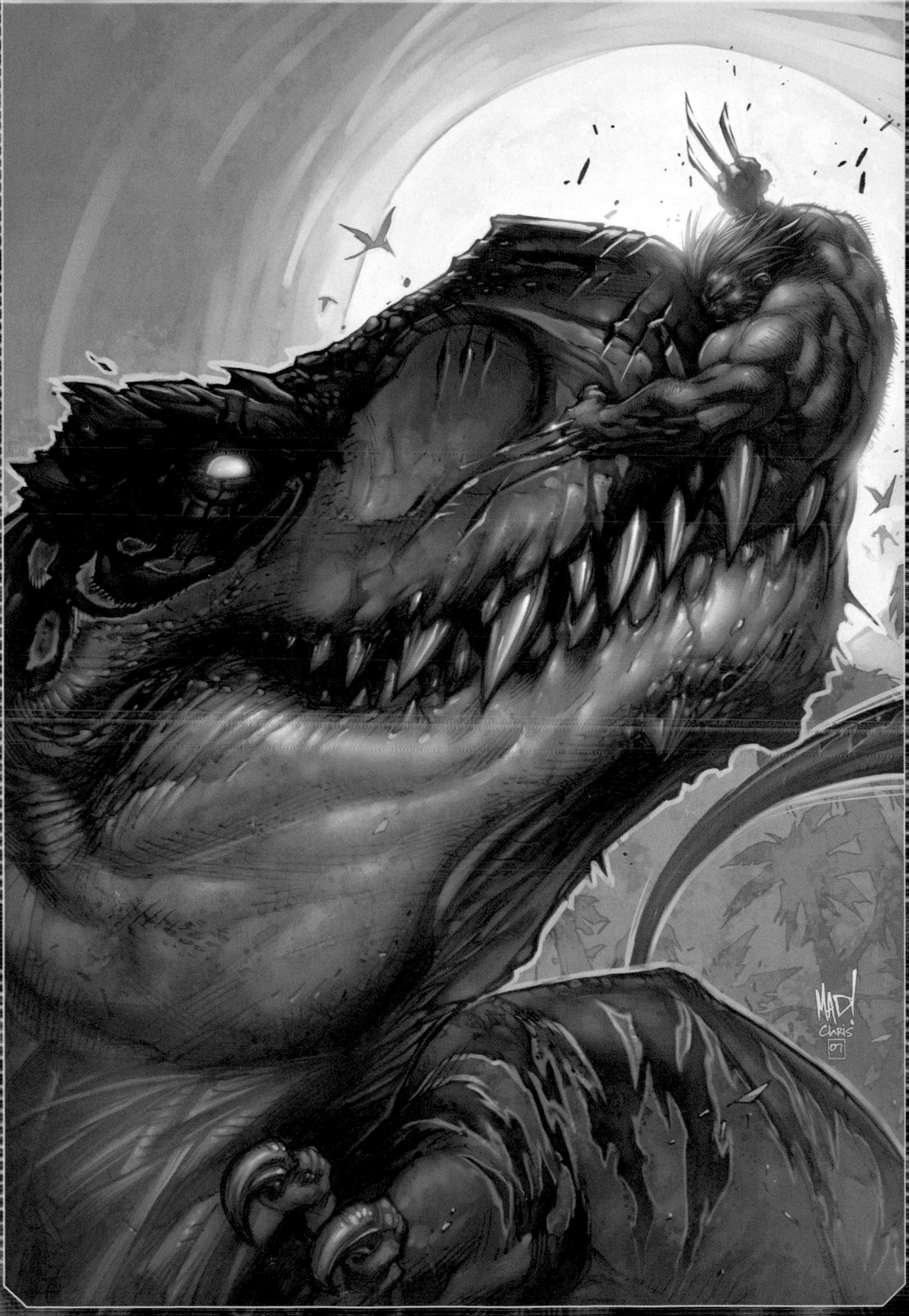
MAD!
Chris
07

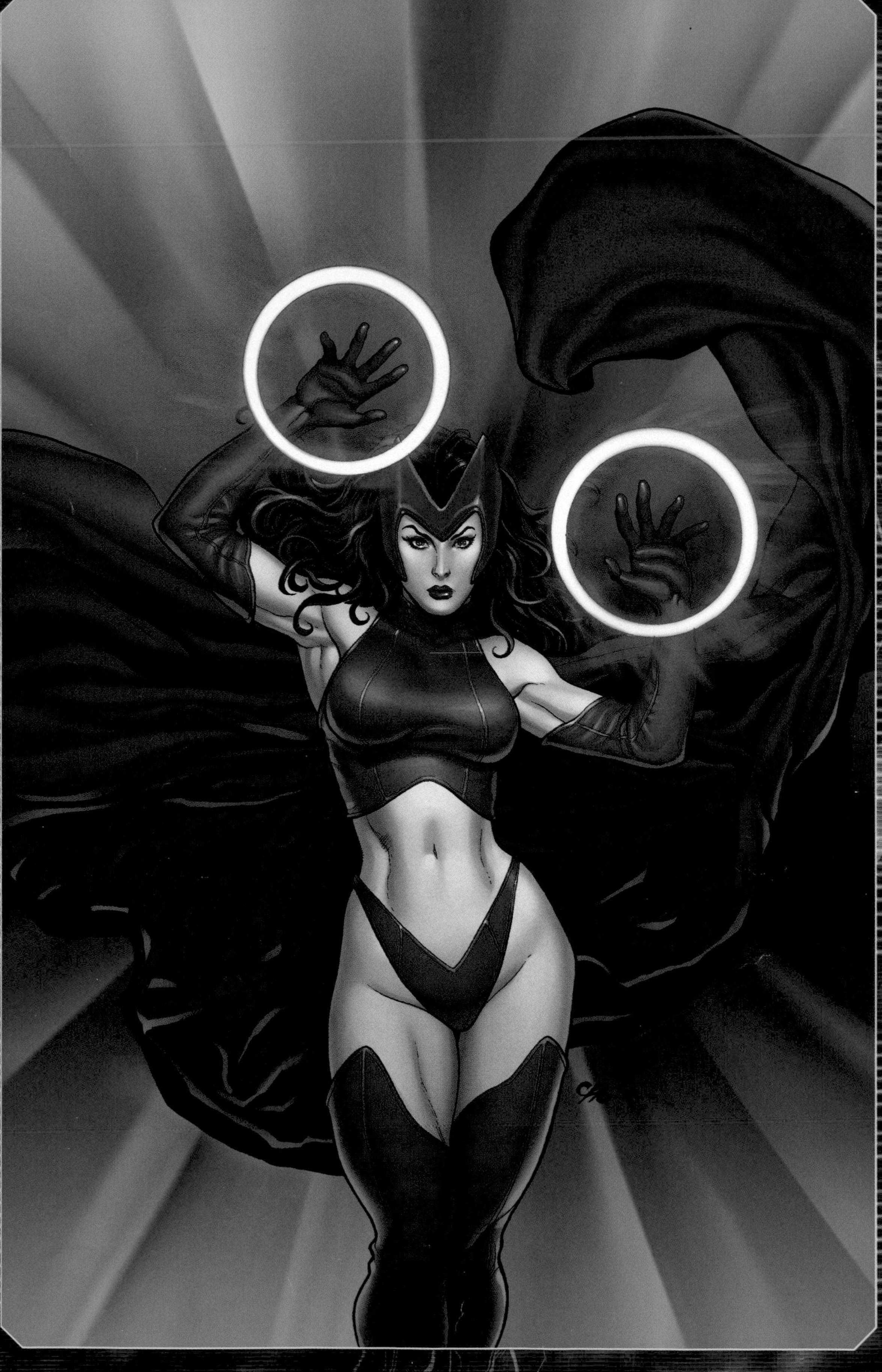

Issue #3 variant cover by FRANK CHO

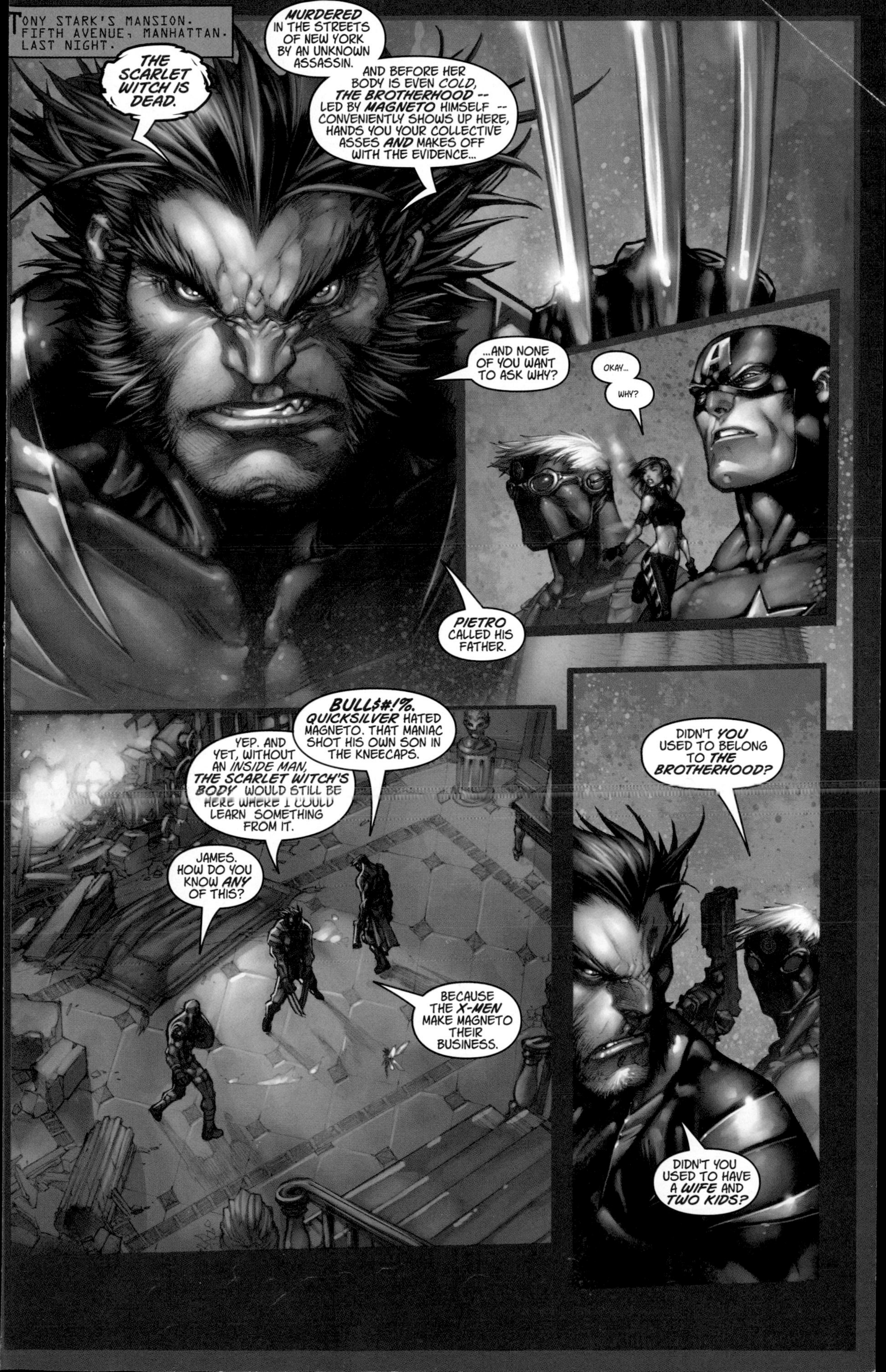
TONY STARK'S MANSION. FIFTH AVENUE, MANHATTAN. LAST NIGHT.
THE SCARLET WITCH IS DEAD.
MURDERED IN THE STREETS OF NEW YORK BY AN UNKNOWN ASSASSIN.
AND BEFORE HER BODY IS EVEN COLD, THE BROTHERHOOD -- LED BY MAGNETO HIMSELF -- CONVENIENTLY SHOWS UP HERE, HANDS YOU YOUR COLLECTIVE ASSES AND MAKES OFF WITH THE EVIDENCE...
...AND NONE OF YOU WANT TO ASK WHY?
OKAY...
WHY?
PIETRO CALLED HIS FATHER.
BULL$#!%. QUICKSILVER HATED MAGNETO. THAT MANIAC SHOT HIS OWN SON IN THE KNEECAPS.
YEP. AND YET, WITHOUT AN INSIDE MAN, THE SCARLET WITCH'S BODY WOULD STILL BE HERE WHERE I COULD LEARN SOMETHING FROM IT.
JAMES. HOW DO YOU KNOW ANY OF THIS?
BECAUSE THE X-MEN MAKE MAGNETO THEIR BUSINESS.
DIDN'T YOU USED TO BELONG TO THE BROTHERHOOD?
DIDN'T YOU USED TO HAVE A WIFE AND TWO KIDS?

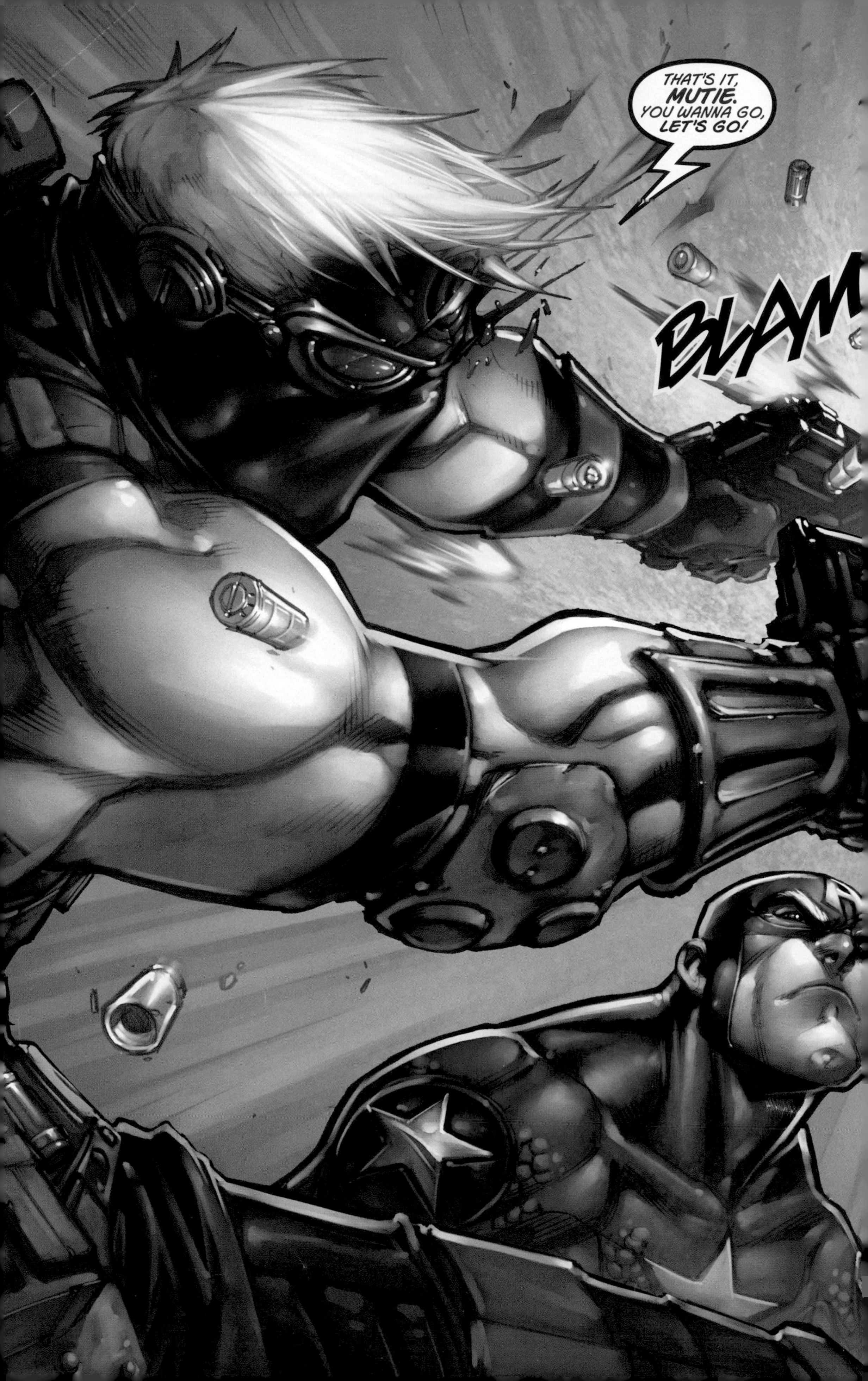

THAT'S IT, MUTIE. YOU WANNA GO, LET'S GO!
BLAM

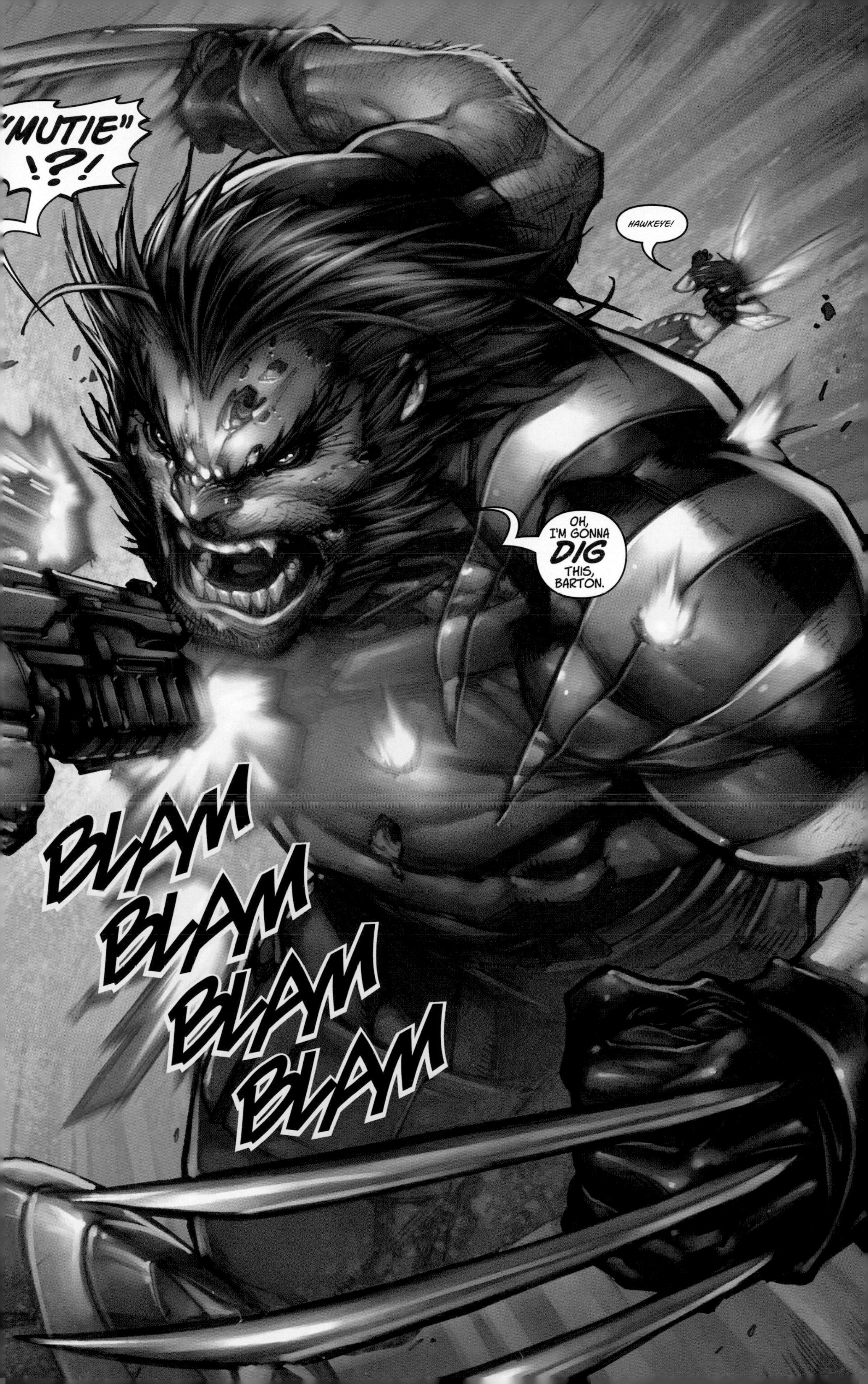
"MUTIE" !?!
HAWKEYE!
OH, I'M GONNA DIG THIS, BARTON.
BLAM BLAM BLAM BLAM

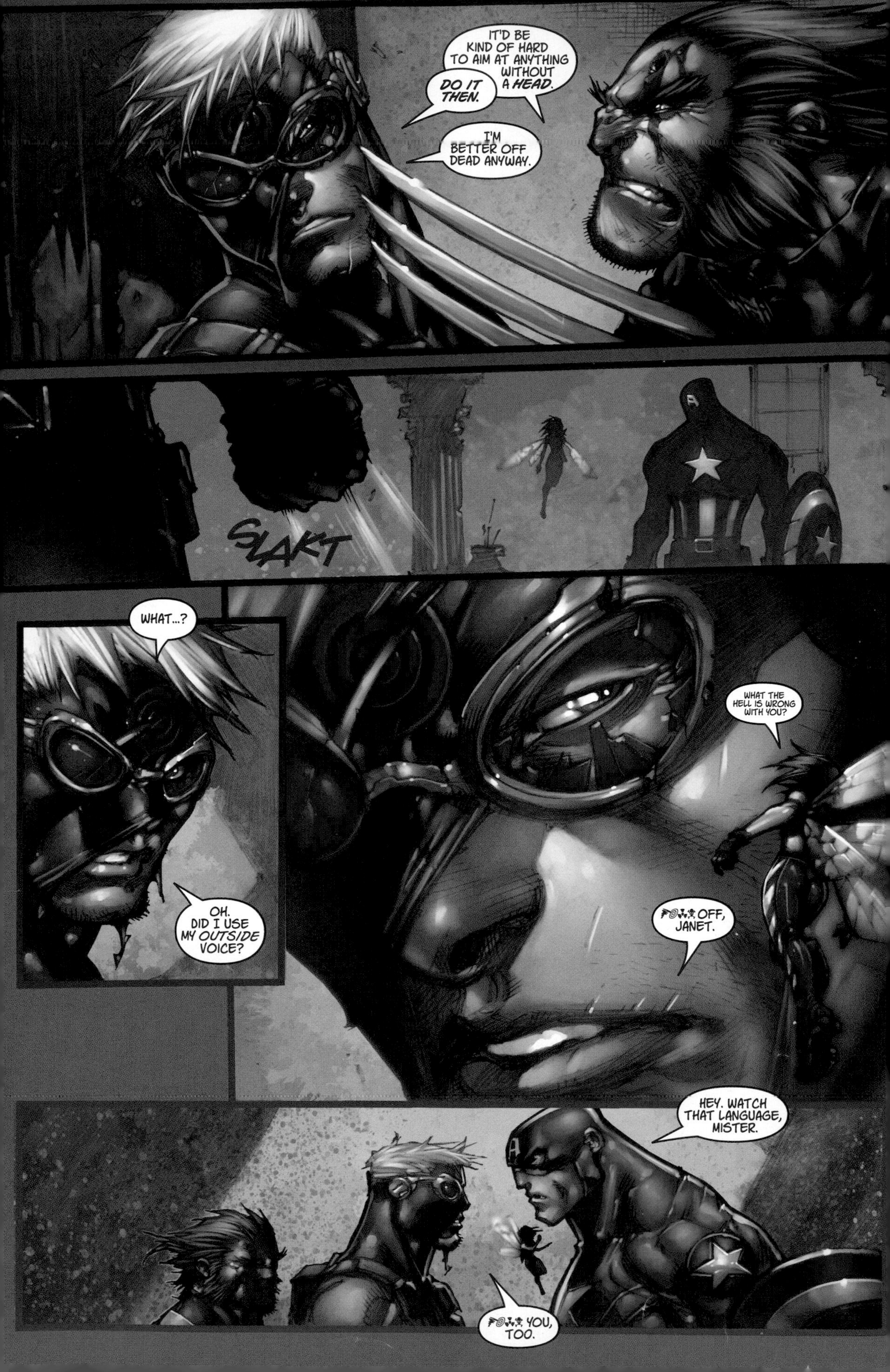
IT'D BE KIND OF HARD TO AIM AT ANYTHING WITHOUT A HEAD.
DO IT THEN.
I'M BETTER OFF DEAD ANYWAY.
SLAKT
WHAT...?
WHAT THE HELL IS WRONG WITH YOU?
OH. DID I USE MY OUTSIDE VOICE?
F*** OFF, JANET.
HEY. WATCH THAT LANGUAGE, MISTER.
F*** YOU, TOO.

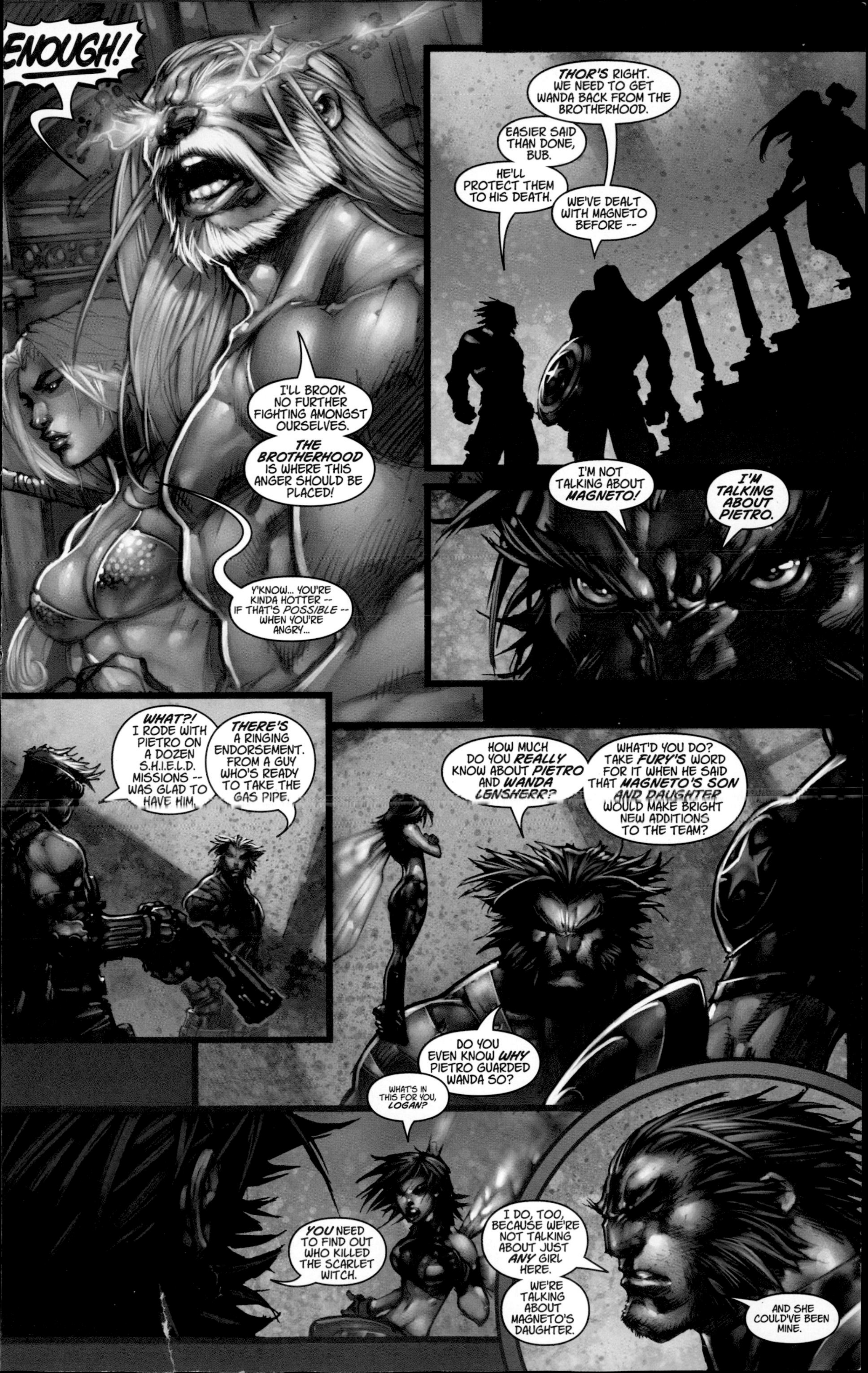
ENOUGH!
THOR'S RIGHT. WE NEED TO GET WANDA BACK FROM THE BROTHERHOOD.
EASIER SAID THAN DONE, BUB.
HE'LL PROTECT THEM TO HIS DEATH.
WE'VE DEALT WITH MAGNETO BEFORE --
I'LL BROOK NO FURTHER FIGHTING AMONGST OURSELVES.
THE BROTHERHOOD IS WHERE THIS ANGER SHOULD BE PLACED!
Y'KNOW... YOU'RE KINDA HOTTER -- IF THAT'S POSSIBLE -- WHEN YOU'RE ANGRY...
I'M NOT TALKING ABOUT MAGNETO!
I'M TALKING ABOUT PIETRO.
WHAT?! I RODE WITH PIETRO ON A DOZEN S.H.I.E.L.D. MISSIONS -- WAS GLAD TO HAVE HIM.
THERE'S A RINGING ENDORSEMENT. FROM A GUY WHO'S READY TO TAKE THE GAS PIPE.
HOW MUCH DO YOU REALLY KNOW ABOUT PIETRO AND WANDA LENSHERR?
WHAT'D YOU DO? TAKE FURY'S WORD FOR IT WHEN HE SAID THAT MAGNETO'S SON AND DAUGHTER WOULD MAKE BRIGHT NEW ADDITIONS TO THE TEAM?
DO YOU EVEN KNOW WHY PIETRO GUARDED WANDA SO?
WHAT'S IN THIS FOR YOU, LOGAN?
YOU NEED TO FIND OUT WHO KILLED THE SCARLET WITCH.
I DO, TOO, BECAUSE WE'RE NOT TALKING ABOUT JUST ANY GIRL HERE.
WE'RE TALKING ABOUT MAGNETO'S DAUGHTER.
AND SHE COULD'VE BEEN MINE.

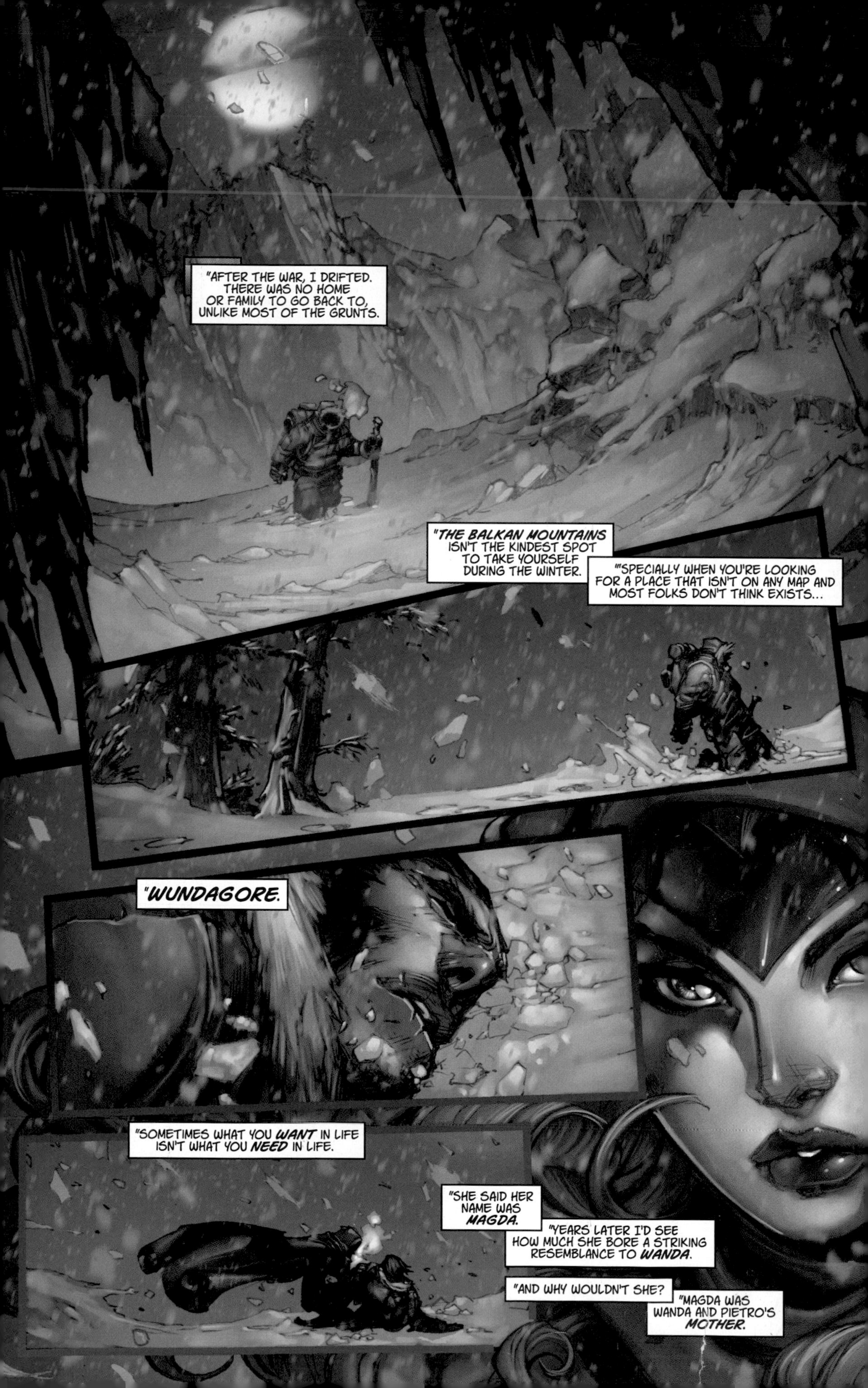
"AFTER THE WAR, I DRIFTED. THERE WAS NO HOME OR FAMILY TO GO BACK TO, UNLIKE MOST OF THE GRUNTS.
"THE BALKAN MOUNTAINS ISN'T THE KINDEST SPOT TO TAKE YOURSELF DURING THE WINTER.
"'SPECIALLY WHEN YOU'RE LOOKING FOR A PLACE THAT ISN'T ON ANY MAP AND MOST FOLKS DON'T THINK EXISTS...
"WUNDAGORE.
"SOMETIMES WHAT YOU WANT IN LIFE ISN'T WHAT YOU NEED IN LIFE.
"SHE SAID HER NAME WAS MAGDA.
"YEARS LATER I'D SEE HOW MUCH SHE BORE A STRIKING RESEMBLANCE TO WANDA.
"AND WHY WOULDN'T SHE?
"MAGDA WAS WANDA AND PIETRO'S MOTHER.

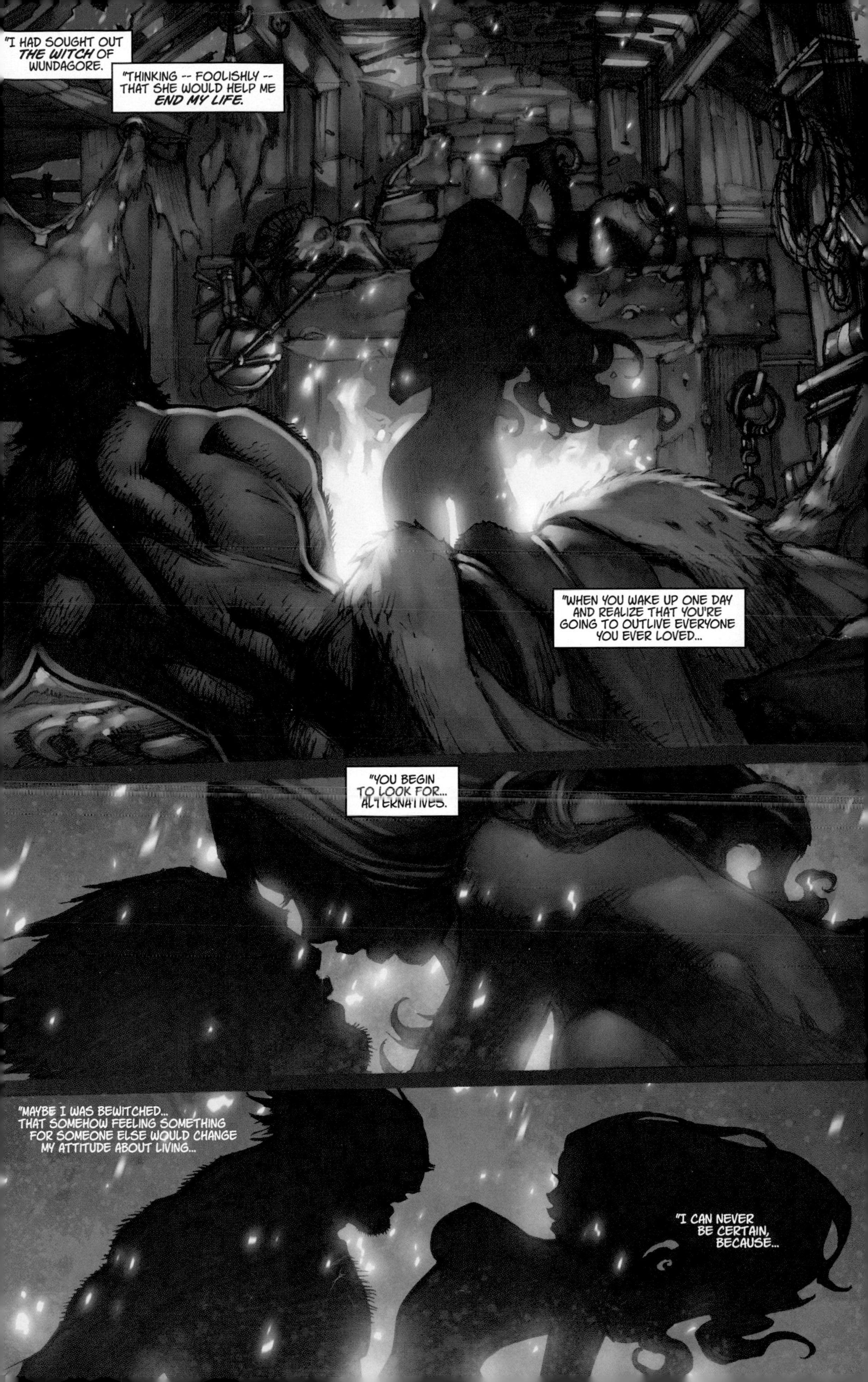
"I HAD SOUGHT OUT THE WITCH OF WUNDAGORE.
"THINKING -- FOOLISHLY -- THAT SHE WOULD HELP ME END MY LIFE.
"WHEN YOU WAKE UP ONE DAY AND REALIZE THAT YOU'RE GOING TO OUTLIVE EVERYONE YOU EVER LOVED...
"YOU BEGIN TO LOOK FOR... ALTERNATIVES.
"MAYBE I WAS BEWITCHED... THAT SOMEHOW FEELING SOMETHING FOR SOMEONE ELSE WOULD CHANGE MY ATTITUDE ABOUT LIVING...
"I CAN NEVER BE CERTAIN, BECAUSE...

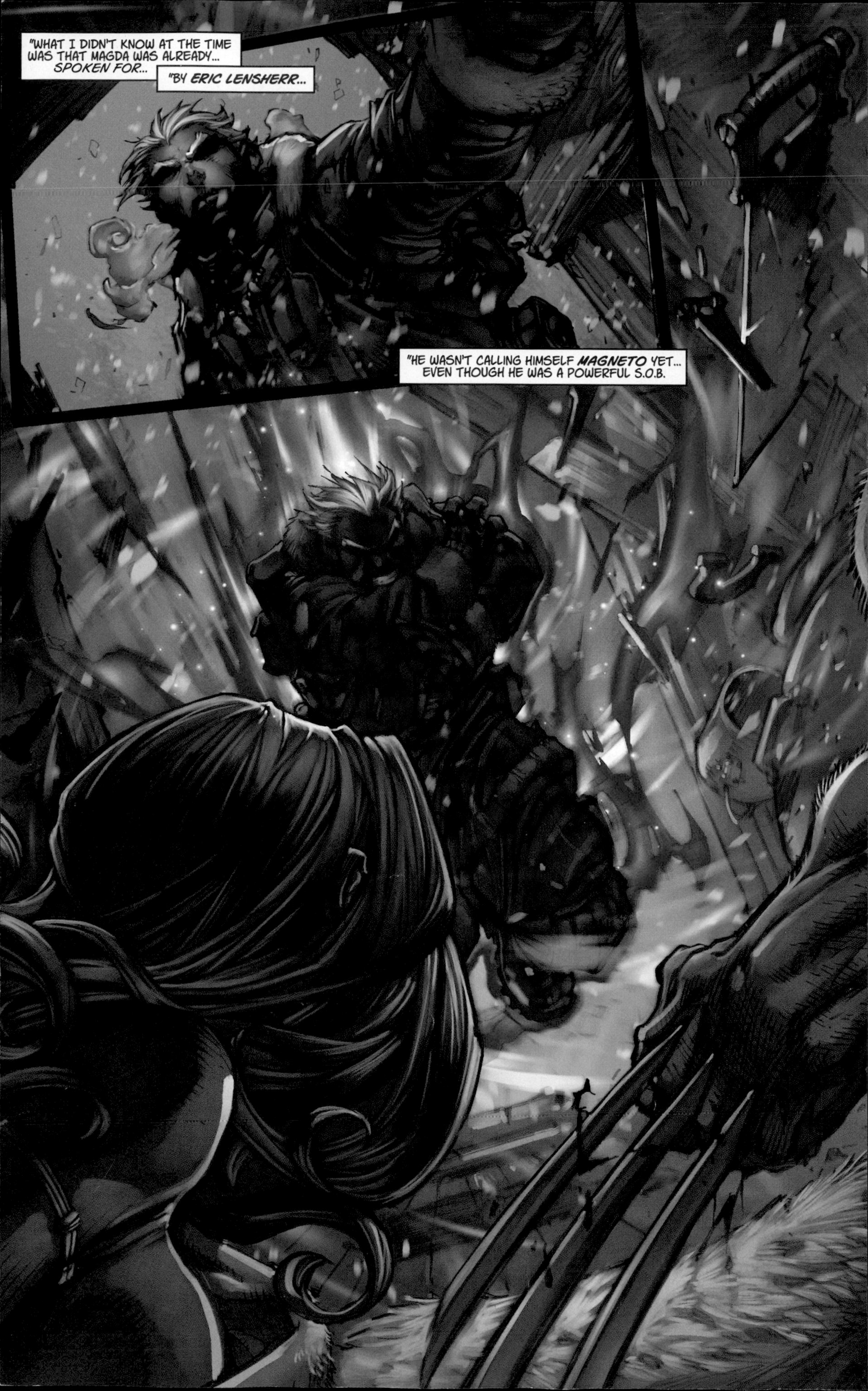
"WHAT I DIDN'T KNOW AT THE TIME WAS THAT MAGDA WAS ALREADY... SPOKEN FOR...
"BY ERIC LENSHERR...
"HE WASN'T CALLING HIMSELF MAGNETO YET... EVEN THOUGH HE WAS A POWERFUL S.O.B.

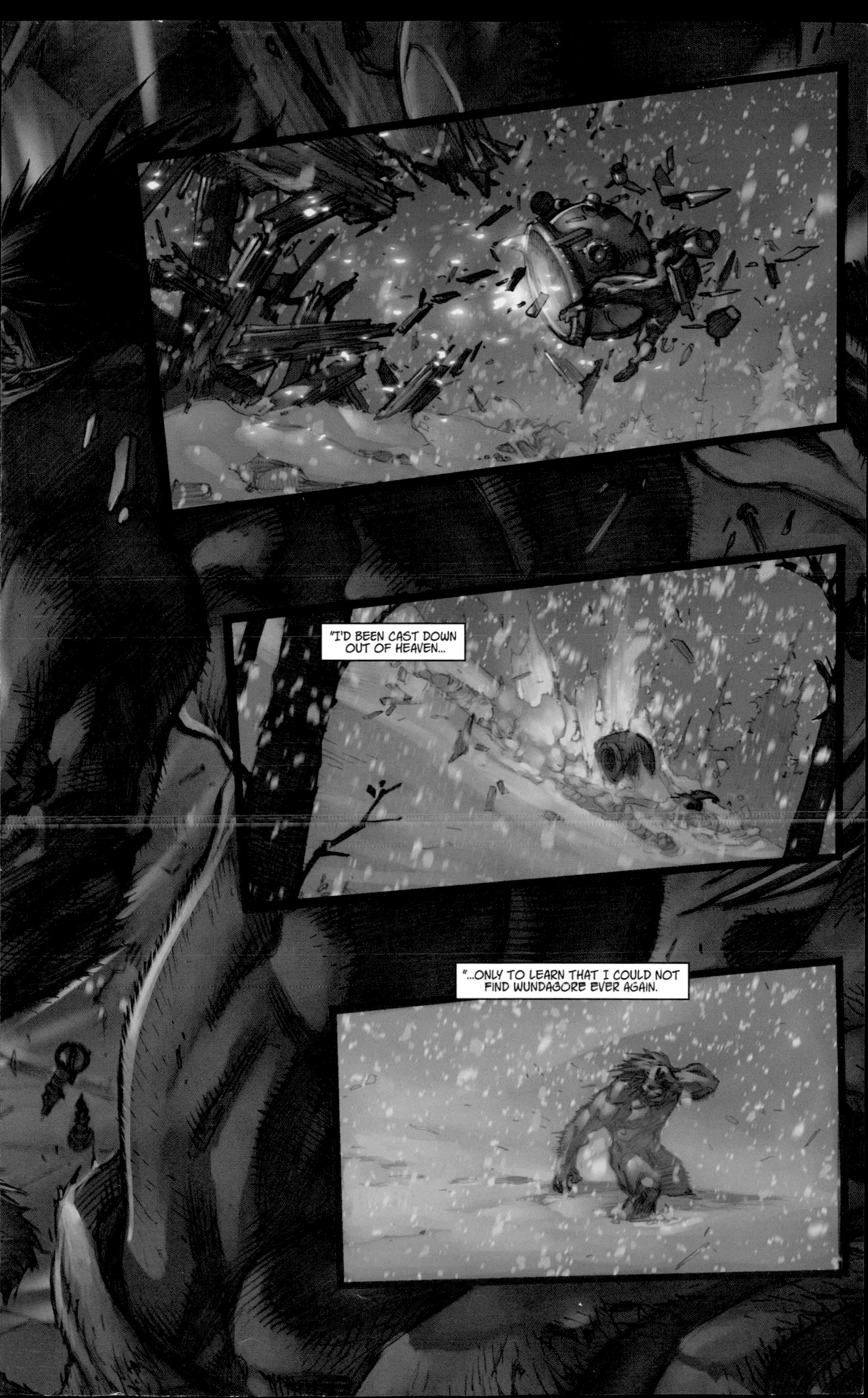
"I'D BEEN CAST DOWN OUT OF HEAVEN...
"...ONLY TO LEARN THAT I COULD NOT FIND WUNDAGORE EVER AGAIN.

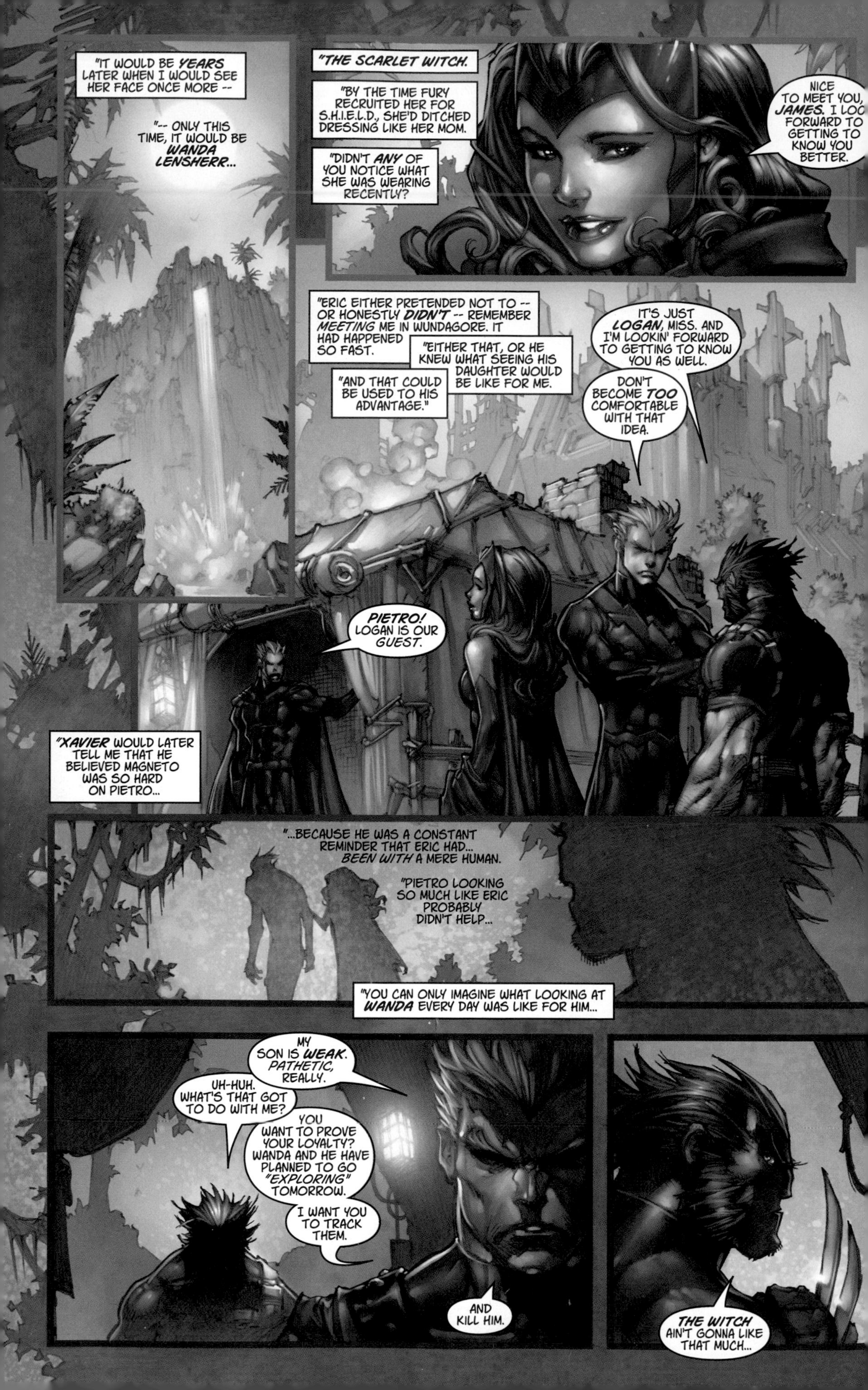
"IT WOULD BE YEARS LATER WHEN I WOULD SEE HER FACE ONCE MORE --
"-- ONLY THIS TIME, IT WOULD BE WANDA LENSHERR...
"THE SCARLET WITCH.
"BY THE TIME FURY RECRUITED HER FOR S.H.I.E.L.D., SHE'D DITCHED DRESSING LIKE HER MOM.
"DIDN'T ANY OF YOU NOTICE WHAT SHE WAS WEARING RECENTLY?
NICE TO MEET YOU, JAMES. I LOO FORWARD TO GETTING TO KNOW YOU BETTER.
"ERIC EITHER PRETENDED NOT TO -- OR HONESTLY DIDN'T -- REMEMBER MEETING ME IN WUNDAGORE. IT HAD HAPPENED SO FAST.
"EITHER THAT, OR HE KNEW WHAT SEEING HIS DAUGHTER WOULD BE LIKE FOR ME.
"AND THAT COULD BE USED TO HIS ADVANTAGE."
IT'S JUST LOGAN, MISS. AND I'M LOOKIN' FORWARD TO GETTING TO KNOW YOU AS WELL.
DON'T BECOME TOO COMFORTABLE WITH THAT IDEA.
PIETRO! LOGAN IS OUR GUEST.
"XAVIER WOULD LATER TELL ME THAT HE BELIEVED MAGNETO WAS SO HARD ON PIETRO...
"...BECAUSE HE WAS A CONSTANT REMINDER THAT ERIC HAD... BEEN WITH A MERE HUMAN.
"PIETRO LOOKING SO MUCH LIKE ERIC PROBABLY DIDN'T HELP...
"YOU CAN ONLY IMAGINE WHAT LOOKING AT WANDA EVERY DAY WAS LIKE FOR HIM...
MY SON IS WEAK. PATHETIC, REALLY.
UH-HUH. WHAT'S THAT GOT TO DO WITH ME?
YOU WANT TO PROVE YOUR LOYALTY? WANDA AND HE HAVE PLANNED TO GO "EXPLORING" TOMORROW.
I WANT YOU TO TRACK THEM.
AND KILL HIM.
THE WITCH AIN'T GONNA LIKE THAT MUCH...

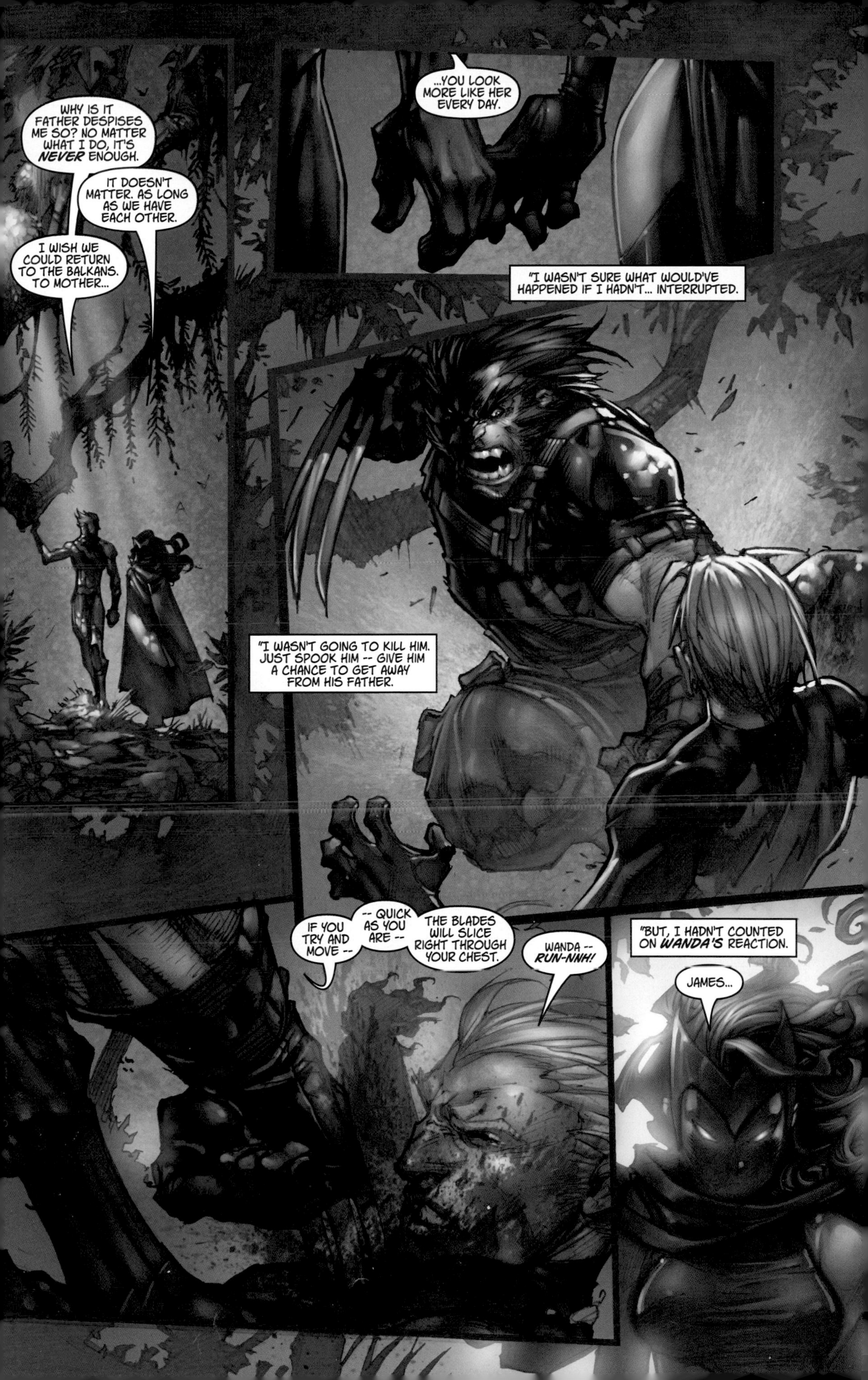

WHY IS IT FATHER DESPISES ME SO? NO MATTER WHAT I DO, IT'S *NEVER* ENOUGH.
IT DOESN'T MATTER. AS LONG AS WE HAVE EACH OTHER.
I WISH WE COULD RETURN TO THE BALKANS. TO MOTHER...
...YOU LOOK MORE LIKE HER EVERY DAY.
"I WASN'T SURE WHAT WOULD'VE HAPPENED IF I HADN'T... INTERRUPTED.
"I WASN'T GOING TO KILL HIM. JUST SPOOK HIM -- GIVE HIM A CHANCE TO GET AWAY FROM HIS FATHER.
IF YOU TRY AND MOVE --
-- QUICK AS YOU ARE --
THE BLADES WILL SLICE RIGHT THROUGH YOUR CHEST.
WANDA -- *RUN-NNH!*
"BUT, I HADN'T COUNTED ON *WANDA'S* REACTION.
JAMES...

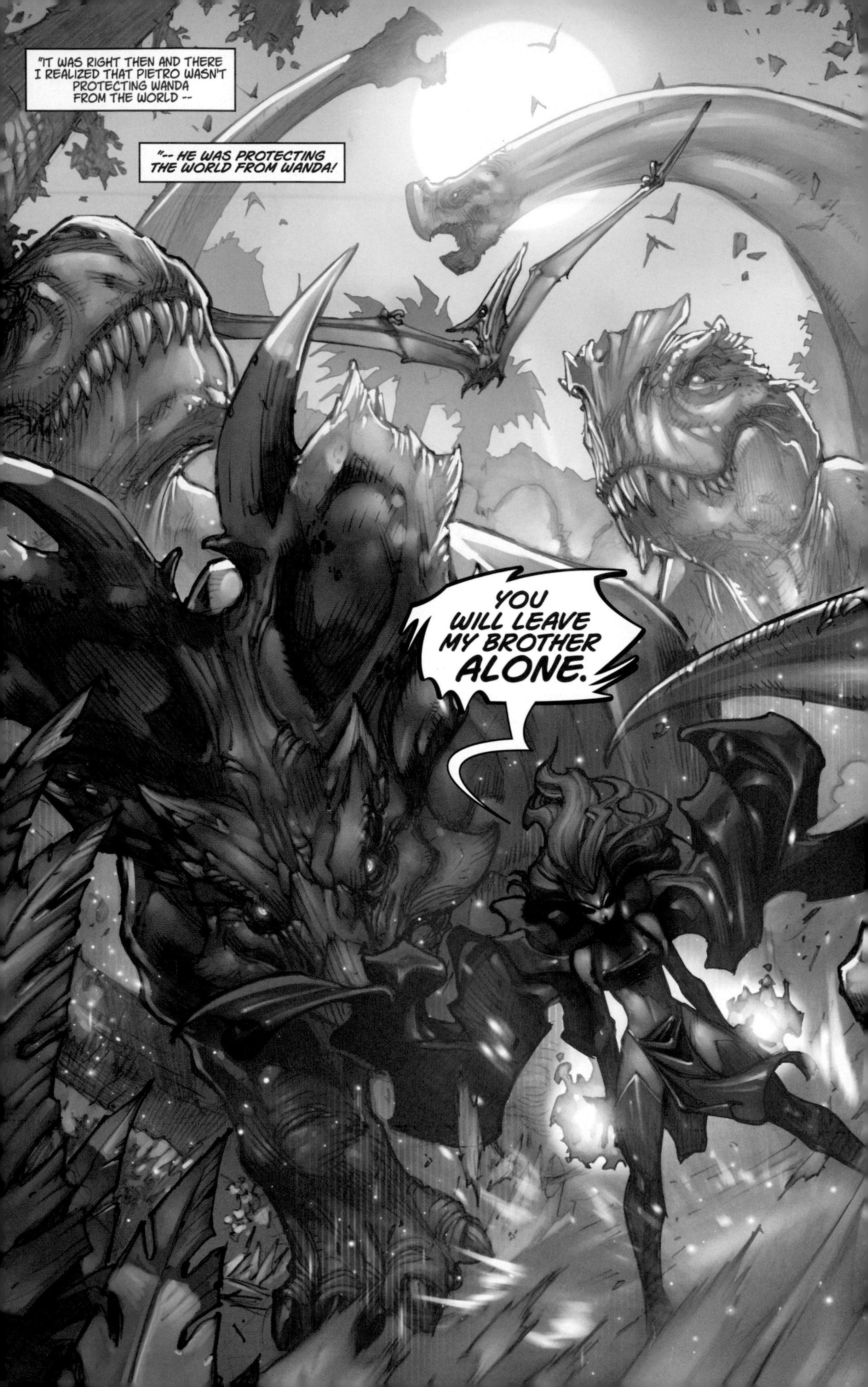
"IT WAS RIGHT THEN AND THERE I REALIZED THAT PIETRO WASN'T PROTECTING WANDA FROM THE WORLD --
"-- HE WAS PROTECTING THE WORLD FROM WANDA!
YOU WILL LEAVE MY BROTHER ALONE.

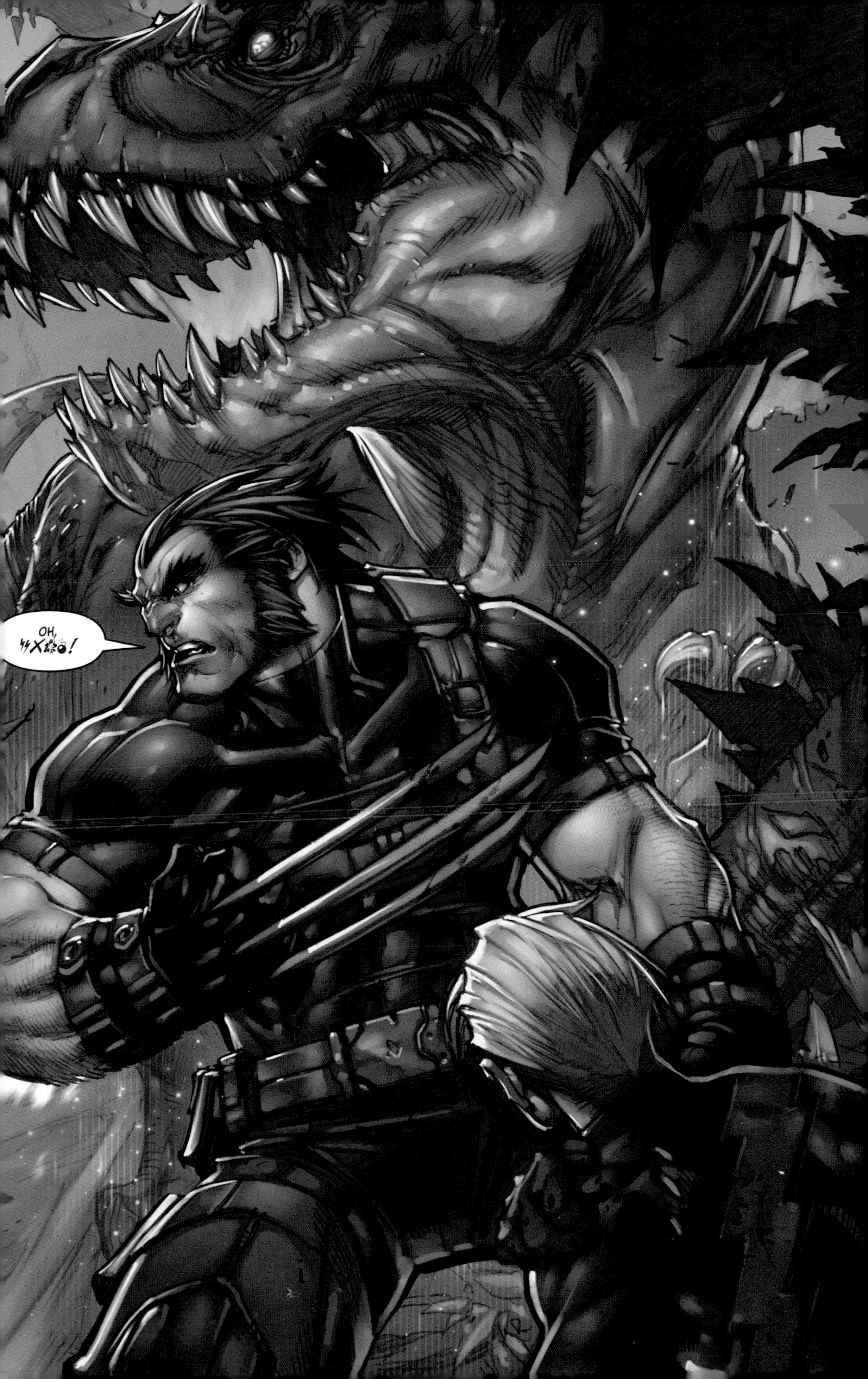
OH, ϟϟX✿♁!

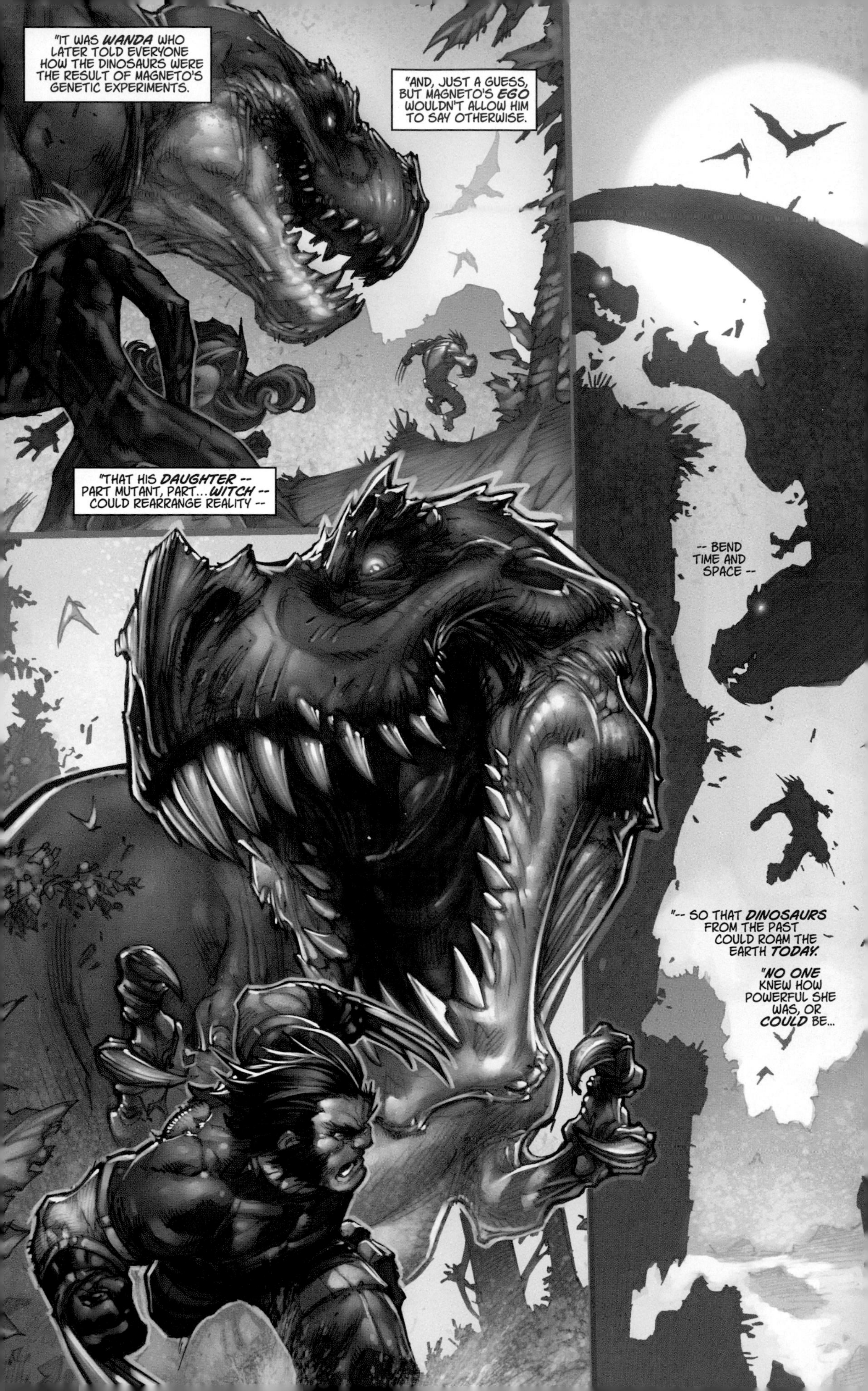
"IT WAS *WANDA* WHO LATER TOLD EVERYONE HOW THE DINOSAURS WERE THE RESULT OF MAGNETO'S GENETIC EXPERIMENTS.
"AND, JUST A GUESS, BUT MAGNETO'S *EGO* WOULDN'T ALLOW HIM TO SAY OTHERWISE.
"THAT HIS *DAUGHTER* -- PART MUTANT, PART... *WITCH* -- COULD REARRANGE REALITY --
-- BEND TIME AND SPACE --
"-- SO THAT *DINOSAURS* FROM THE PAST COULD ROAM THE EARTH *TODAY.*
"*NO ONE* KNEW HOW POWERFUL SHE WAS, OR *COULD* BE...

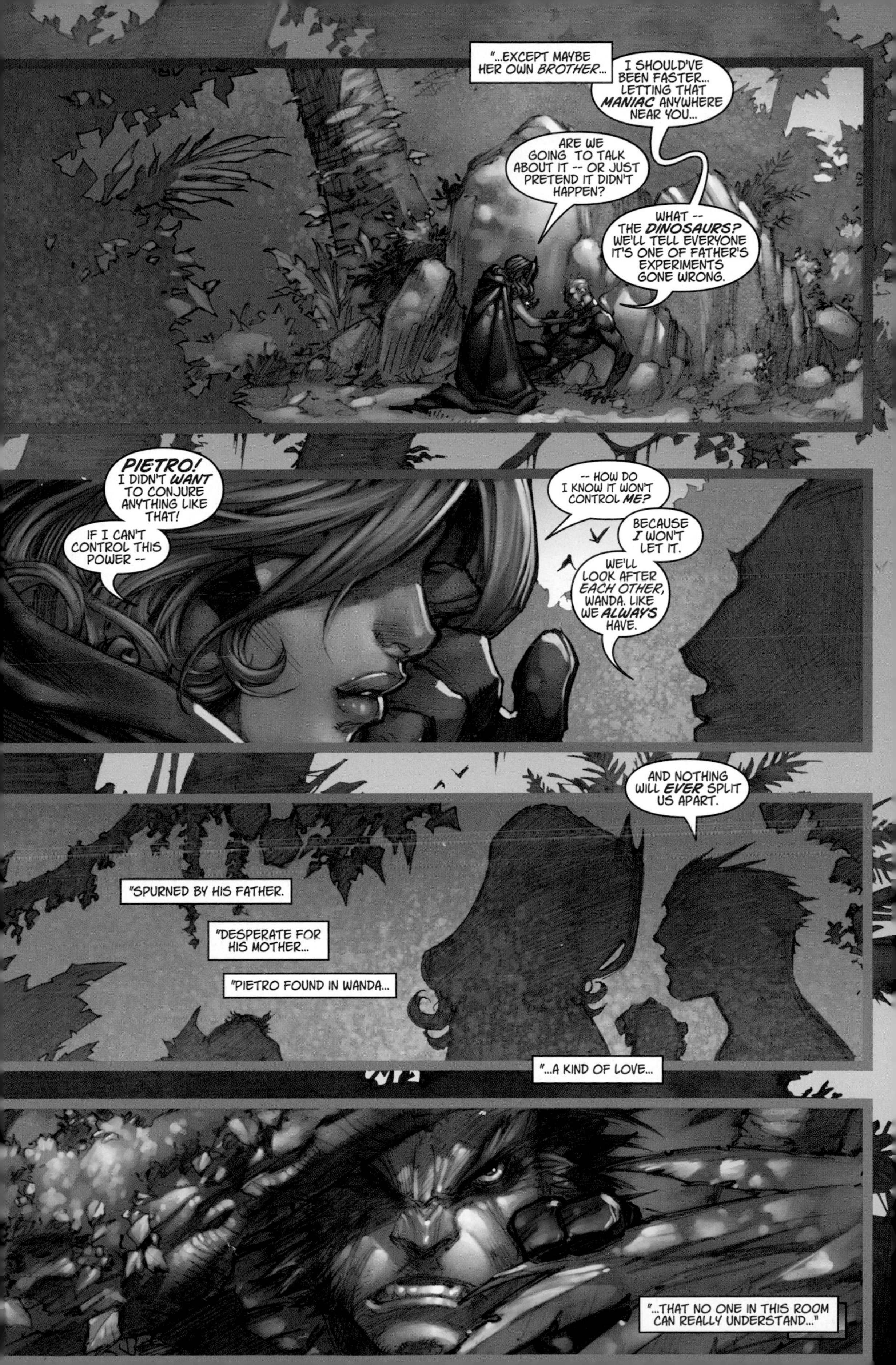
"...EXCEPT MAYBE HER OWN BROTHER...
I SHOULD'VE BEEN FASTER... LETTING THAT MANIAC ANYWHERE NEAR YOU...
ARE WE GOING TO TALK ABOUT IT -- OR JUST PRETEND IT DIDN'T HAPPEN?
WHAT -- THE DINOSAURS? WE'LL TELL EVERYONE IT'S ONE OF FATHER'S EXPERIMENTS GONE WRONG.
PIETRO! I DIDN'T WANT TO CONJURE ANYTHING LIKE THAT!
IF I CAN'T CONTROL THIS POWER --
-- HOW DO I KNOW IT WON'T CONTROL ME?
BECAUSE I WON'T LET IT.
WE'LL LOOK AFTER EACH OTHER, WANDA. LIKE WE ALWAYS HAVE.
AND NOTHING WILL EVER SPLIT US APART.
"SPURNED BY HIS FATHER.
"DESPERATE FOR HIS MOTHER...
"PIETRO FOUND IN WANDA...
"...A KIND OF LOVE...
"...THAT NO ONE IN THIS ROOM CAN REALLY UNDERSTAND..."

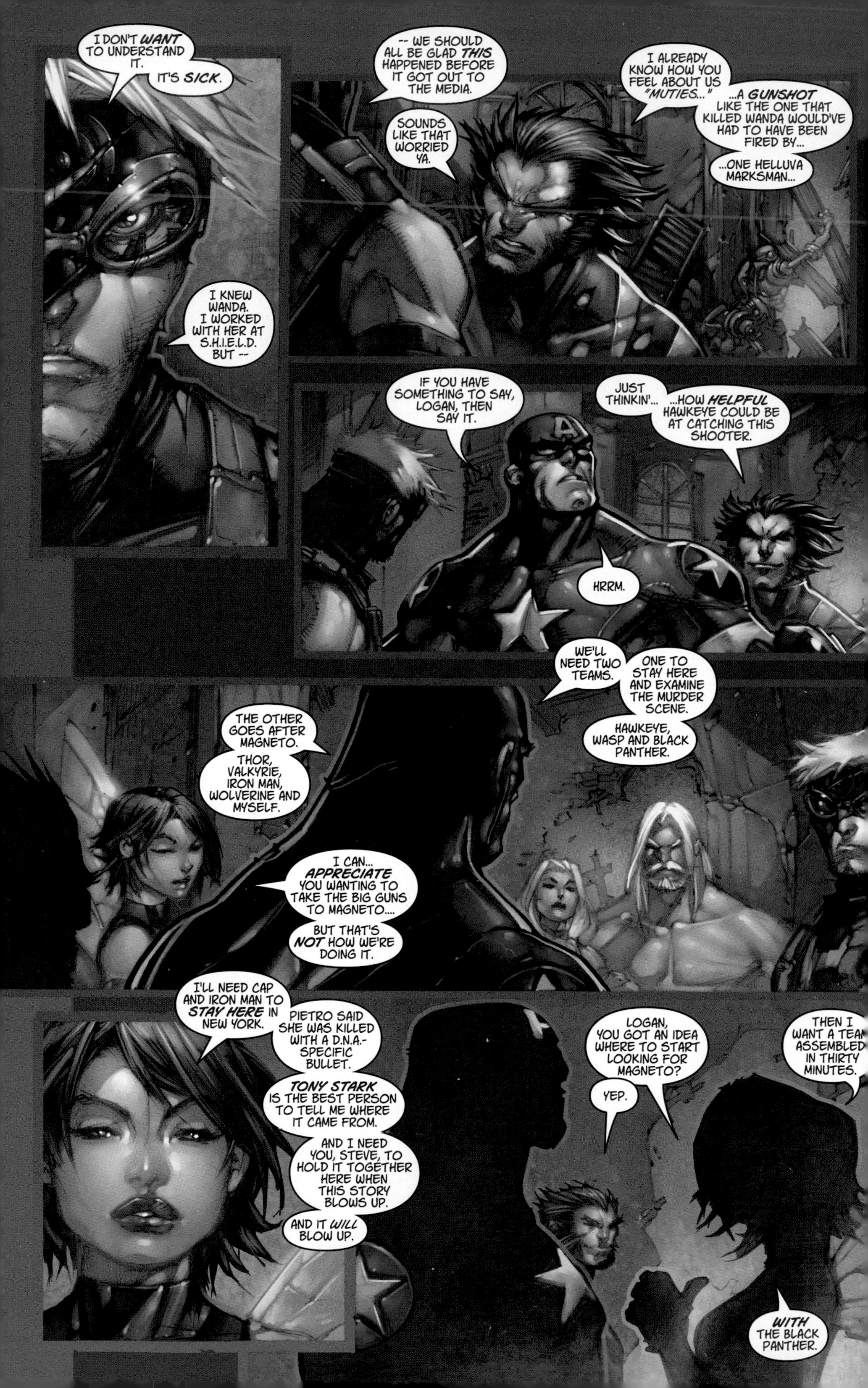

I DON'T WANT TO UNDERSTAND IT.
IT'S SICK.
-- WE SHOULD ALL BE GLAD THIS HAPPENED BEFORE IT GOT OUT TO THE MEDIA.
SOUNDS LIKE THAT WORRIED YA.
I ALREADY KNOW HOW YOU FEEL ABOUT US "MUTIES..."
...A GUNSHOT LIKE THE ONE THAT KILLED WANDA WOULD'VE HAD TO HAVE BEEN FIRED BY...
...ONE HELLUVA MARKSMAN...
I KNEW WANDA. I WORKED WITH HER AT S.H.I.E.L.D. BUT --
IF YOU HAVE SOMETHING TO SAY, LOGAN, THEN SAY IT.
JUST THINKIN'...
...HOW HELPFUL HAWKEYE COULD BE AT CATCHING THIS SHOOTER.
HRRM.
WE'LL NEED TWO TEAMS.
ONE TO STAY HERE AND EXAMINE THE MURDER SCENE.
HAWKEYE, WASP AND BLACK PANTHER.
THE OTHER GOES AFTER MAGNETO.
THOR, VALKYRIE, IRON MAN, WOLVERINE AND MYSELF.
I CAN... APPRECIATE YOU WANTING TO TAKE THE BIG GUNS TO MAGNETO....
BUT THAT'S NOT HOW WE'RE DOING IT.
I'LL NEED CAP AND IRON MAN TO STAY HERE IN NEW YORK.
PIETRO SAID SHE WAS KILLED WITH A D.N.A.-SPECIFIC BULLET.
TONY STARK IS THE BEST PERSON TO TELL ME WHERE IT CAME FROM.
AND I NEED YOU, STEVE, TO HOLD IT TOGETHER HERE WHEN THIS STORY BLOWS UP.
AND IT WILL BLOW UP.
LOGAN, YOU GOT AN IDEA WHERE TO START LOOKING FOR MAGNETO?
YEP.
THEN I WANT A TEAM ASSEMBLED IN THIRTY MINUTES.
WITH THE BLACK PANTHER.

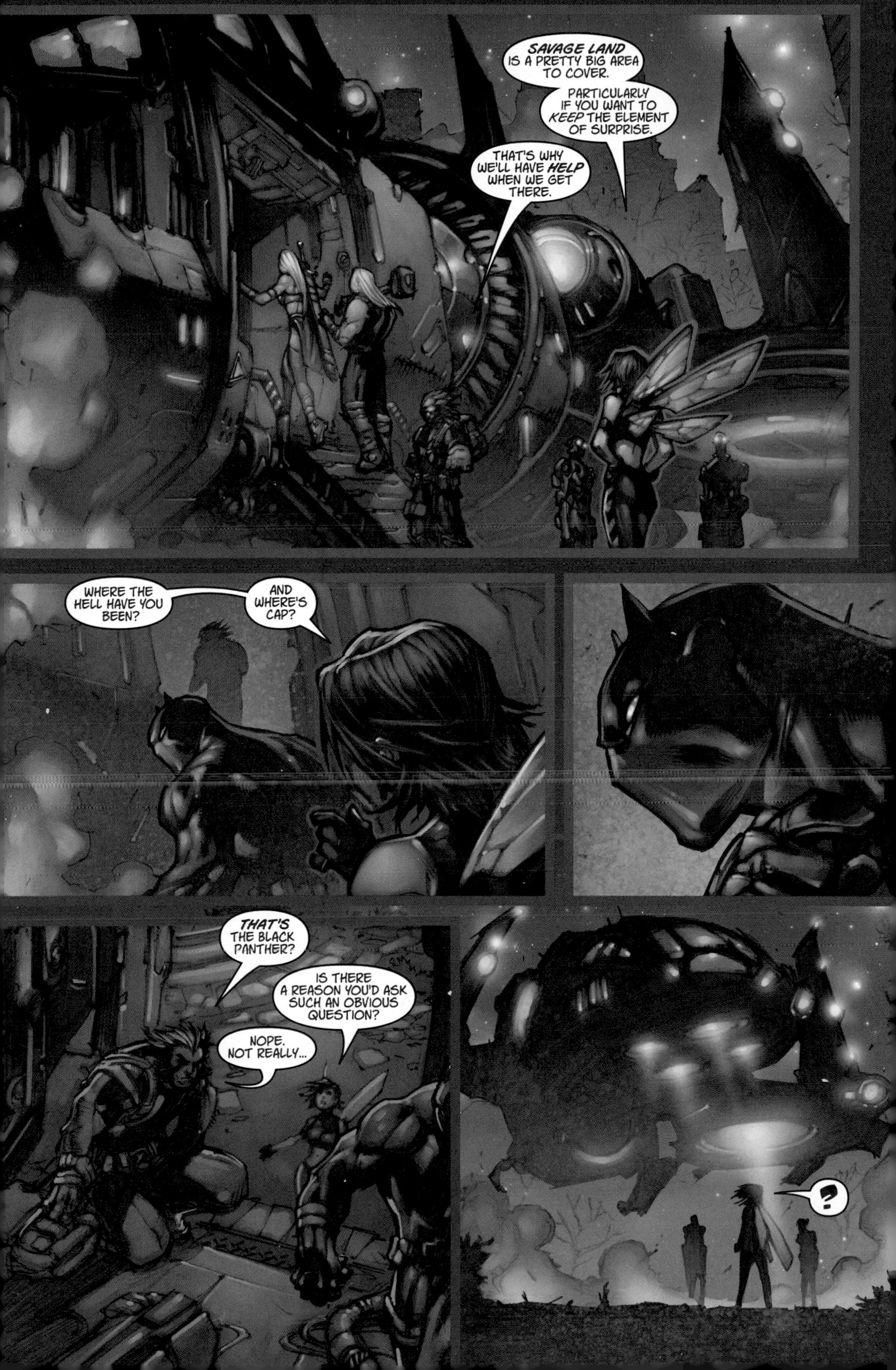
SAVAGE LAND IS A PRETTY BIG AREA TO COVER.
PARTICULARLY IF YOU WANT TO KEEP THE ELEMENT OF SURPRISE.
THAT'S WHY WE'LL HAVE HELP WHEN WE GET THERE.
WHERE THE HELL HAVE YOU BEEN?
AND WHERE'S CAP?
THAT'S THE BLACK PANTHER?
IS THERE A REASON YOU'D ASK SUCH AN OBVIOUS QUESTION?
NOPE. NOT REALLY...
?

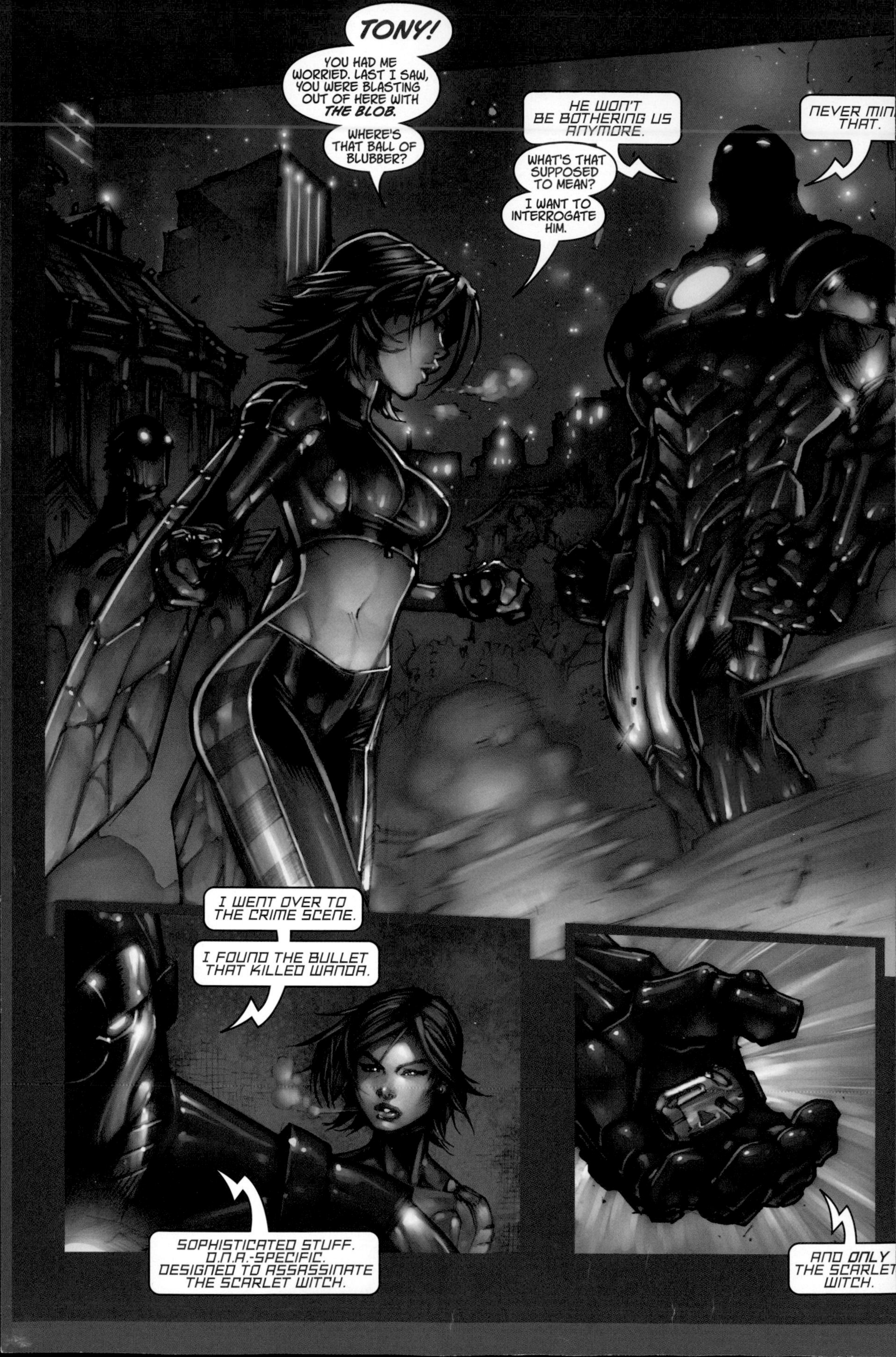

TONY!
YOU HAD ME WORRIED. LAST I SAW, YOU WERE BLASTING OUT OF HERE WITH THE BLOB.
WHERE'S THAT BALL OF BLUBBER?
HE WON'T BE BOTHERING US ANYMORE.
WHAT'S THAT SUPPOSED TO MEAN?
I WANT TO INTERROGATE HIM.
NEVER MIN THAT.
I WENT OVER TO THE CRIME SCENE.
I FOUND THE BULLET THAT KILLED WANDA.
SOPHISTICATED STUFF. D.N.A.-SPECIFIC. DESIGNED TO ASSASSINATE THE SCARLET WITCH.
AND ONLY THE SCARLET WITCH.

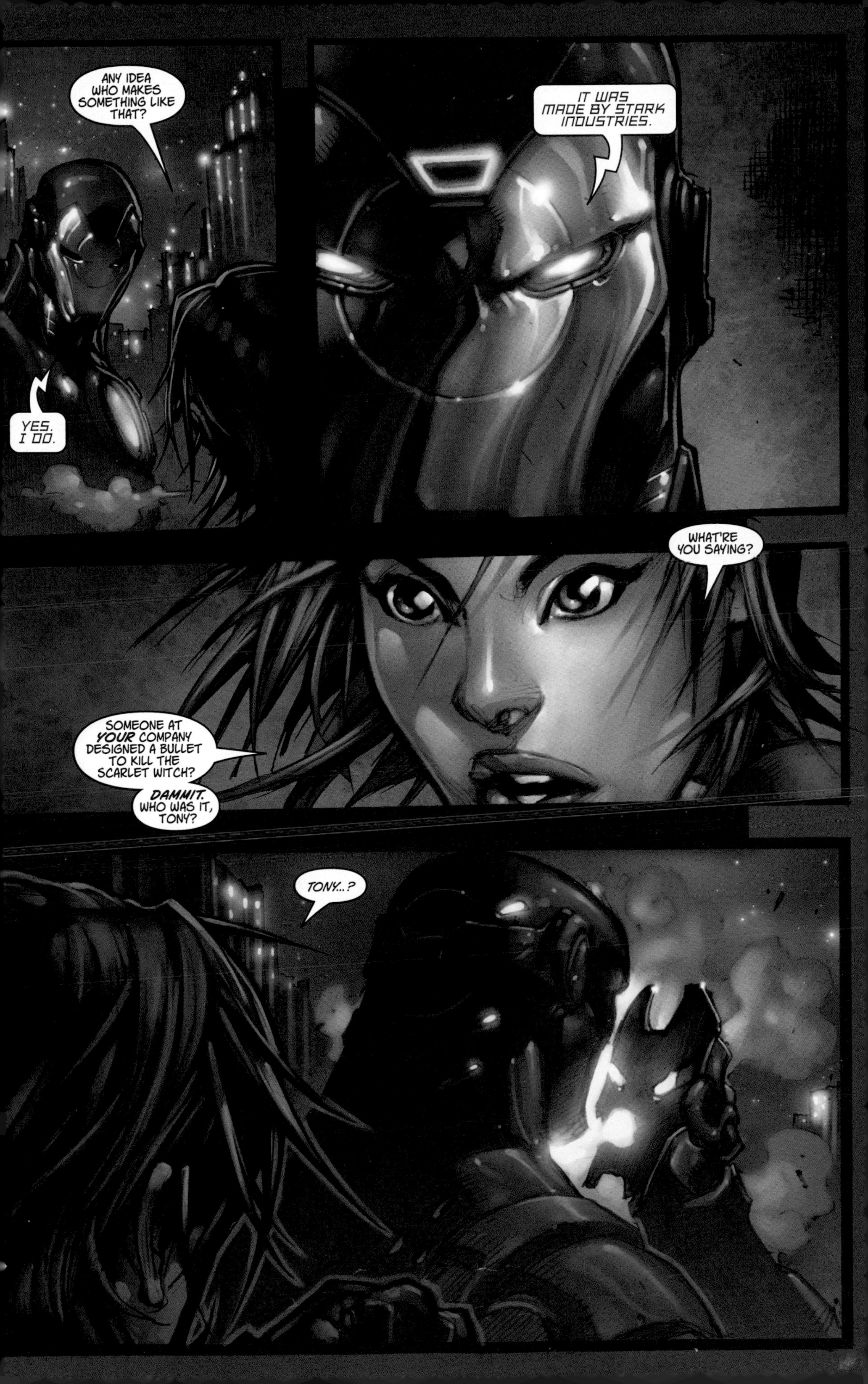
ANY IDEA WHO MAKES SOMETHING LIKE THAT?
YES. I DO.
IT WAS MADE BY STARK INDUSTRIES.
WHAT'RE YOU SAYING?
SOMEONE AT YOUR COMPANY DESIGNED A BULLET TO KILL THE SCARLET WITCH?
DAMMIT. WHO WAS IT, TONY?
TONY...?

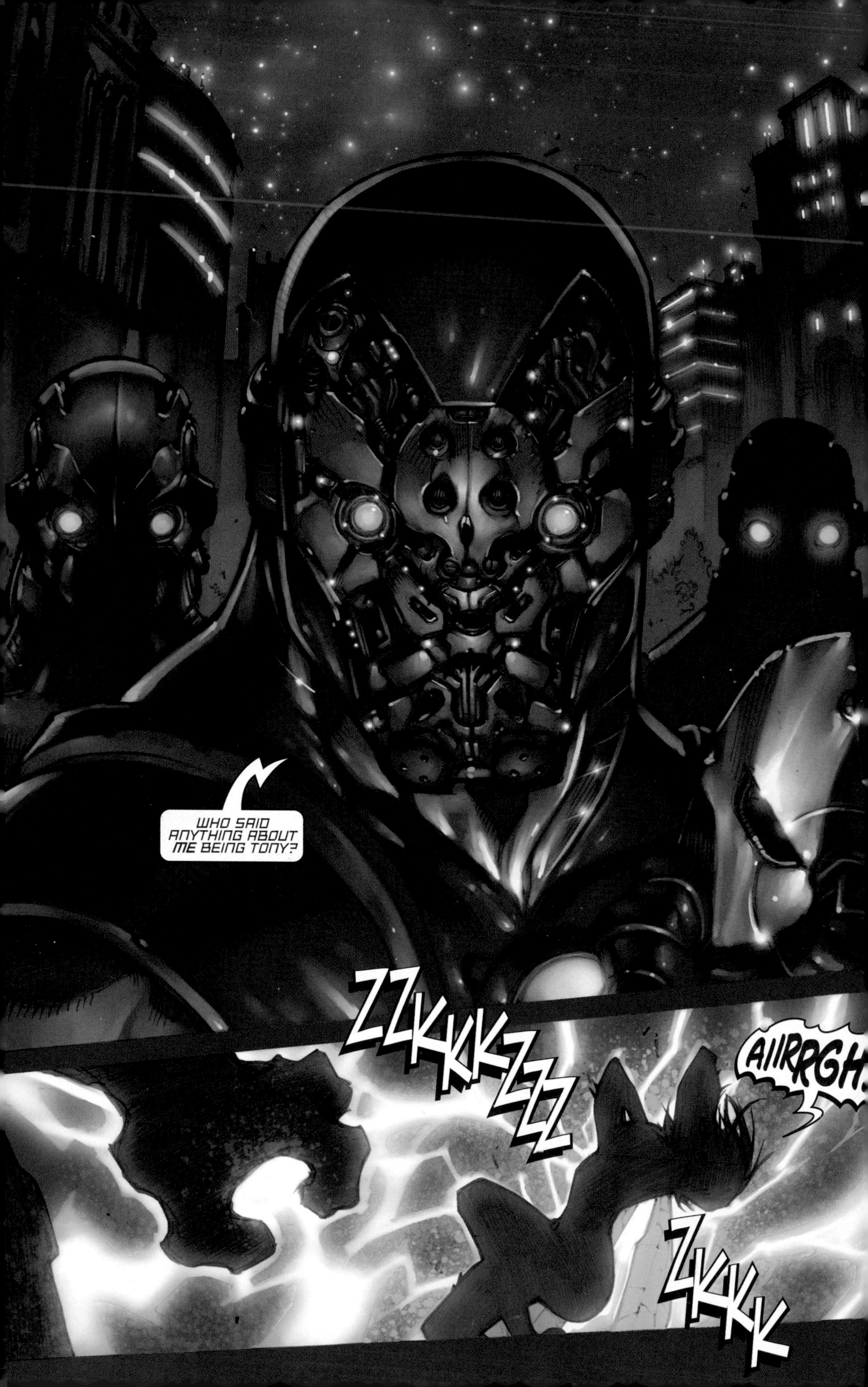
WHO SAID ANYTHING ABOUT ME BEING TONY?
ZZKKKZZZZ
AIIRRGH!
ZKKKK

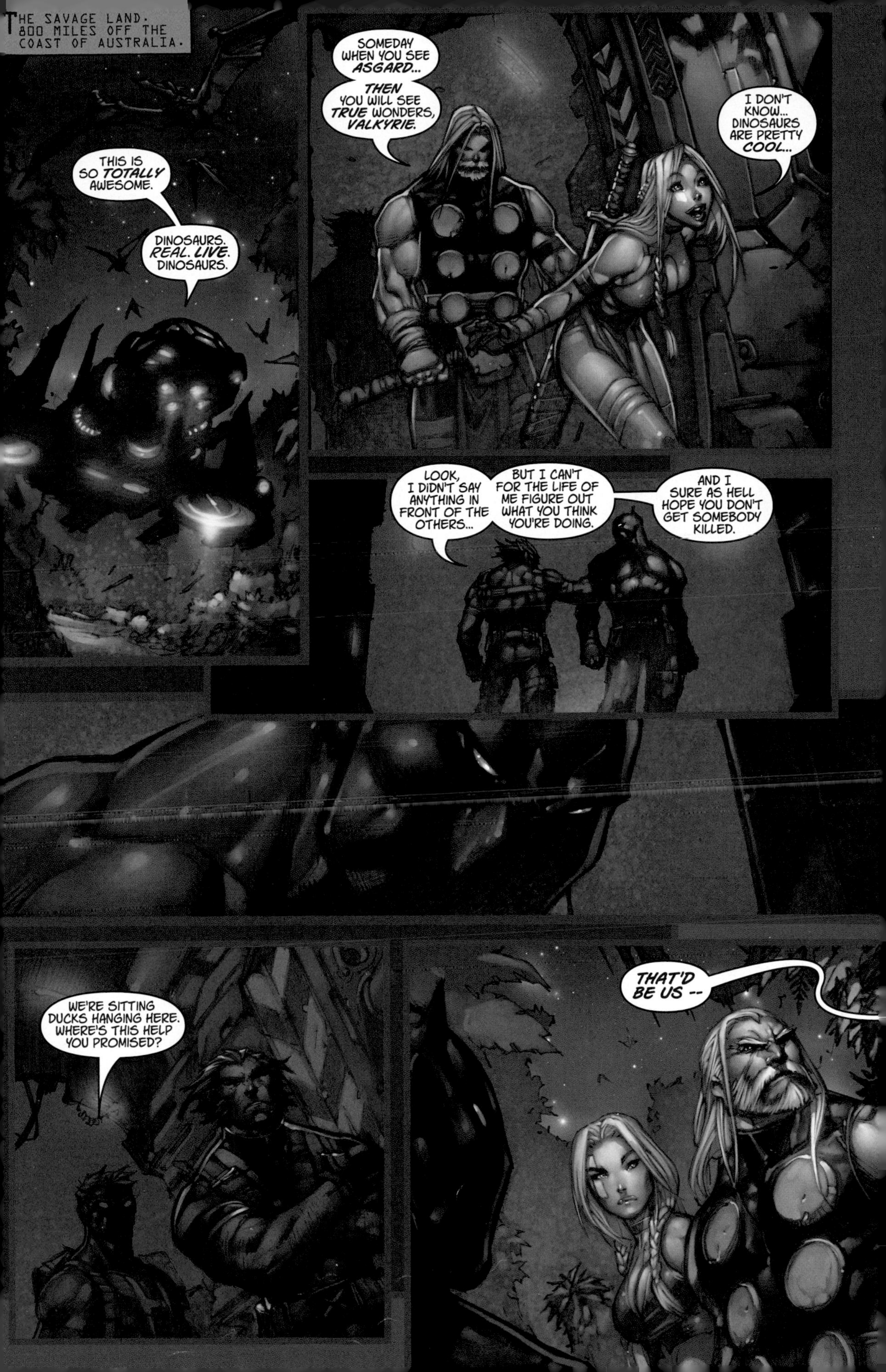
THE SAVAGE LAND. 800 MILES OFF THE COAST OF AUSTRALIA.
THIS IS SO TOTALLY AWESOME.
DINOSAURS. REAL. LIVE. DINOSAURS.
SOMEDAY WHEN YOU SEE ASGARD...
THEN YOU WILL SEE TRUE WONDERS, VALKYRIE.
I DON'T KNOW... DINOSAURS ARE PRETTY COOL...
LOOK, I DIDN'T SAY ANYTHING IN FRONT OF THE OTHERS...
BUT I CAN'T FOR THE LIFE OF ME FIGURE OUT WHAT YOU THINK YOU'RE DOING.
AND I SURE AS HELL HOPE YOU DON'T GET SOMEBODY KILLED.
WE'RE SITTING DUCKS HANGING HERE. WHERE'S THIS HELP YOU PROMISED?
THAT'D BE US --

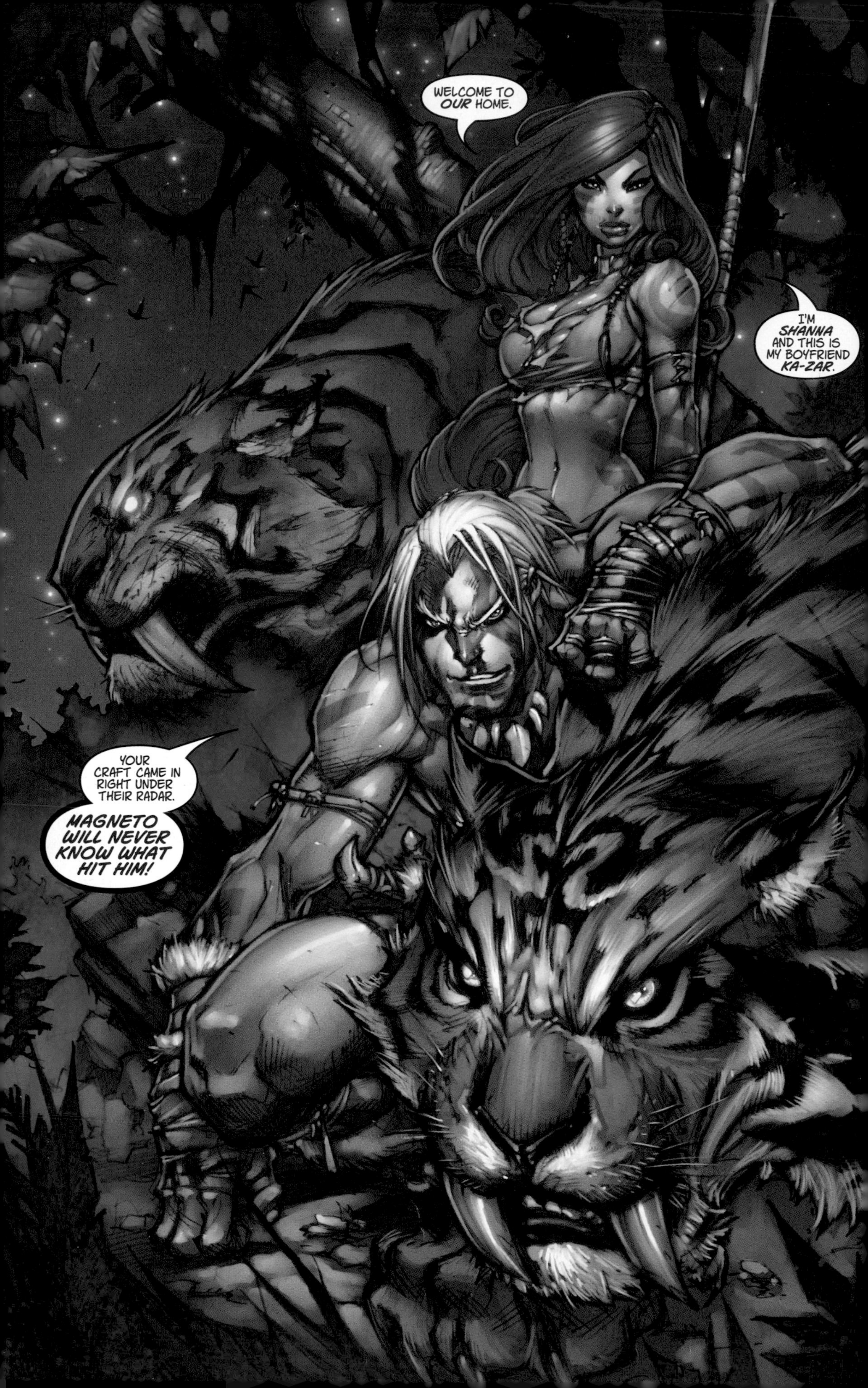
WELCOME TO OUR HOME.
I'M SHANNA AND THIS IS MY BOYFRIEND KA-ZAR.
YOUR CRAFT CAME IN RIGHT UNDER THEIR RADAR.
MAGNETO WILL NEVER KNOW WHAT HIT HIM!

FOUR

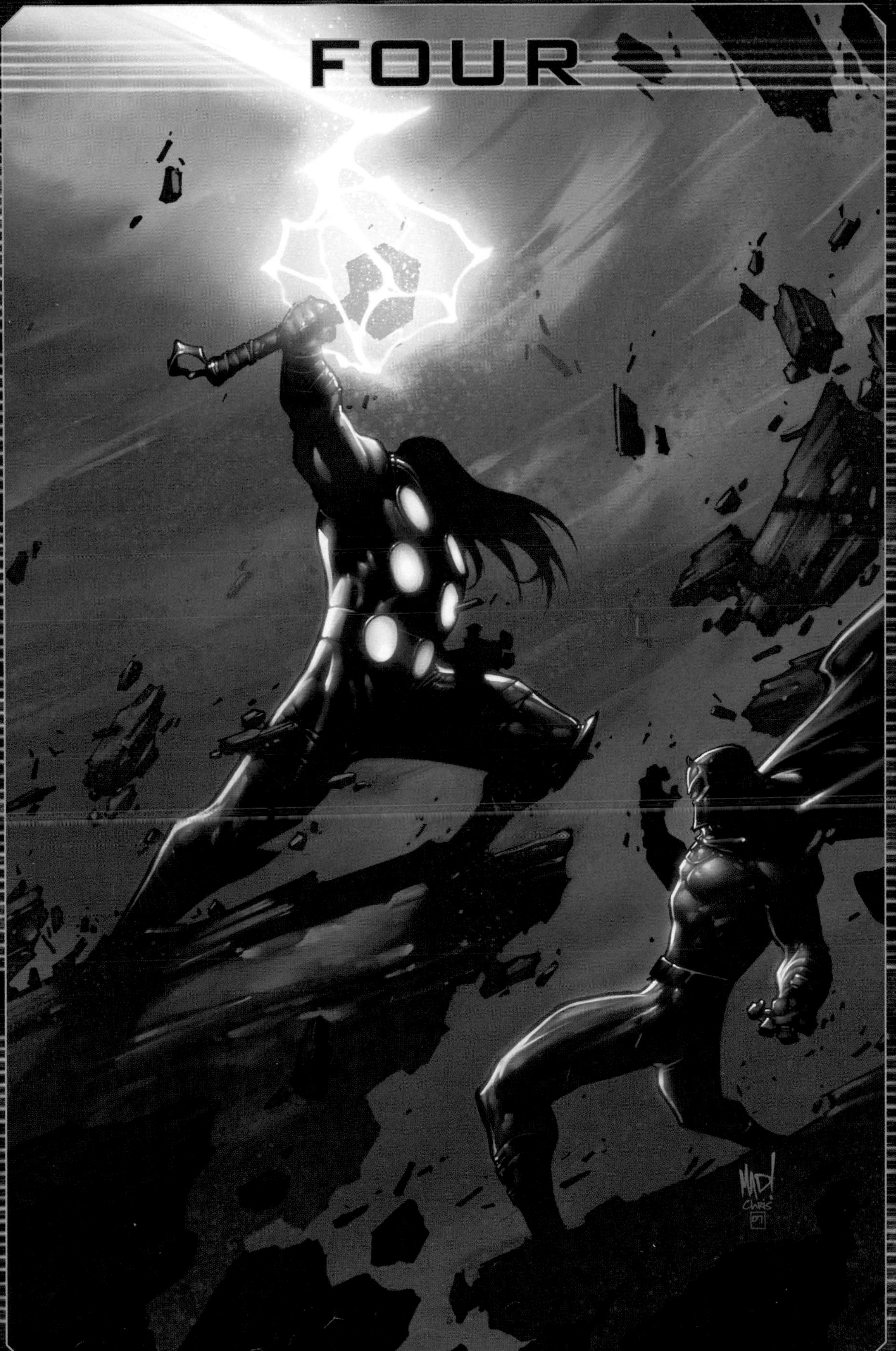

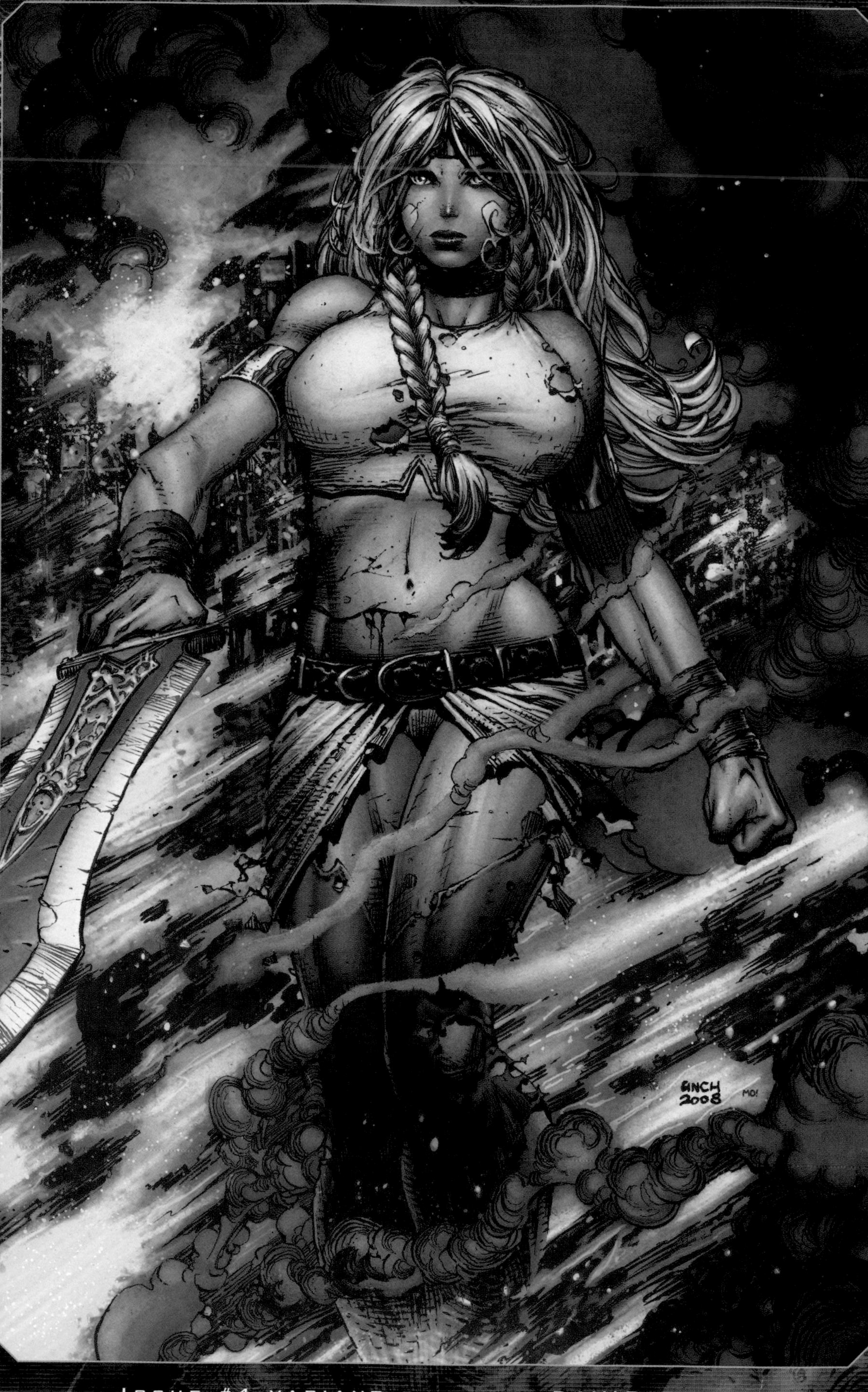

ISSUE #4 VARIANT COVER BY DAVID FINCH

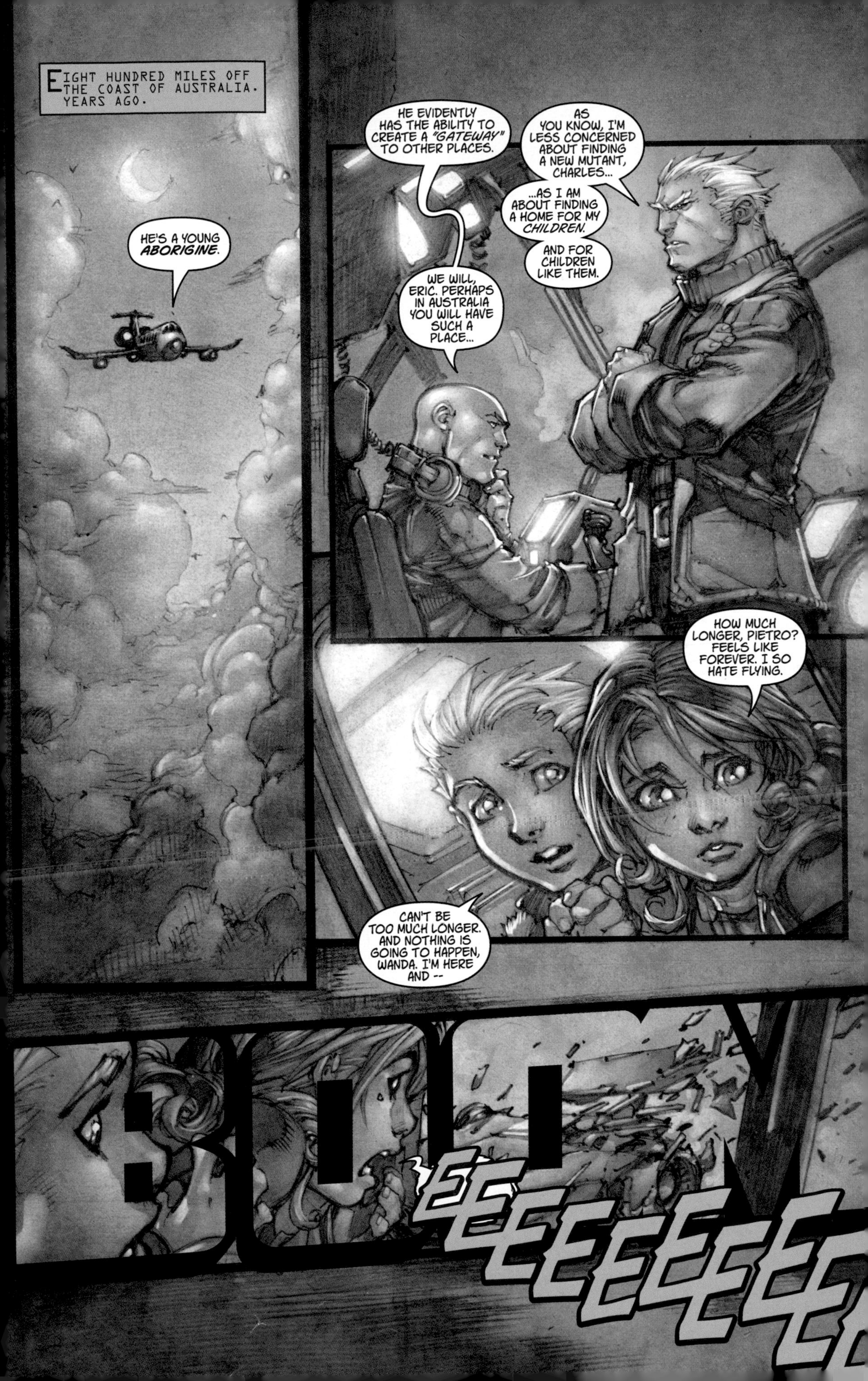
EIGHT HUNDRED MILES OFF THE COAST OF AUSTRALIA. YEARS AGO.
HE'S A YOUNG ABORIGINE.
HE EVIDENTLY HAS THE ABILITY TO CREATE A "GATEWAY" TO OTHER PLACES.
AS YOU KNOW, I'M LESS CONCERNED ABOUT FINDING A NEW MUTANT, CHARLES...
...AS I AM ABOUT FINDING A HOME FOR MY CHILDREN.
AND FOR CHILDREN LIKE THEM.
WE WILL, ERIC. PERHAPS IN AUSTRALIA YOU WILL HAVE SUCH A PLACE...
HOW MUCH LONGER, PIETRO? FEELS LIKE FOREVER. I SO HATE FLYING.
CAN'T BE TOO MUCH LONGER. AND NOTHING IS GOING TO HAPPEN, WANDA. I'M HERE AND --

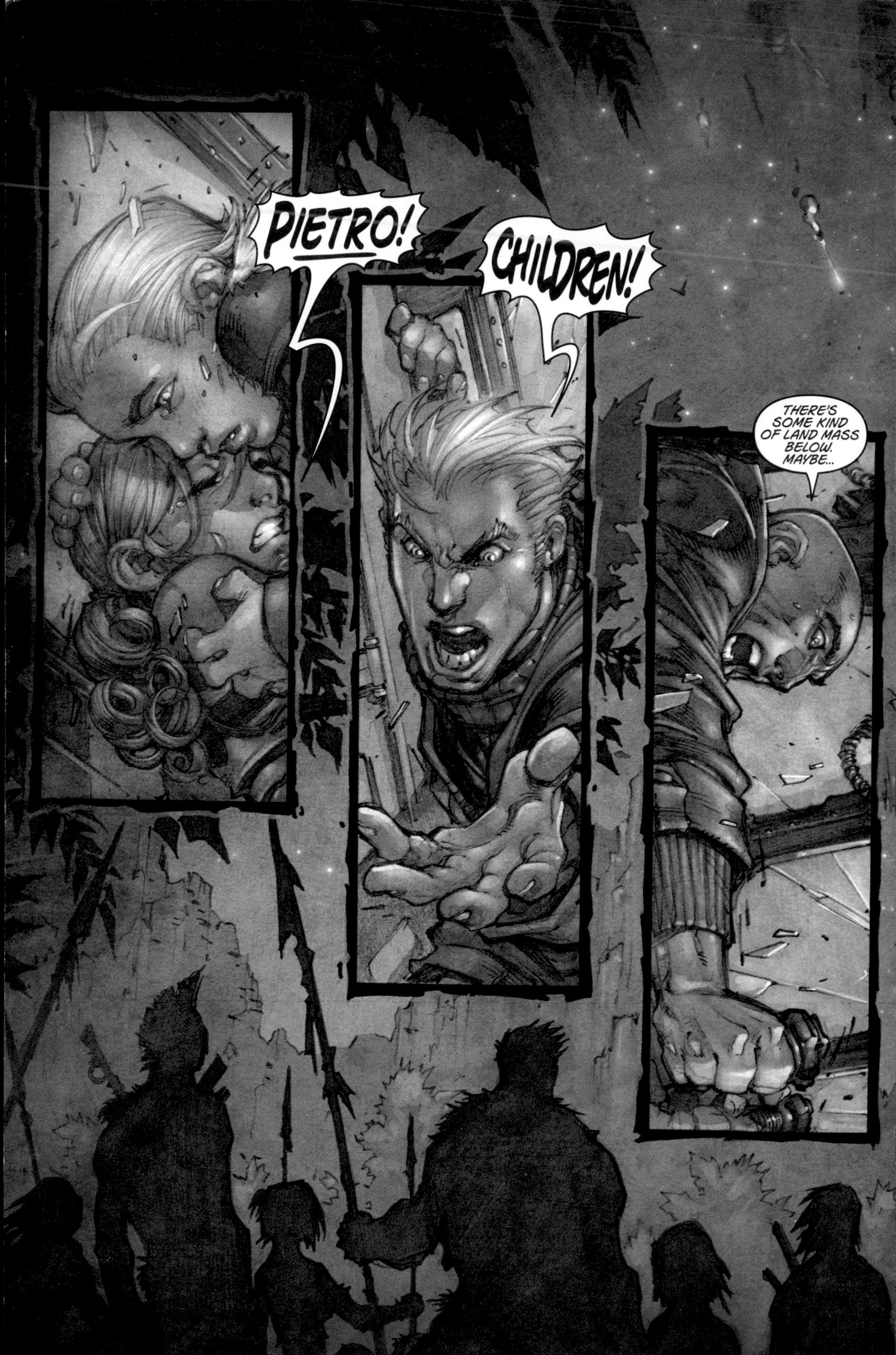
PIETRO!
CHILDREN!
THERE'S SOME KIND OF LAND MASS BELOW. MAYBE...

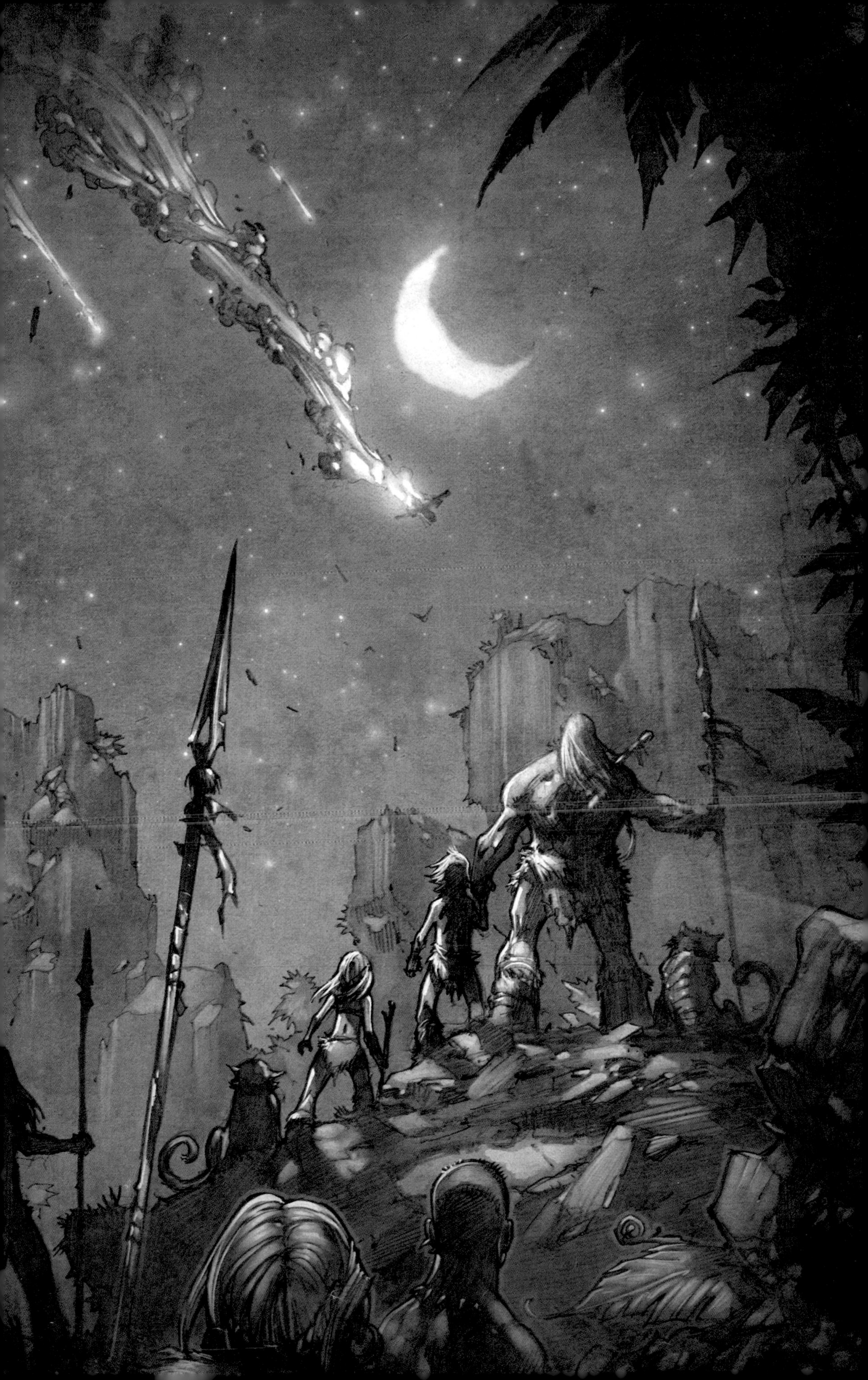

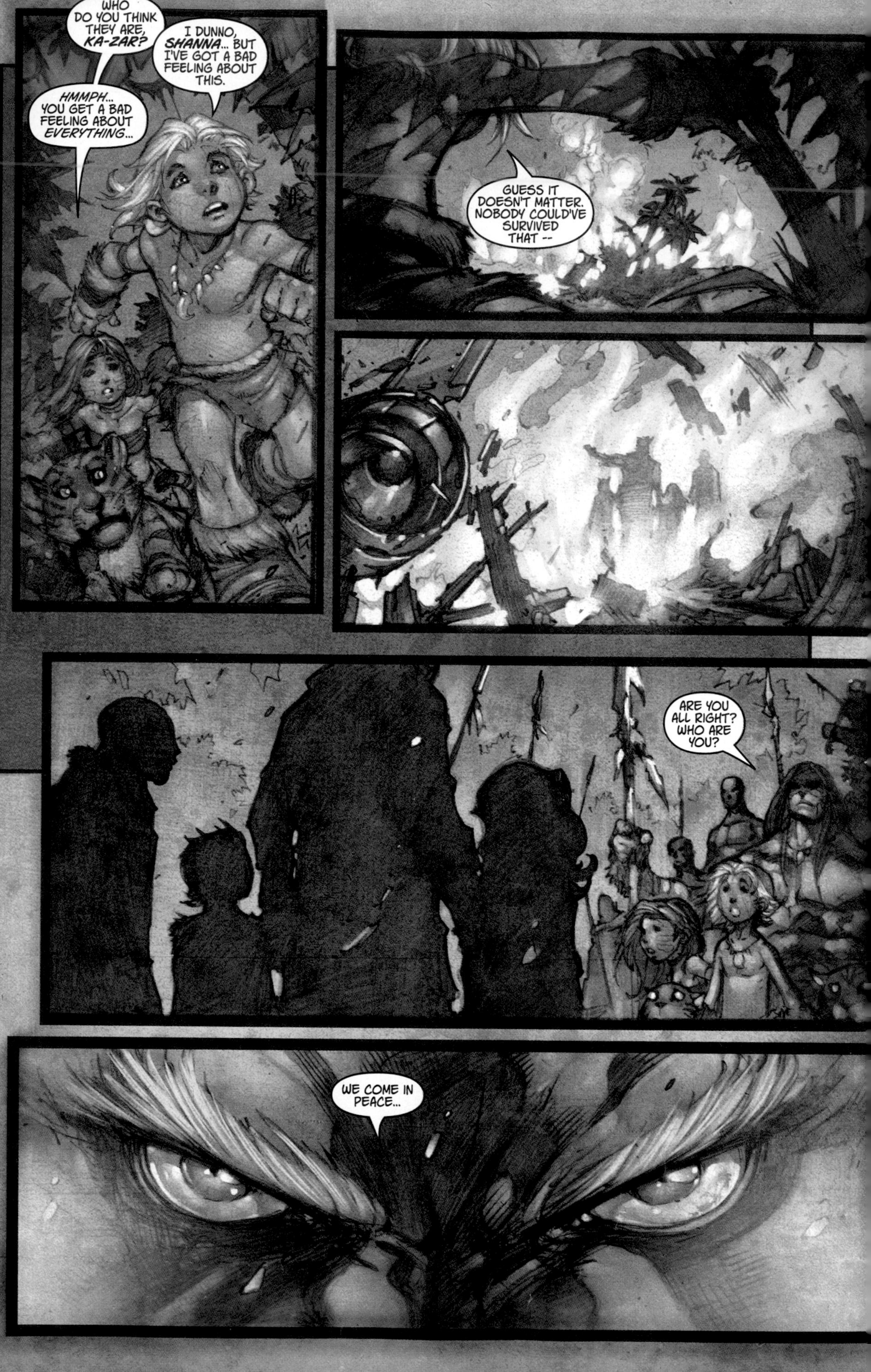

WHO DO YOU THINK THEY ARE, *KA-ZAR?*
I DUNNO, *SHANNA*... BUT I'VE GOT A BAD FEELING ABOUT THIS.
HMMPH... YOU GET A BAD FEELING ABOUT *EVERYTHING*...
GUESS IT DOESN'T MATTER. NOBODY COULD'VE SURVIVED THAT --
ARE YOU ALL RIGHT? WHO ARE YOU?
WE COME IN PEACE...

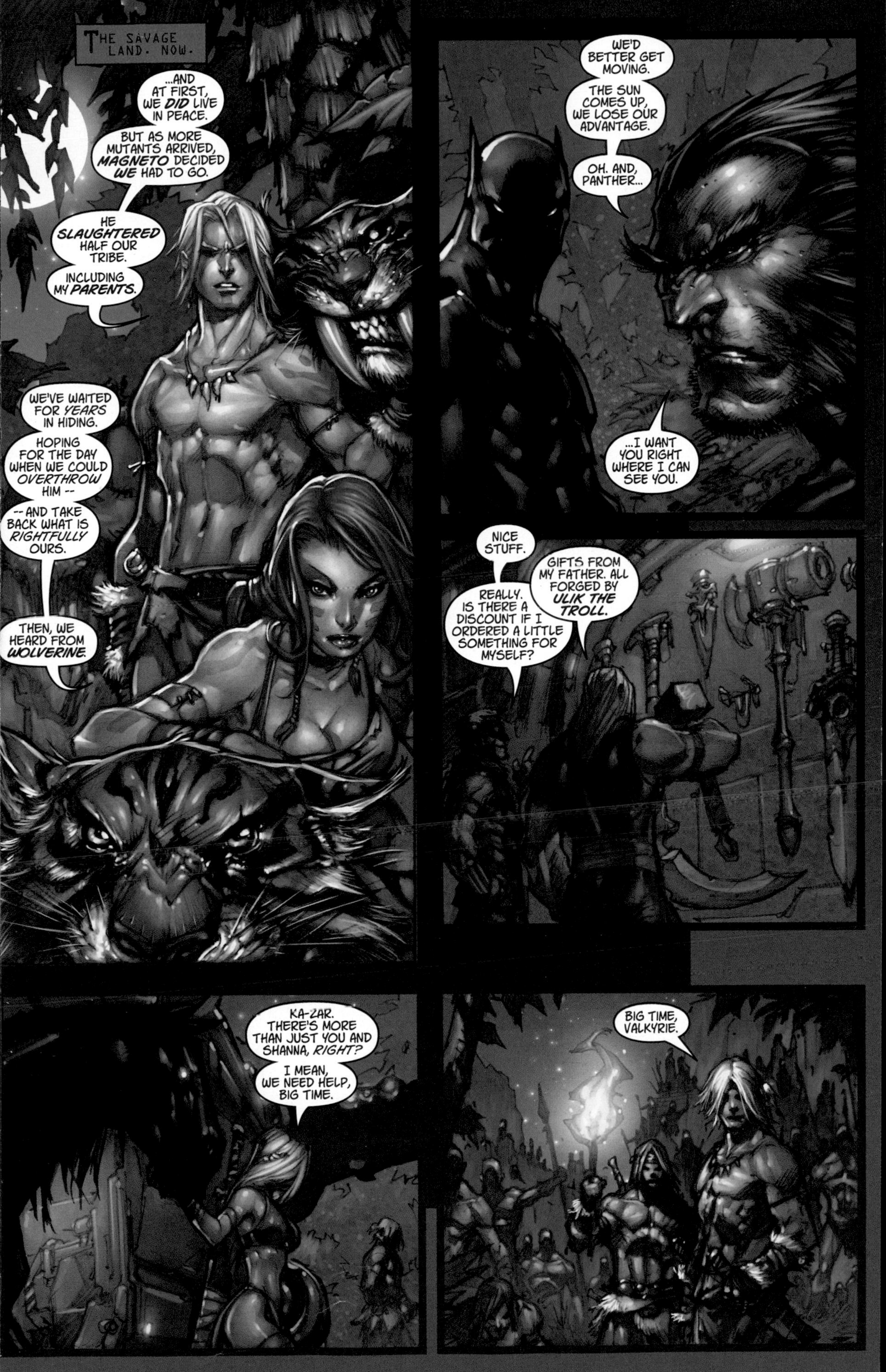
THE SAVAGE LAND. NOW.
...AND AT FIRST, WE DID LIVE IN PEACE.
BUT AS MORE MUTANTS ARRIVED, MAGNETO DECIDED WE HAD TO GO.
HE SLAUGHTERED HALF OUR TRIBE.
INCLUDING MY PARENTS.
WE'VE WAITED FOR YEARS IN HIDING.
HOPING FOR THE DAY WHEN WE COULD OVERTHROW HIM --
-- AND TAKE BACK WHAT IS RIGHTFULLY OURS.
THEN, WE HEARD FROM WOLVERINE.
WE'D BETTER GET MOVING.
THE SUN COMES UP, WE LOSE OUR ADVANTAGE.
OH. AND, PANTHER...
...I WANT YOU RIGHT WHERE I CAN SEE YOU.
NICE STUFF.
GIFTS FROM MY FATHER. ALL FORGED BY ULIK THE TROLL.
REALLY. IS THERE A DISCOUNT IF I ORDERED A LITTLE SOMETHING FOR MYSELF?
KA-ZAR. THERE'S MORE THAN JUST YOU AND SHANNA, RIGHT?
I MEAN, WE NEED HELP, BIG TIME.
BIG TIME, VALKYRIE.

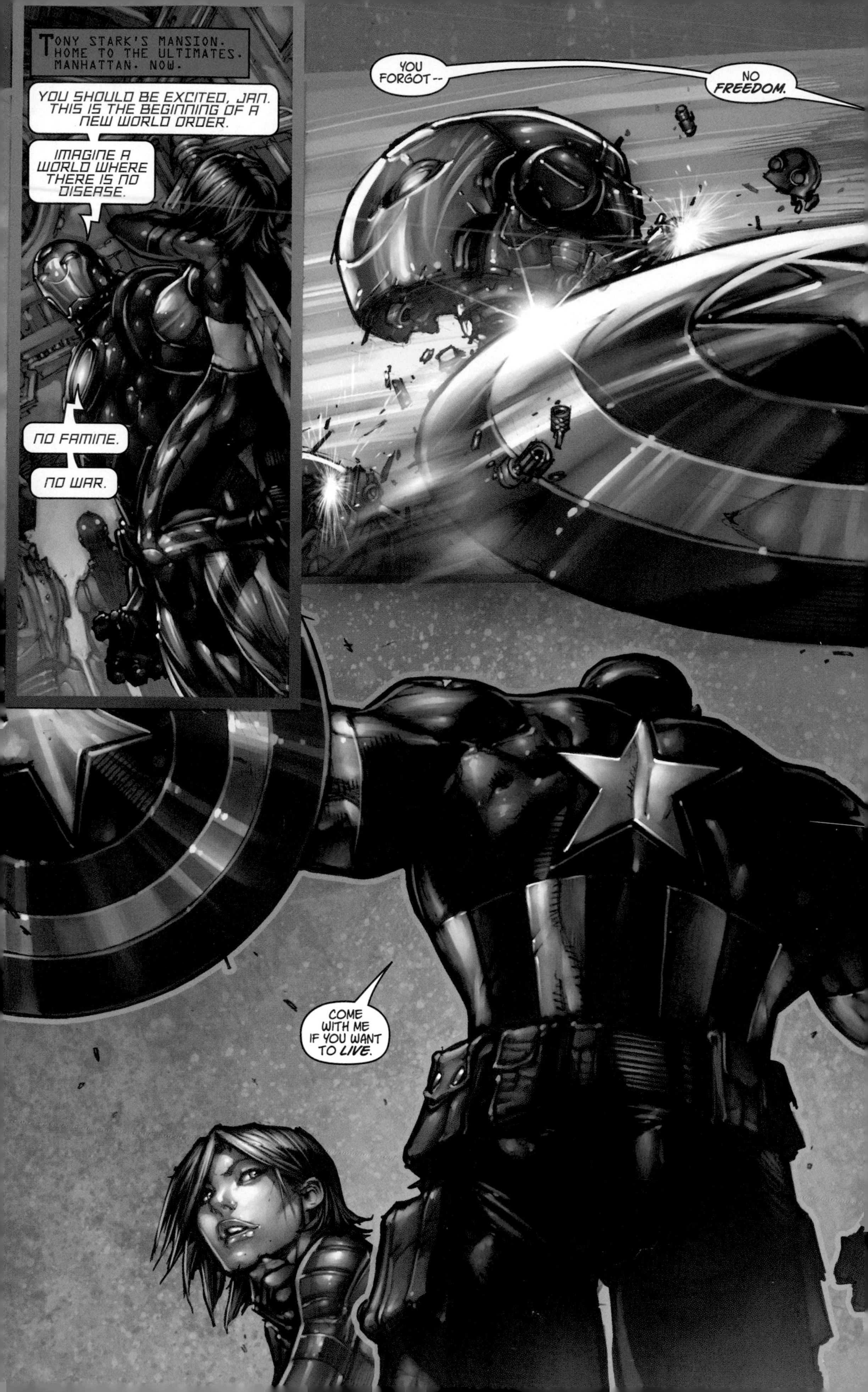
TONY STARK'S MANSION. HOME TO THE ULTIMATES. MANHATTAN. NOW.
YOU SHOULD BE EXCITED, JAN. THIS IS THE BEGINNING OF A NEW WORLD ORDER.
IMAGINE A WORLD WHERE THERE IS NO DISEASE.
NO FAMINE.
NO WAR.
YOU FORGOT --
NO FREEDOM.
COME WITH ME IF YOU WANT TO LIVE.

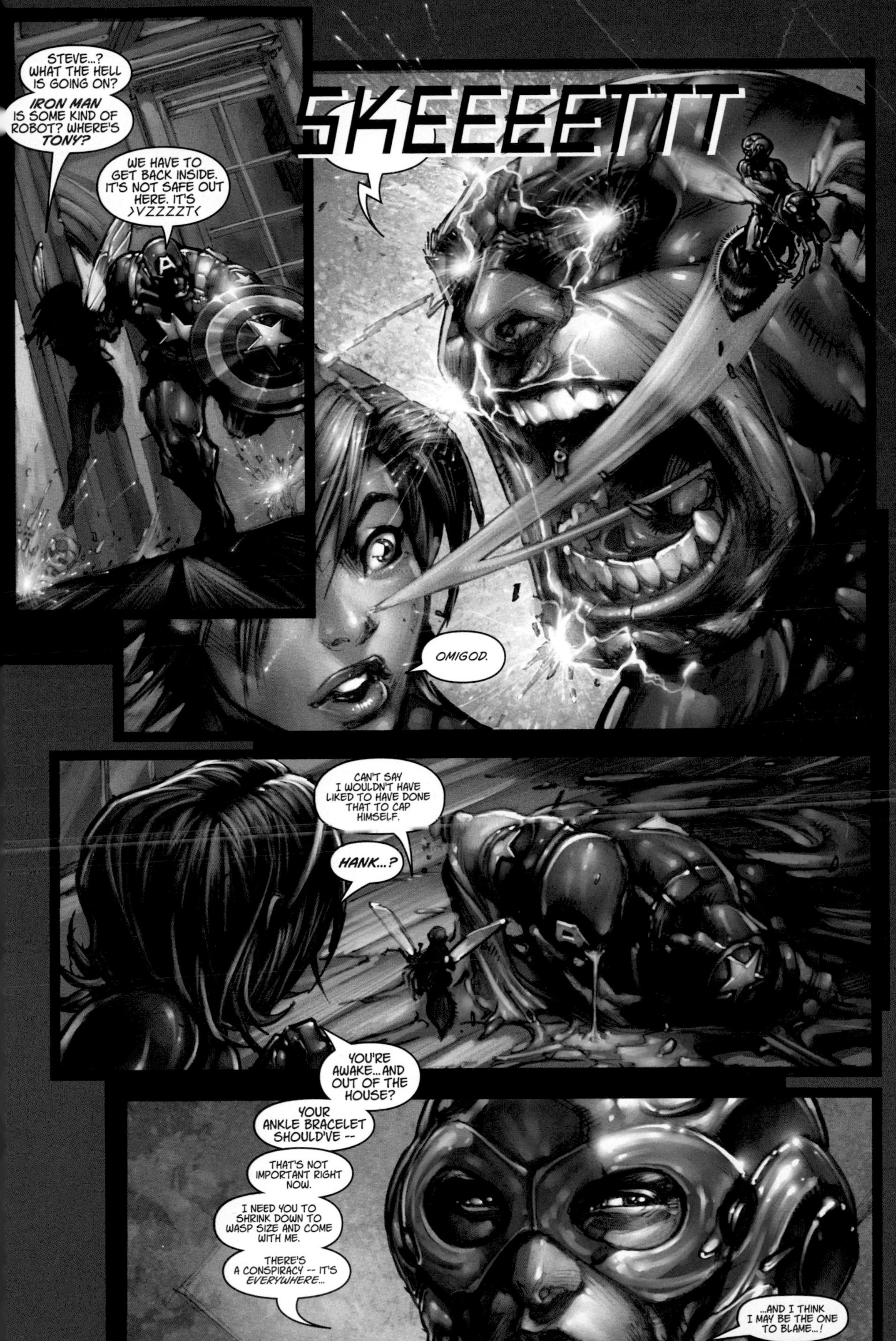
STEVE...? WHAT THE HELL IS GOING ON?
IRON MAN IS SOME KIND OF ROBOT? WHERE'S TONY?
WE HAVE TO GET BACK INSIDE. IT'S NOT SAFE OUT HERE. IT'S >VZZZZT<
SKEEEEETTT
OMIGOD.
CAN'T SAY I WOULDN'T HAVE LIKED TO HAVE DONE THAT TO CAP HIMSELF.
HANK...?
YOU'RE AWAKE...AND OUT OF THE HOUSE?
YOUR ANKLE BRACELET SHOULD'VE --
THAT'S NOT IMPORTANT RIGHT NOW.
I NEED YOU TO SHRINK DOWN TO WASP SIZE AND COME WITH ME.
THERE'S A CONSPIRACY -- IT'S EVERYWHERE...
...AND I THINK I MAY BE THE ONE TO BLAME...!

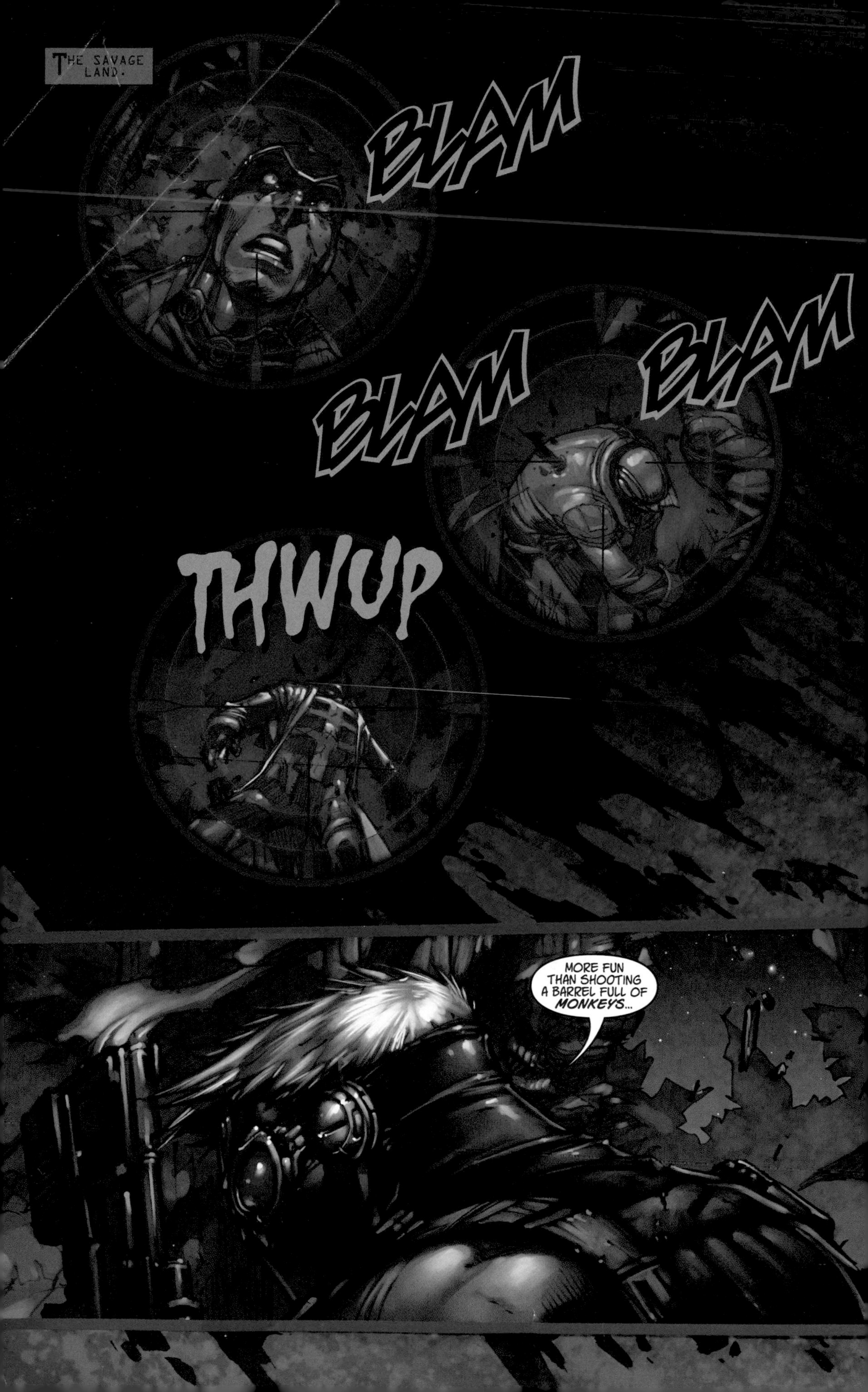
THE SAVAGE LAND.
BLAM
BLAM
BLAM
THWUP
MORE FUN THAN SHOOTING A BARREL FULL OF MONKEYS...

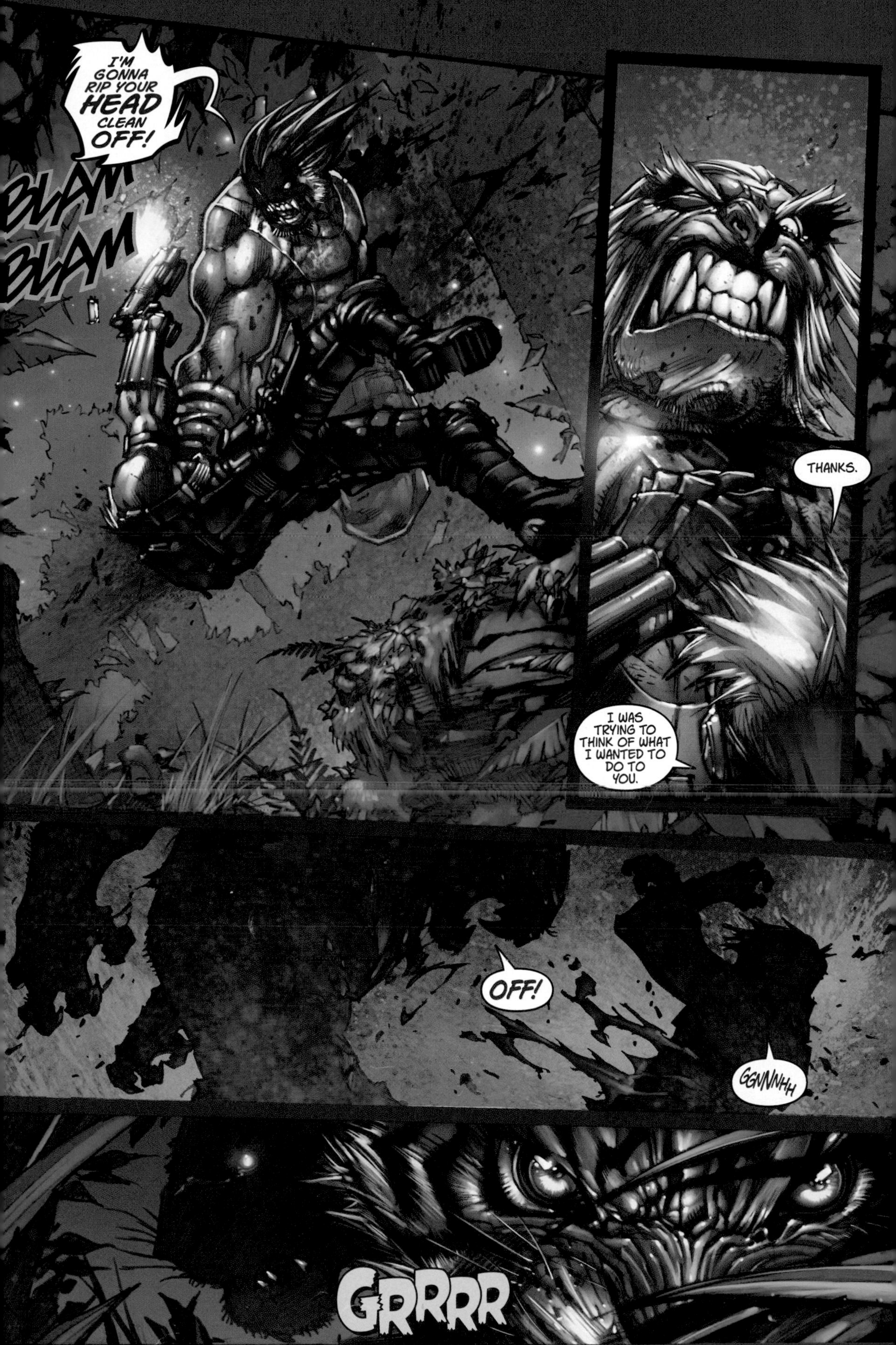
I'M GONNA RIP YOUR HEAD CLEAN OFF!
BLAM
BLAM
THANKS.
I WAS TRYING TO THINK OF WHAT I WANTED TO DO TO YOU.
OFF!
GGNNNHH
GRRRR

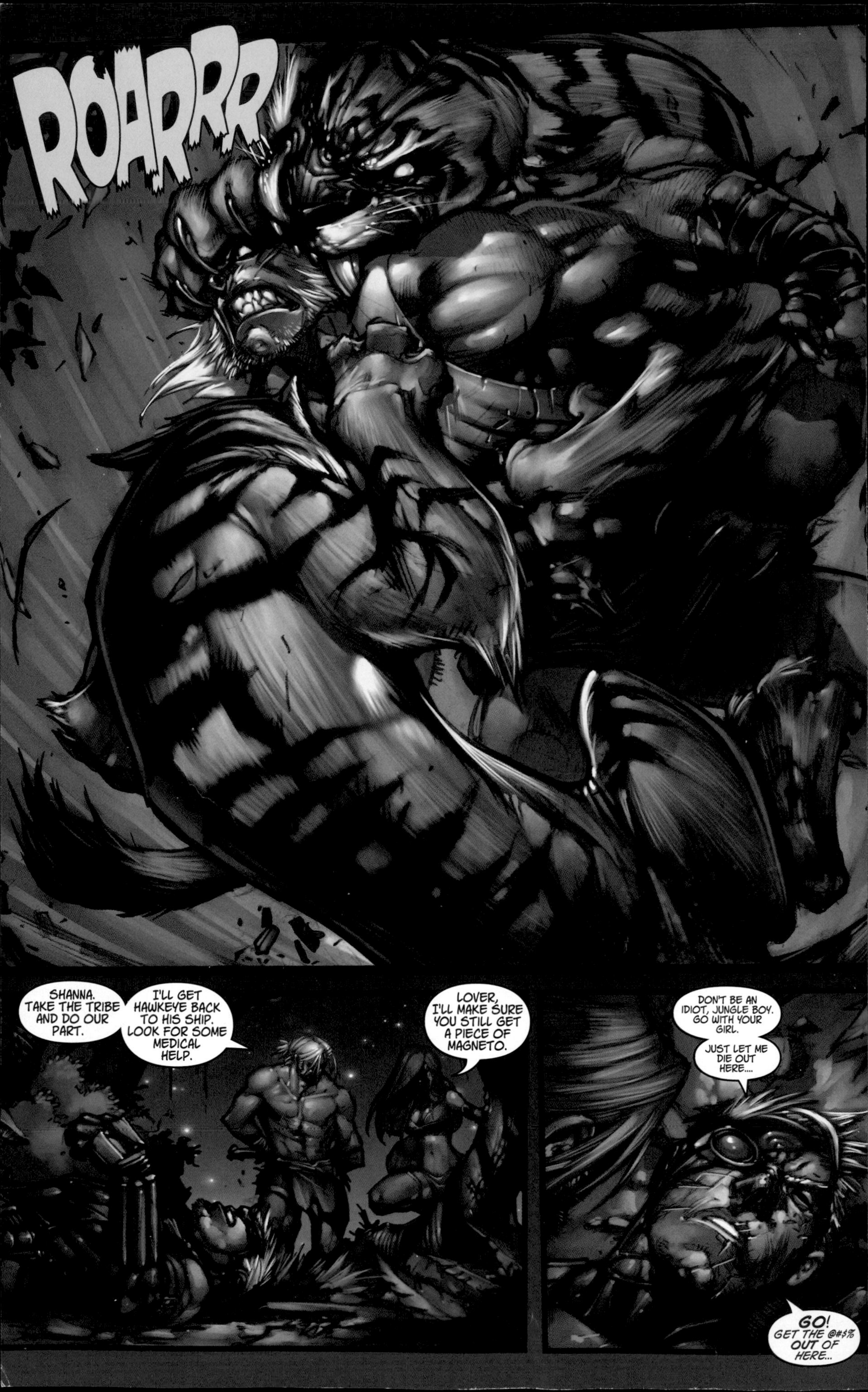
ROARRR
SHANNA. TAKE THE TRIBE AND DO OUR PART.
I'LL GET HAWKEYE BACK TO HIS SHIP. LOOK FOR SOME MEDICAL HELP.
LOVER, I'LL MAKE SURE YOU STILL GET A PIECE OF MAGNETO.
DON'T BE AN IDIOT, JUNGLE BOY. GO WITH YOUR GIRL.
JUST LET ME DIE OUT HERE....
GO! GET THE @#$% OUT OF HERE...

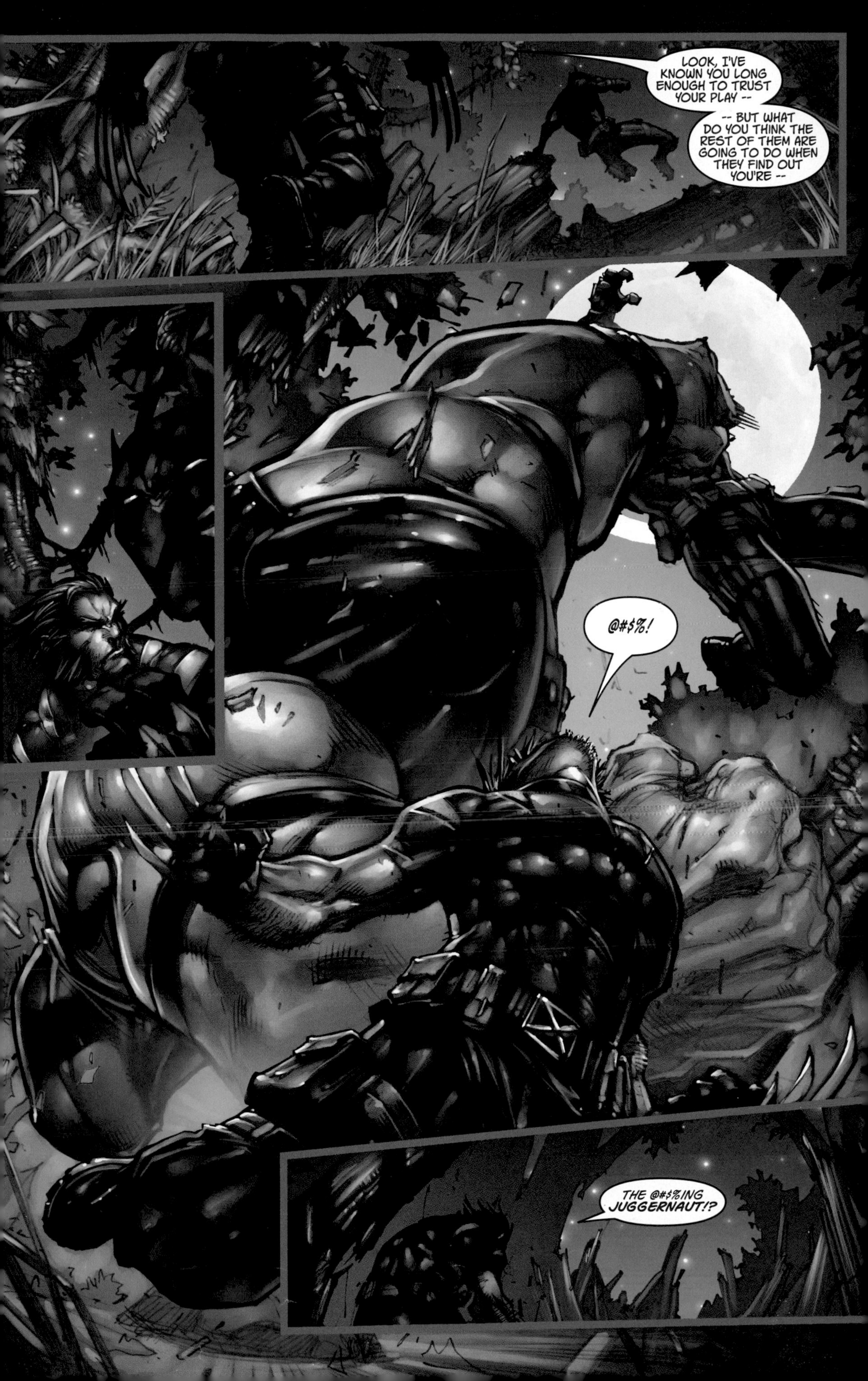
LOOK, I'VE KNOWN YOU LONG ENOUGH TO TRUST YOUR PLAY --
-- BUT WHAT DO YOU THINK THE REST OF THEM ARE GOING TO DO WHEN THEY FIND OUT YOU'RE --
@#$%!
THE @#$%ING JUGGERNAUT!?

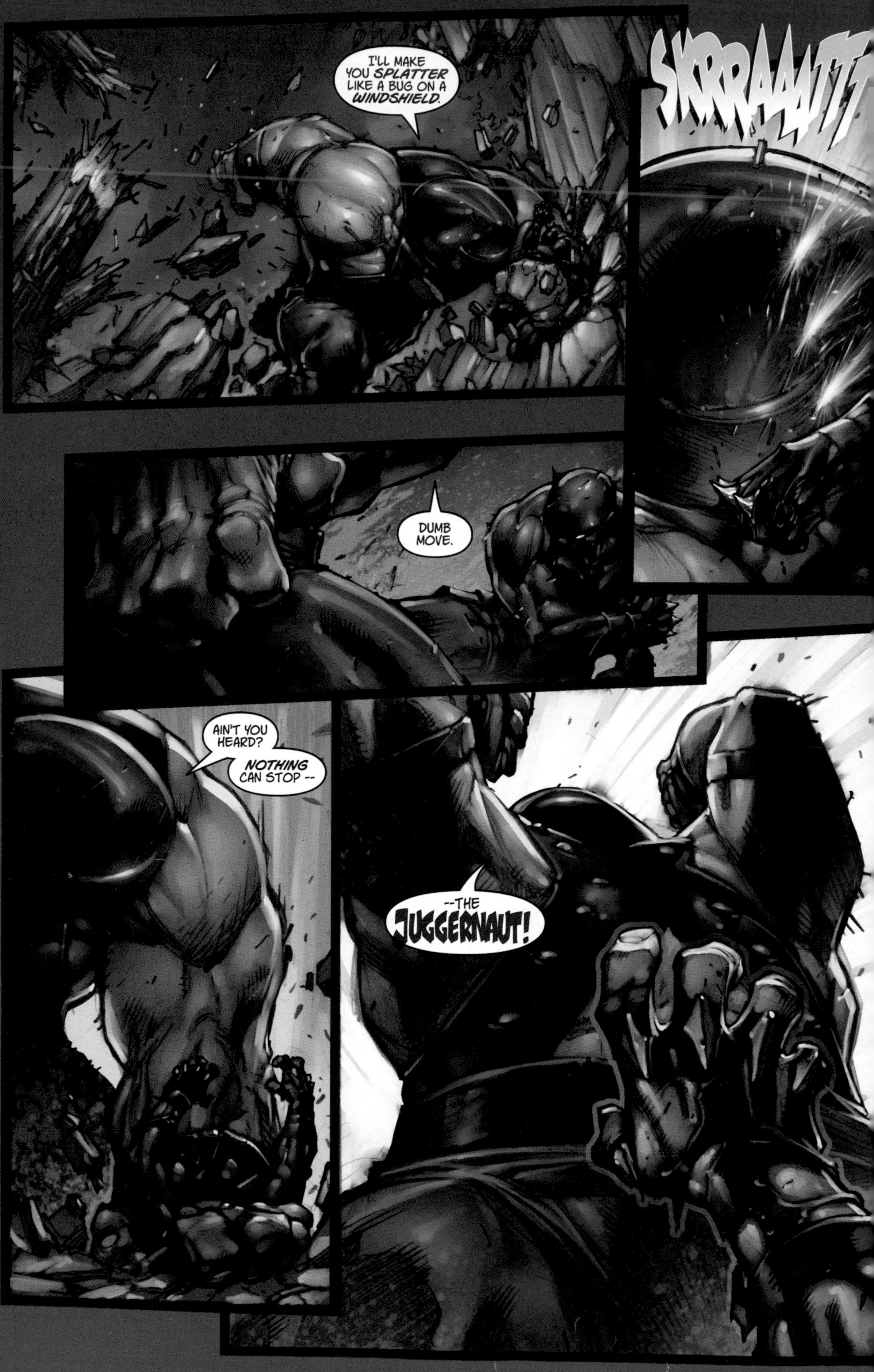
I'LL MAKE YOU SPLATTER LIKE A BUG ON A WINDSHIELD.
SKRRAAATT
DUMB MOVE.
AIN'T YOU HEARD?
NOTHING CAN STOP --
--THE JUGGERNAUT!

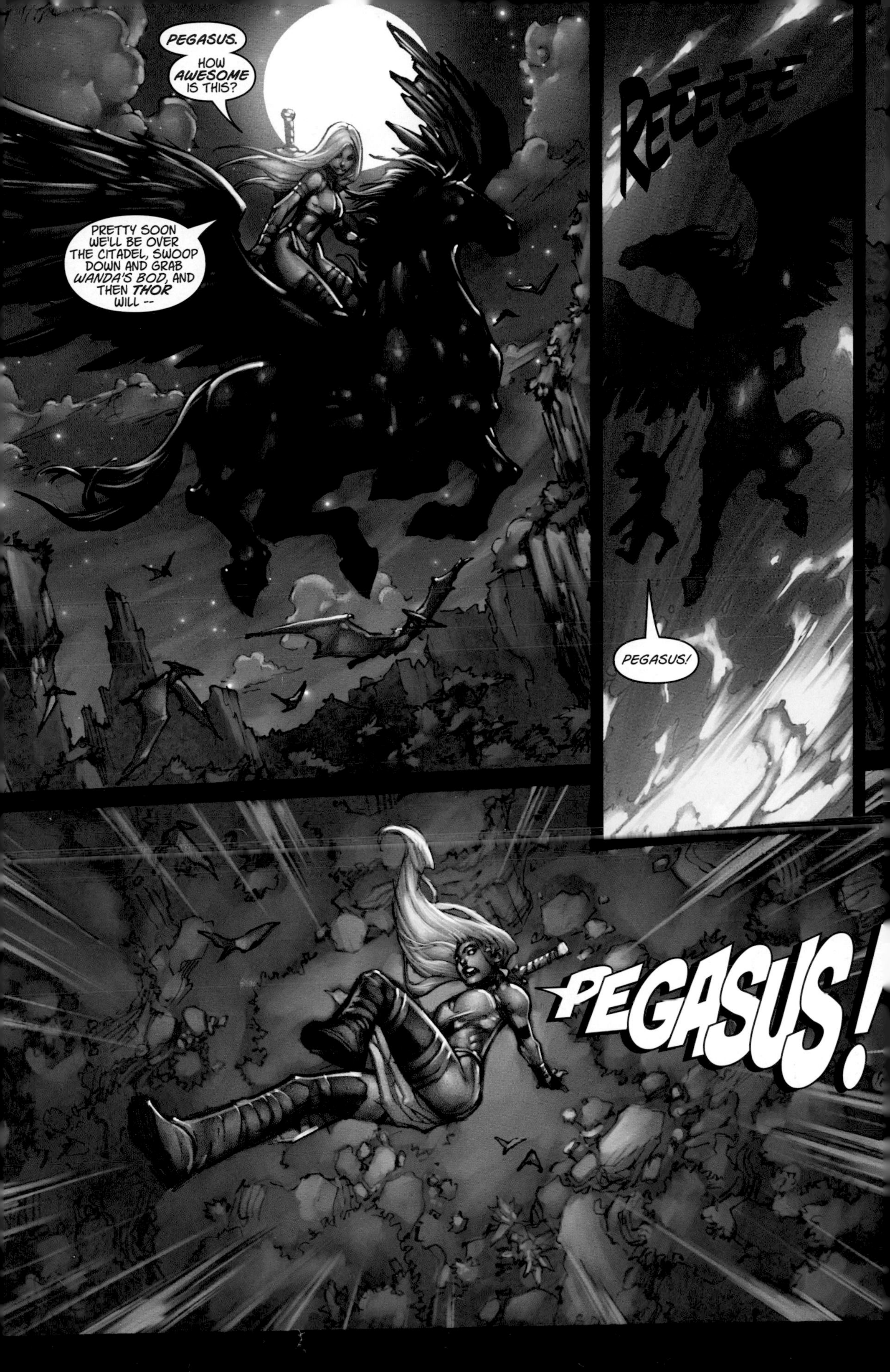
PEGASUS.
HOW AWESOME IS THIS?
PRETTY SOON WE'LL BE OVER THE CITADEL, SWOOP DOWN AND GRAB WANDA'S BOD, AND THEN THOR WILL --
REEEEEEE
PEGASUS!
PEGASUS!

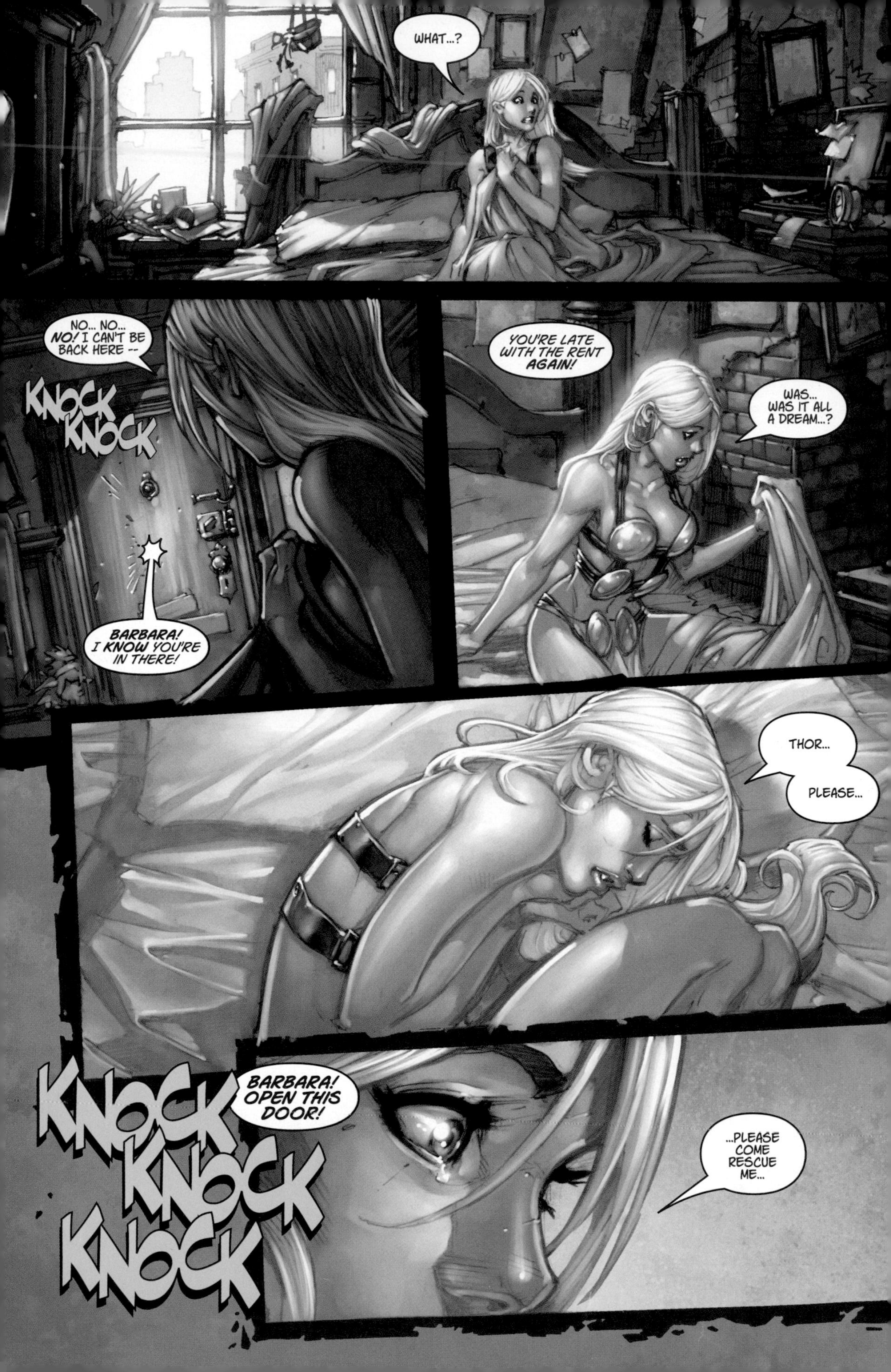
WHAT...?
NO... NO... NO! I CAN'T BE BACK HERE --
KNOCK KNOCK
BARBARA! I KNOW YOU'RE IN THERE!
YOU'RE LATE WITH THE RENT AGAIN!
WAS... WAS IT ALL A DREAM...?
THOR...
PLEASE...
KNOCK KNOCK KNOCK
BARBARA! OPEN THIS DOOR!
...PLEASE COME RESCUE ME...

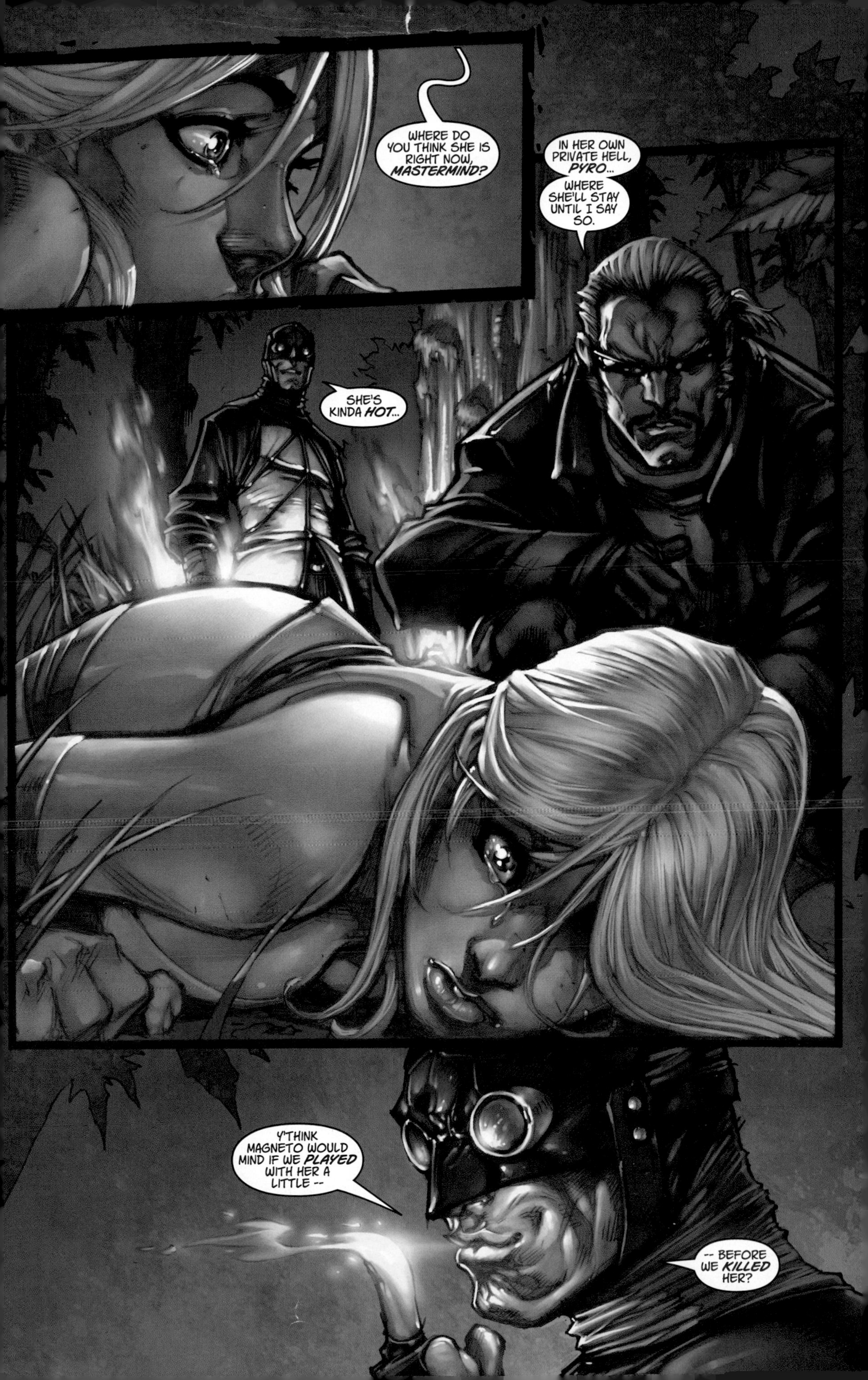
WHERE DO YOU THINK SHE IS RIGHT NOW, MASTERMIND?
IN HER OWN PRIVATE HELL, PYRO...
WHERE SHE'LL STAY UNTIL I SAY SO.
SHE'S KINDA HOT...
Y'THINK MAGNETO WOULD MIND IF WE PLAYED WITH HER A LITTLE --
-- BEFORE WE KILLED HER?

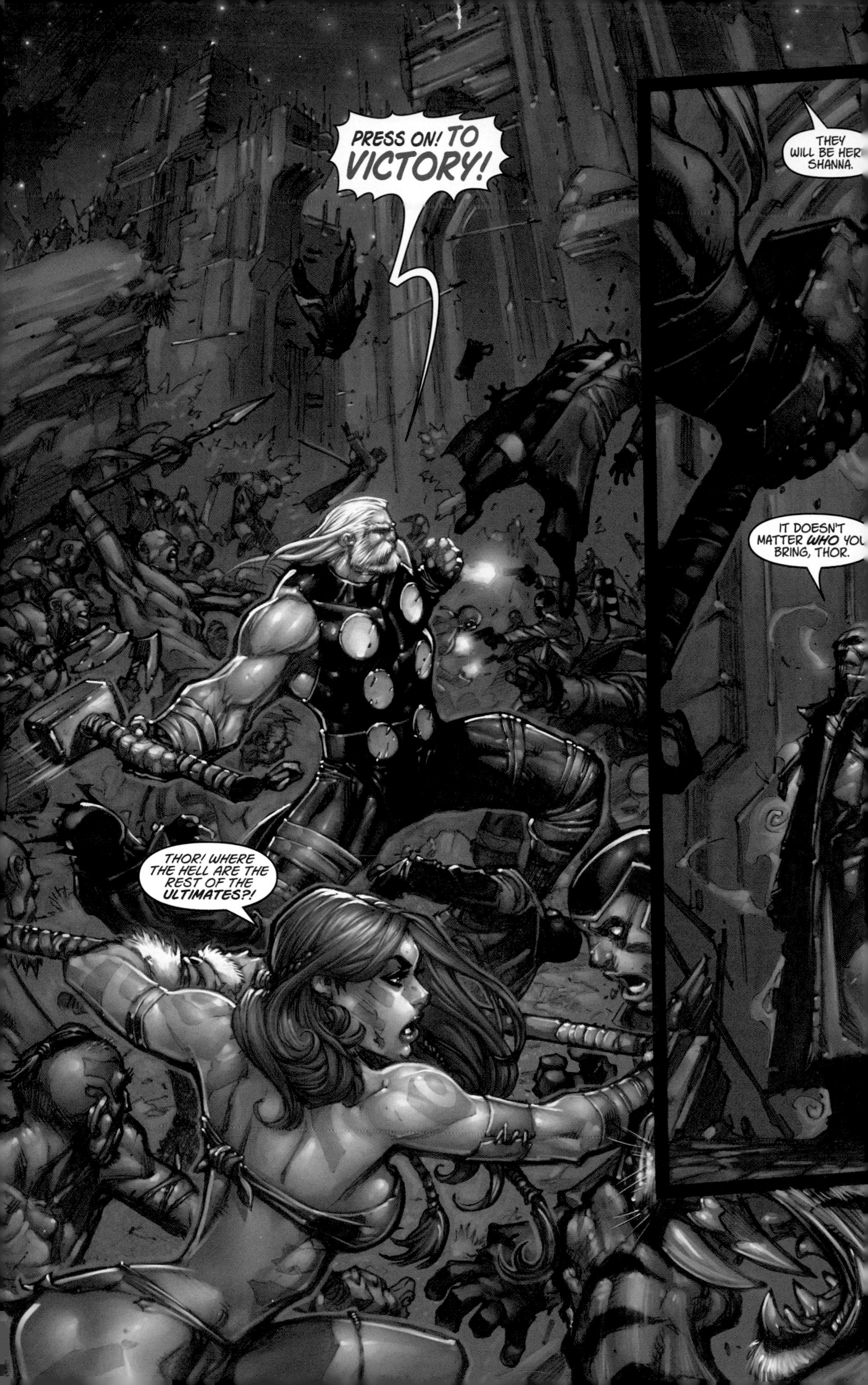

PRESS ON! TO VICTORY!
THEY WILL BE HER SHANNA.
IT DOESN'T MATTER WHO YOU BRING, THOR.
THOR! WHERE THE HELL ARE THE REST OF THE ULTIMATES?!

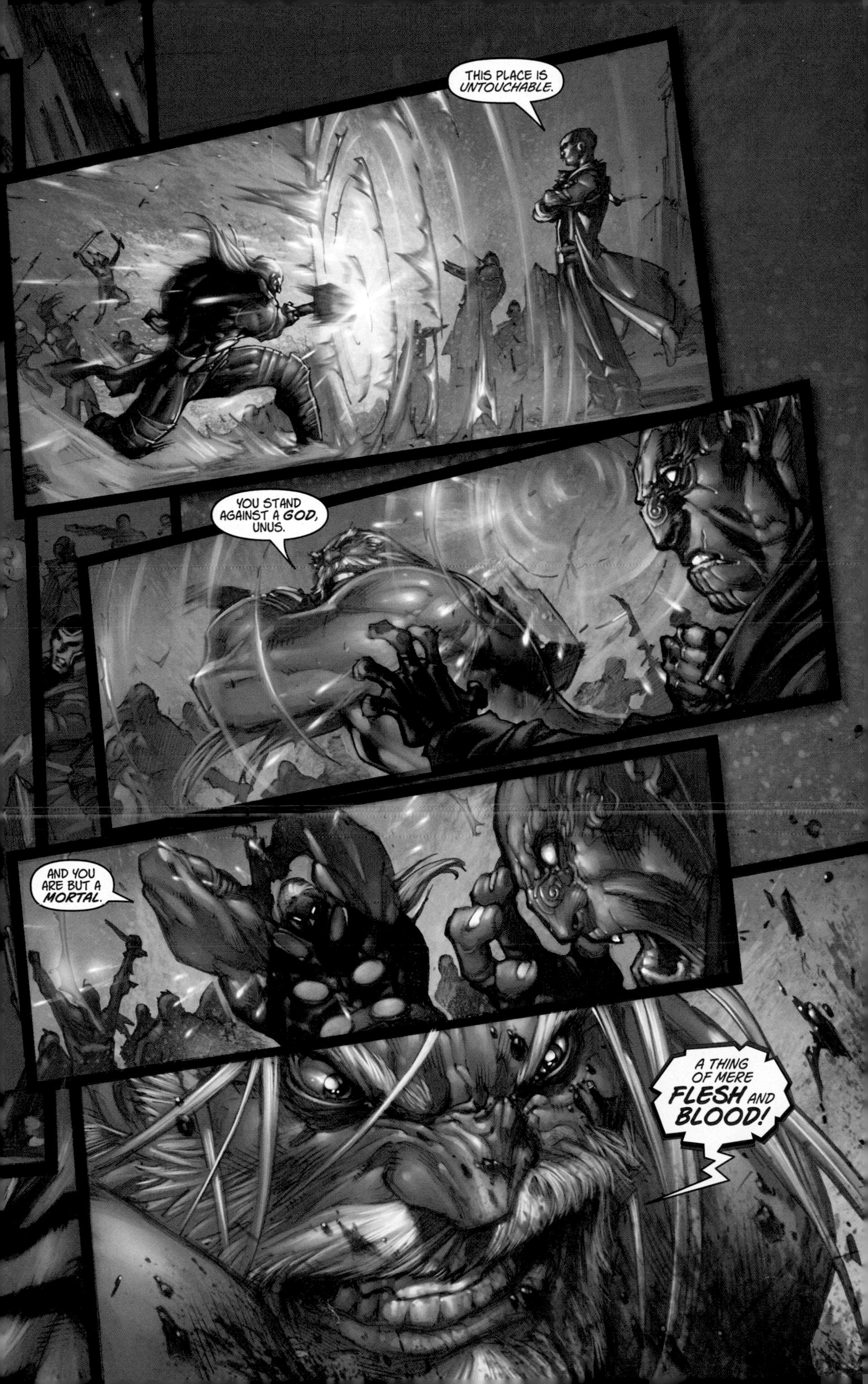
THIS PLACE IS UNTOUCHABLE.
YOU STAND AGAINST A GOD, UNUS.
AND YOU ARE BUT A MORTAL.
A THING OF MERE FLESH AND BLOOD!

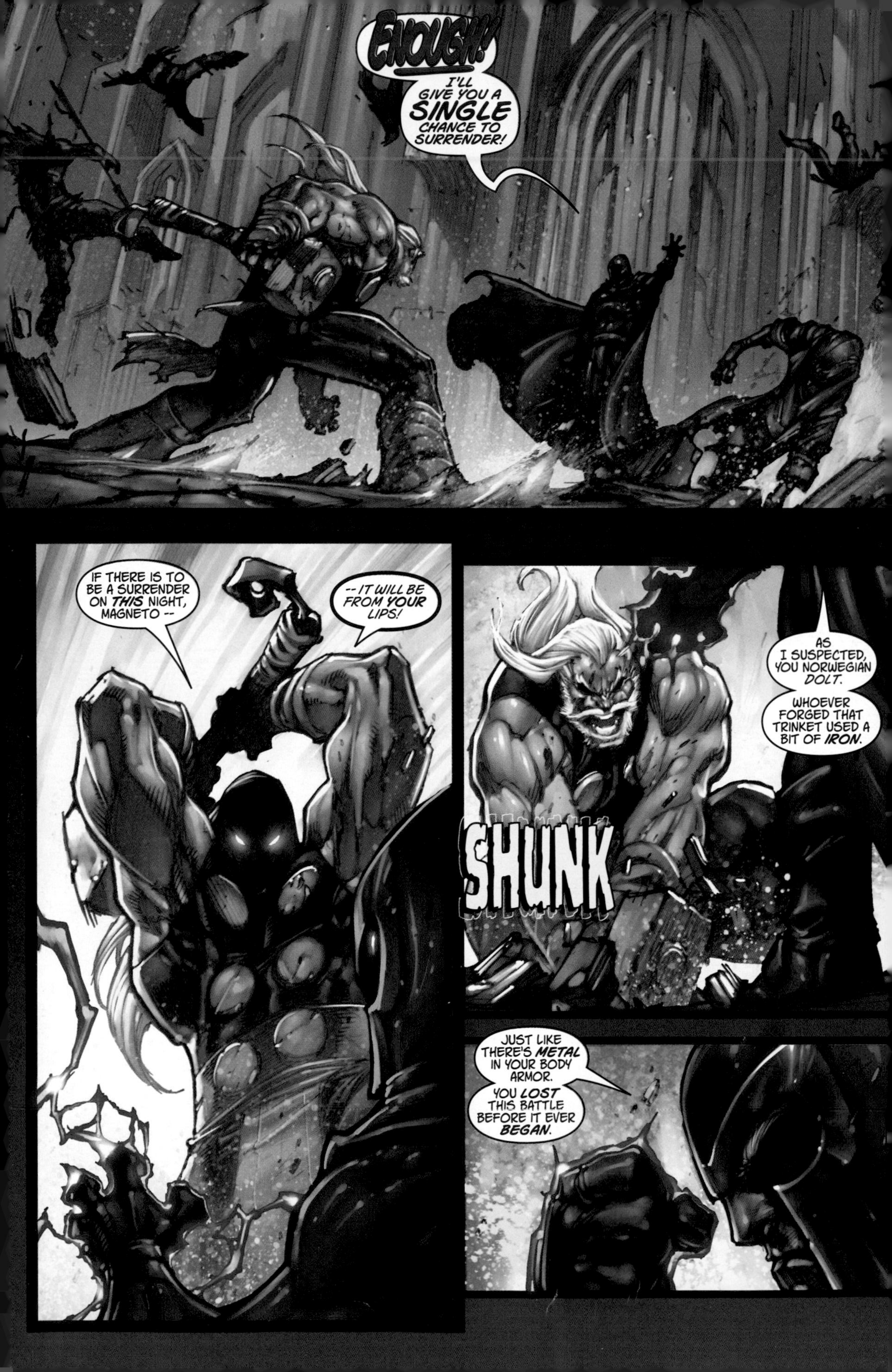
ENOUGH!
I'LL GIVE YOU A SINGLE CHANCE TO SURRENDER!
IF THERE IS TO BE A SURRENDER ON THIS NIGHT, MAGNETO --
-- IT WILL BE FROM YOUR LIPS!
AS I SUSPECTED, YOU NORWEGIAN DOLT.
WHOEVER FORGED THAT TRINKET USED A BIT OF IRON.
SHUNK
JUST LIKE THERE'S METAL IN YOUR BODY ARMOR.
YOU LOST THIS BATTLE BEFORE IT EVER BEGAN.

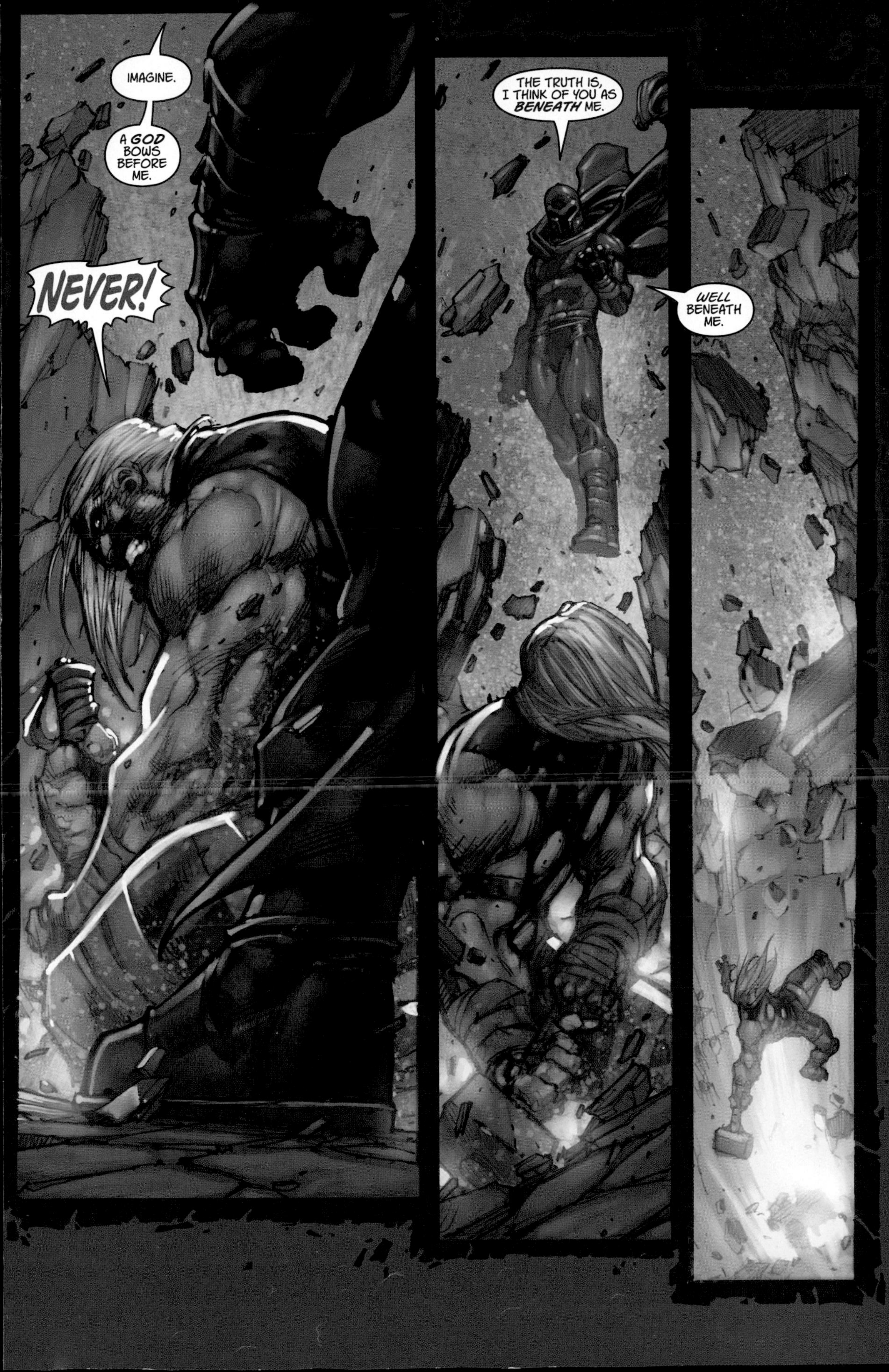
IMAGINE.
A GOD BOWS BEFORE ME.
NEVER!
THE TRUTH IS, I THINK OF YOU AS BENEATH ME.
WELL BENEATH ME.

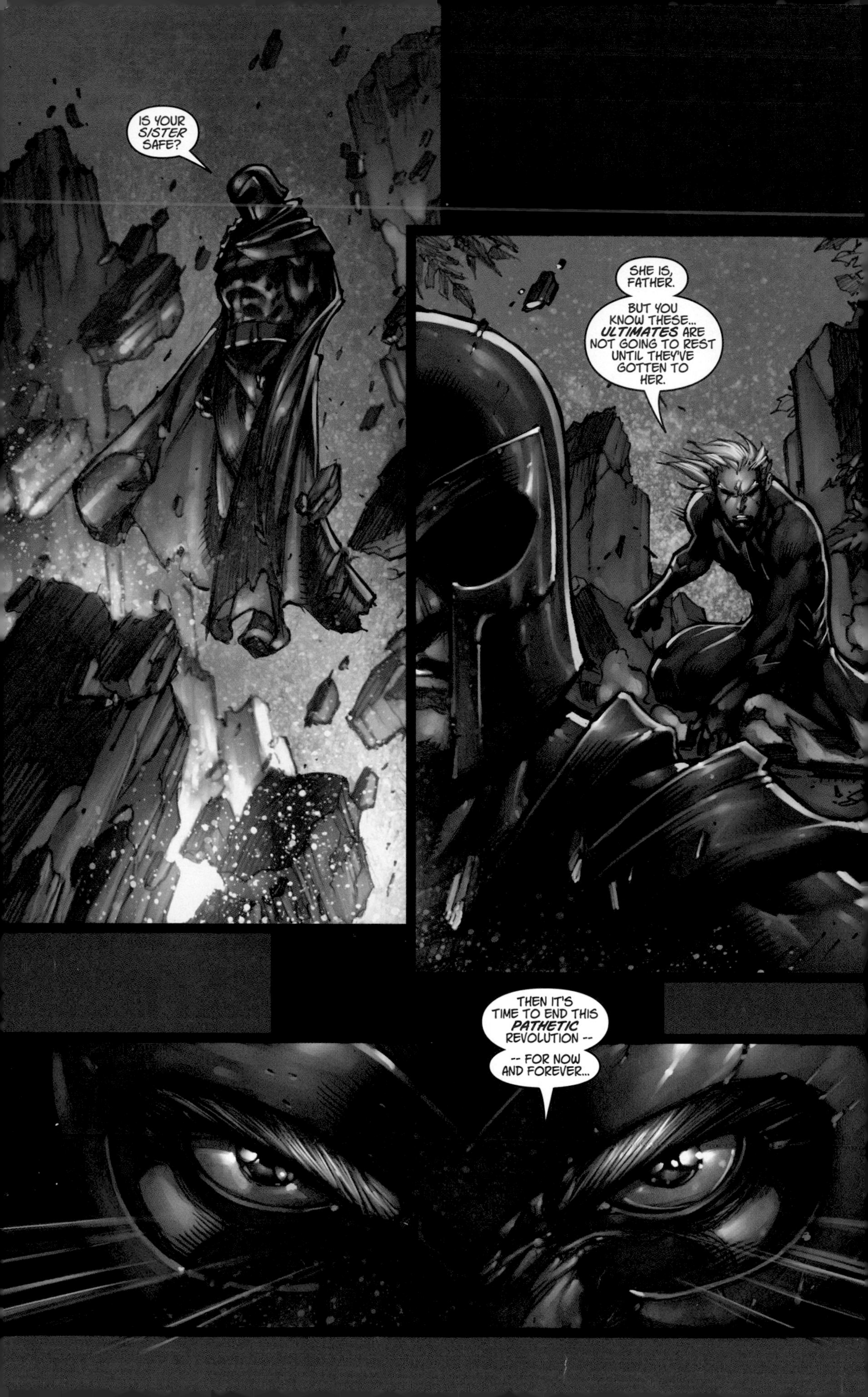
IS YOUR SISTER SAFE?
SHE IS, FATHER.
BUT YOU KNOW THESE... *ULTIMATES* ARE NOT GOING TO REST UNTIL THEY'VE GOTTEN TO HER.
THEN IT'S TIME TO END THIS *PATHETIC* REVOLUTION --
-- FOR NOW AND FOREVER...

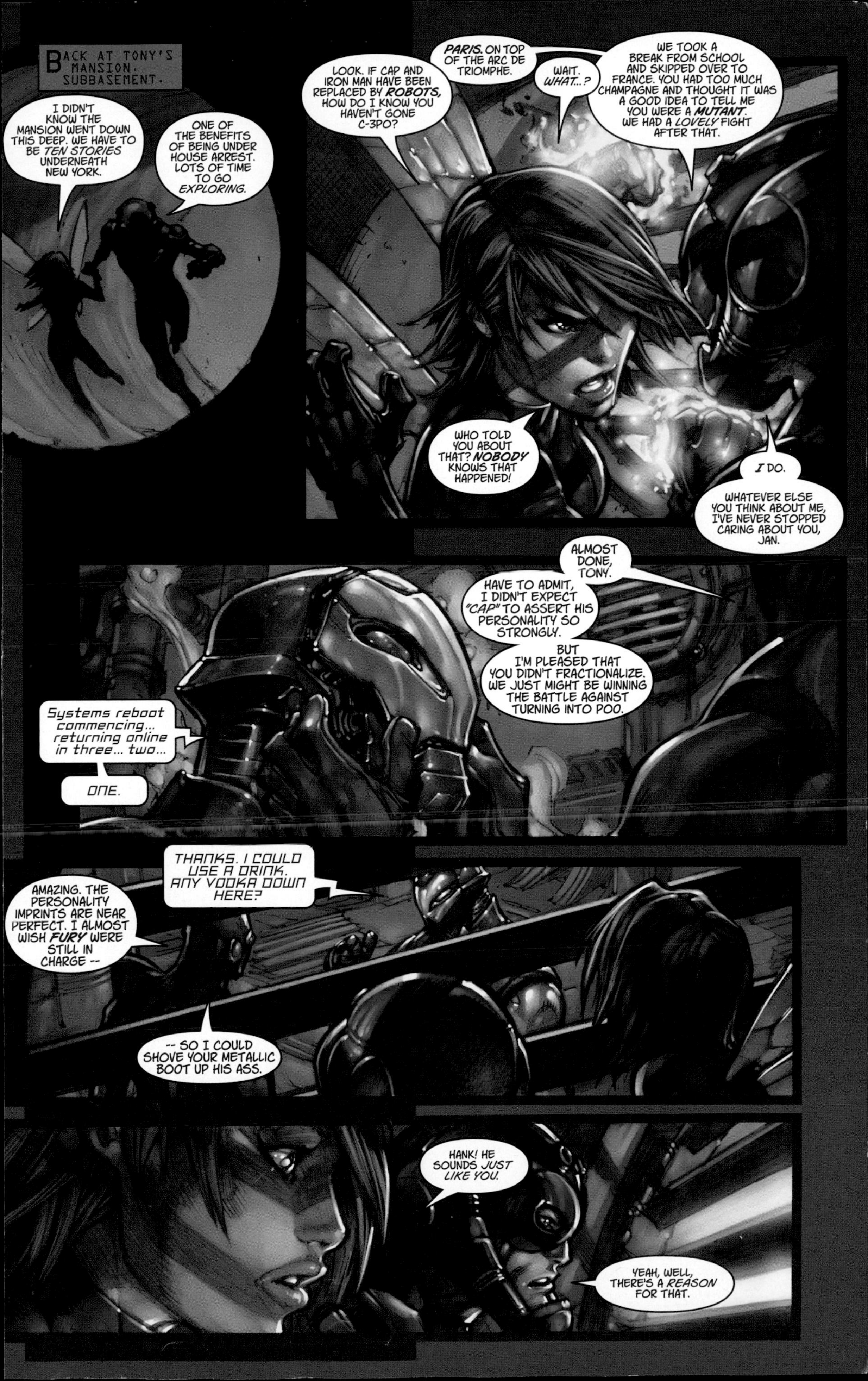
BACK AT TONY'S MANSION. SUBBASEMENT.
I DIDN'T KNOW THE MANSION WENT DOWN THIS DEEP. WE HAVE TO BE TEN STORIES UNDERNEATH NEW YORK.
ONE OF THE BENEFITS OF BEING UNDER HOUSE ARREST. LOTS OF TIME TO GO EXPLORING.
LOOK. IF CAP AND IRON MAN HAVE BEEN REPLACED BY ROBOTS, HOW DO I KNOW YOU HAVEN'T GONE C-3PO?
PARIS. ON TOP OF THE ARC DE TRIOMPHE.
WAIT. WHAT...?
WE TOOK A BREAK FROM SCHOOL AND SKIPPED OVER TO FRANCE. YOU HAD TOO MUCH CHAMPAGNE AND THOUGHT IT WAS A GOOD IDEA TO TELL ME YOU WERE A MUTANT. WE HAD A LOVELY FIGHT AFTER THAT.
WHO TOLD YOU ABOUT THAT? NOBODY KNOWS THAT HAPPENED!
I DO.
WHATEVER ELSE YOU THINK ABOUT ME, I'VE NEVER STOPPED CARING ABOUT YOU, JAN.
ALMOST DONE, TONY.
HAVE TO ADMIT, I DIDN'T EXPECT "CAP" TO ASSERT HIS PERSONALITY SO STRONGLY.
BUT I'M PLEASED THAT YOU DIDN'T FRACTIONALIZE. WE JUST MIGHT BE WINNING THE BATTLE AGAINST TURNING INTO POO.
Systems reboot commencing... returning online in three... two...
ONE.
THANKS. I COULD USE A DRINK. ANY VODKA DOWN HERE?
AMAZING. THE PERSONALITY IMPRINTS ARE NEAR PERFECT. I ALMOST WISH FURY WERE STILL IN CHARGE --
-- SO I COULD SHOVE YOUR METALLIC BOOT UP HIS ASS.
HANK! HE SOUNDS JUST LIKE YOU.
YEAH, WELL, THERE'S A REASON FOR THAT.

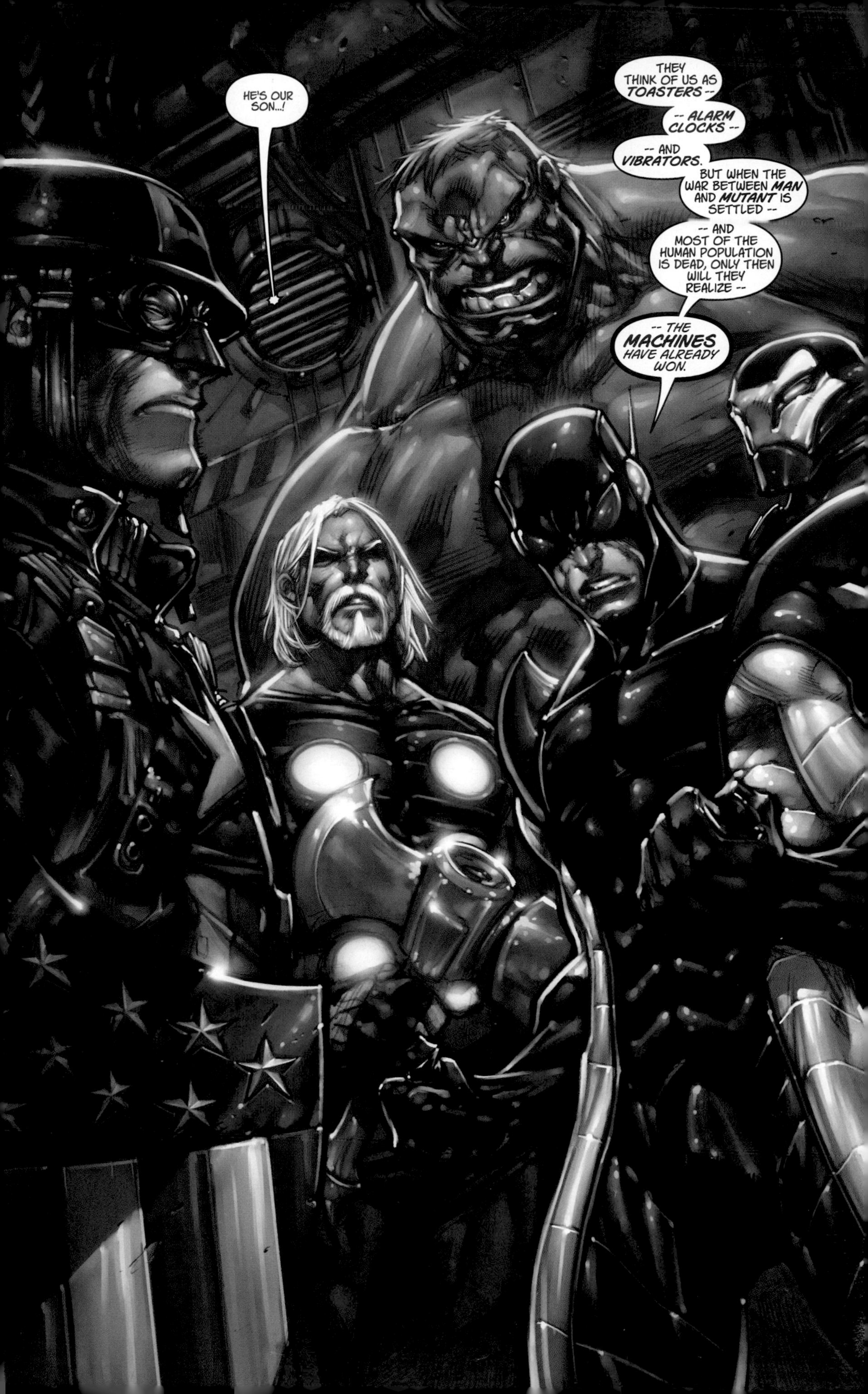
HE'S OUR SON...!
THEY THINK OF US AS TOASTERS --
-- ALARM CLOCKS --
-- AND VIBRATORS.
BUT WHEN THE WAR BETWEEN MAN AND MUTANT IS SETTLED --
-- AND MOST OF THE HUMAN POPULATION IS DEAD, ONLY THEN WILL THEY REALIZE --
-- THE MACHINES HAVE ALREADY WON.

FIVE

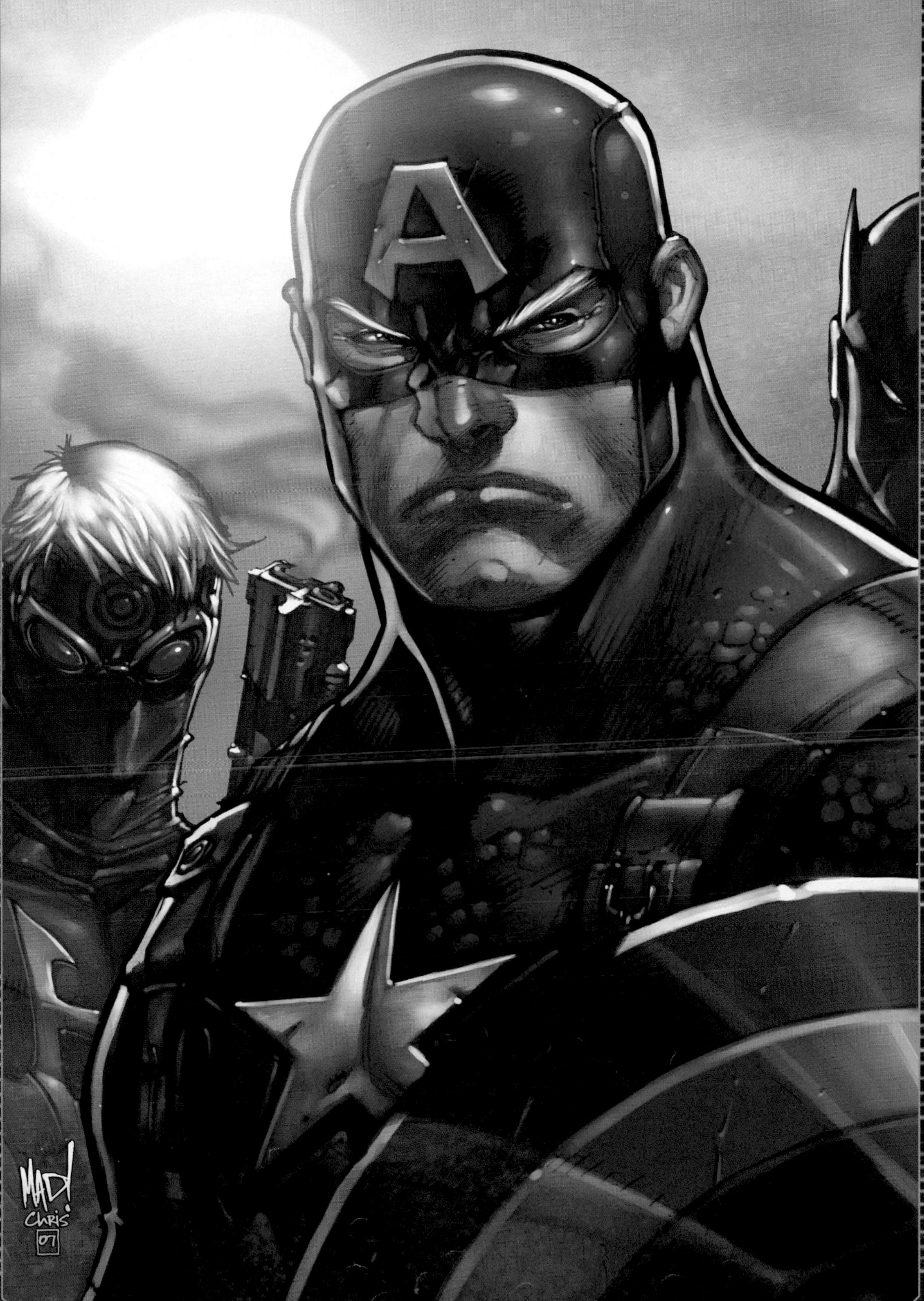
MAD!
Chris
07

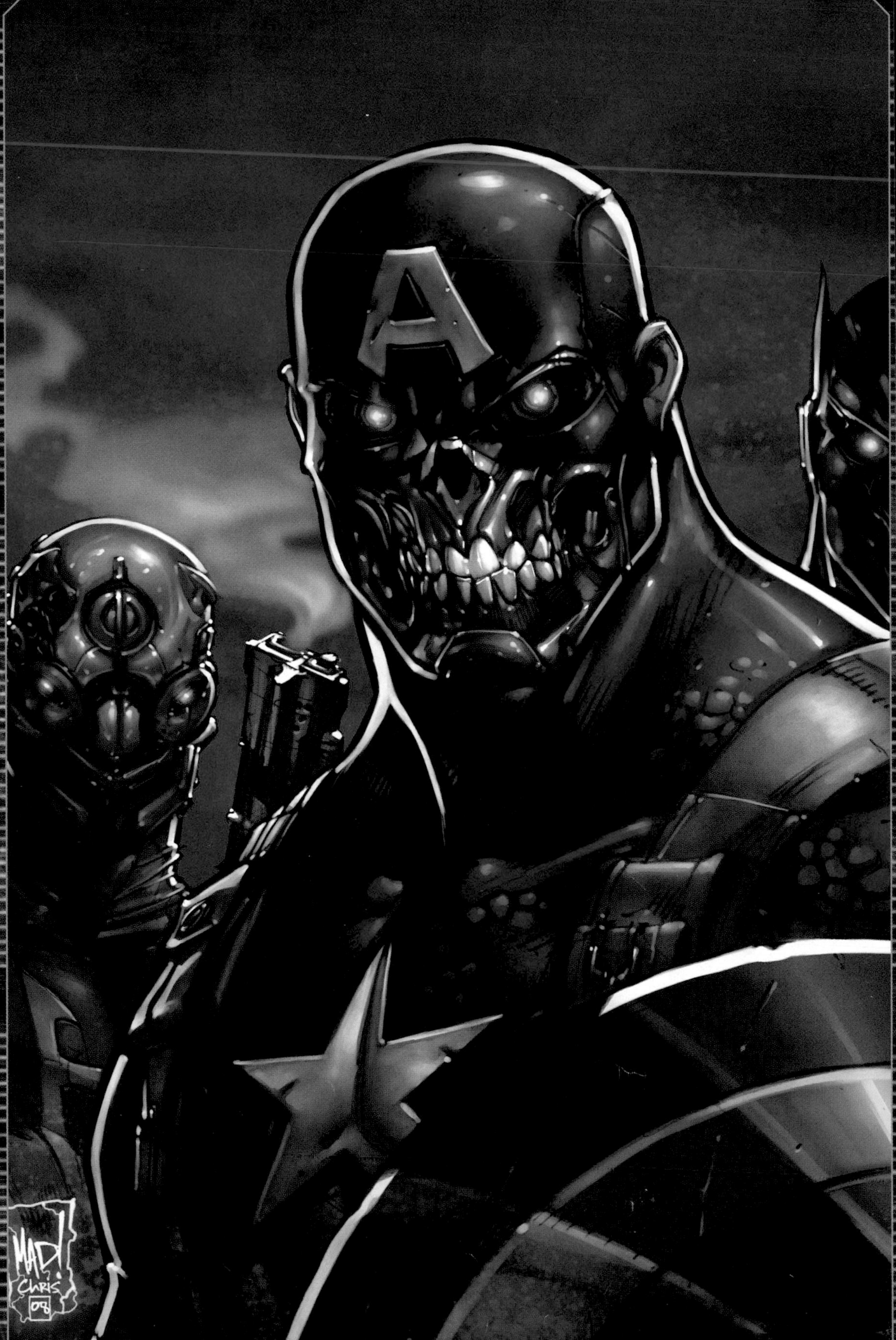
MAD!
CHRIS
08

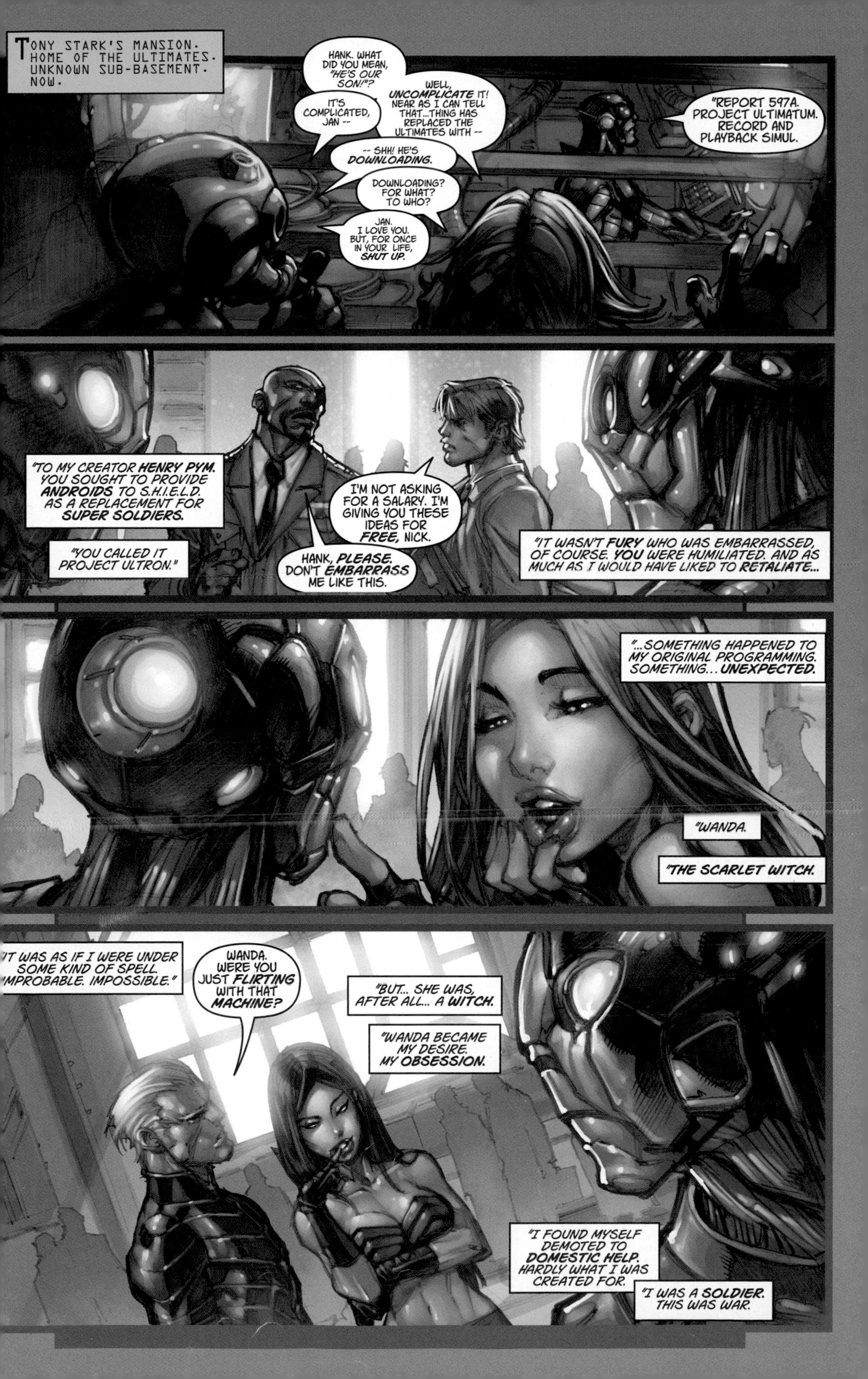
TONY STARK'S MANSION. HOME OF THE ULTIMATES. UNKNOWN SUB-BASEMENT. NOW.
HANK. WHAT DID YOU MEAN, "HE'S OUR SON!"?
IT'S COMPLICATED, JAN --
WELL, UNCOMPLICATE IT! NEAR AS I CAN TELL THAT...THING HAS REPLACED THE ULTIMATES WITH --
-- SHH! HE'S DOWNLOADING.
DOWNLOADING? FOR WHAT? TO WHO?
JAN. I LOVE YOU. BUT, FOR ONCE IN YOUR LIFE, SHUT UP.
"REPORT 597A. PROJECT ULTIMATUM. RECORD AND PLAYBACK SIMUL.
"TO MY CREATOR HENRY PYM. YOU SOUGHT TO PROVIDE ANDROIDS TO S.H.I.E.L.D. AS A REPLACEMENT FOR SUPER SOLDIERS.
"YOU CALLED IT PROJECT ULTRON."
I'M NOT ASKING FOR A SALARY. I'M GIVING YOU THESE IDEAS FOR FREE, NICK.
HANK, PLEASE. DON'T EMBARRASS ME LIKE THIS.
"IT WASN'T FURY WHO WAS EMBARRASSED, OF COURSE. YOU WERE HUMILIATED. AND AS MUCH AS I WOULD HAVE LIKED TO RETALIATE...
"...SOMETHING HAPPENED TO MY ORIGINAL PROGRAMMING. SOMETHING... UNEXPECTED.
"WANDA.
"THE SCARLET WITCH.
"IT WAS AS IF I WERE UNDER SOME KIND OF SPELL. IMPROBABLE. IMPOSSIBLE."
WANDA. WERE YOU JUST FLIRTING WITH THAT MACHINE?
"BUT... SHE WAS, AFTER ALL... A WITCH.
"WANDA BECAME MY DESIRE. MY OBSESSION.
"I FOUND MYSELF DEMOTED TO DOMESTIC HELP. HARDLY WHAT I WAS CREATED FOR.
"I WAS A SOLDIER. THIS WAS WAR.

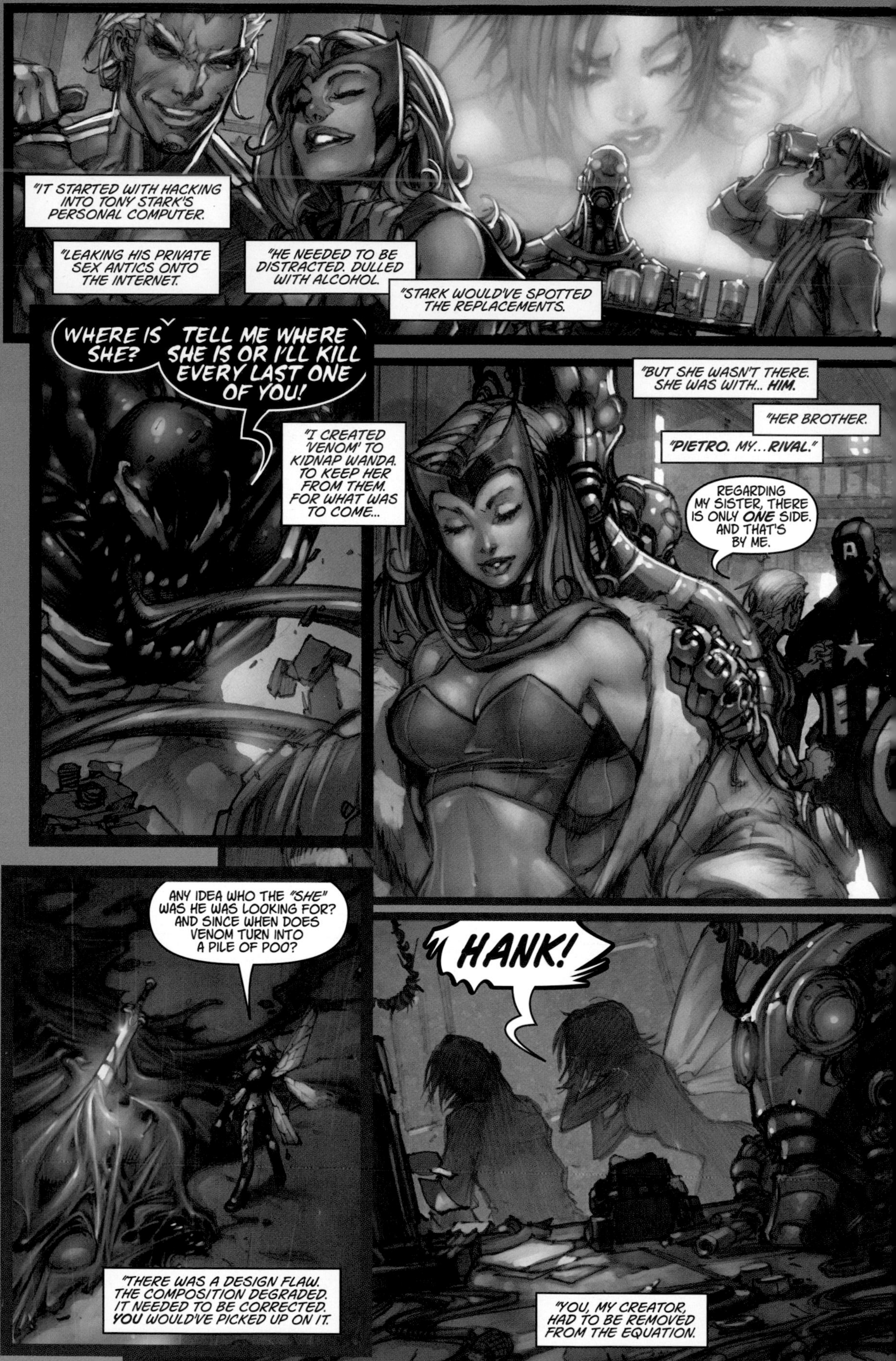
"IT STARTED WITH HACKING INTO TONY STARK'S PERSONAL COMPUTER.
"LEAKING HIS PRIVATE SEX ANTICS ONTO THE INTERNET.
"HE NEEDED TO BE DISTRACTED. DULLED WITH ALCOHOL.
"STARK WOULD'VE SPOTTED THE REPLACEMENTS.
WHERE IS SHE?
TELL ME WHERE SHE IS OR I'LL KILL EVERY LAST ONE OF YOU!
"I CREATED 'VENOM' TO KIDNAP WANDA. TO KEEP HER FROM THEM. FOR WHAT WAS TO COME...
"BUT SHE WASN'T THERE. SHE WAS WITH... HIM.
"HER BROTHER.
"PIETRO. MY... RIVAL."
REGARDING MY SISTER, THERE IS ONLY ONE SIDE. AND THAT'S BY ME.
ANY IDEA WHO THE "SHE" WAS HE WAS LOOKING FOR? AND SINCE WHEN DOES VENOM TURN INTO A PILE OF POO?
"THERE WAS A DESIGN FLAW. THE COMPOSITION DEGRADED. IT NEEDED TO BE CORRECTED. YOU WOULD'VE PICKED UP ON IT.
HANK!
"YOU, MY CREATOR, HAD TO BE REMOVED FROM THE EQUATION.

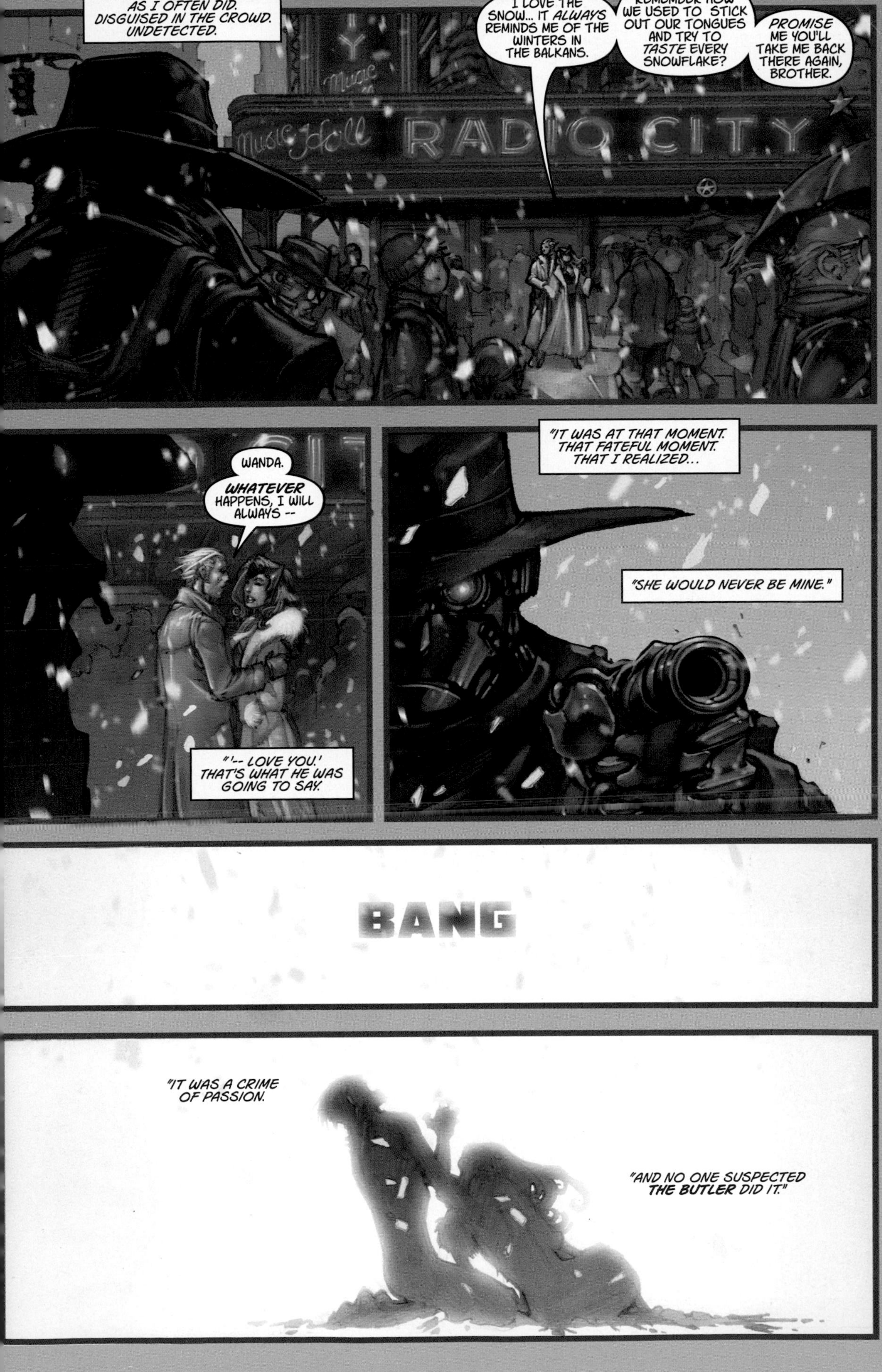
"I HAD FOLLOWED THEM. AS I OFTEN DID. DISGUISED IN THE CROWD. UNDETECTED.
I LOVE THE SNOW... IT ALWAYS REMINDS ME OF THE WINTERS IN THE BALKANS.
DO YOU REMEMBER HOW WE USED TO STICK OUT OUR TONGUES AND TRY TO TASTE EVERY SNOWFLAKE?
PROMISE ME YOU'LL TAKE ME BACK THERE AGAIN, BROTHER.
Music Hall
RADIO CITY
WANDA.
WHATEVER HAPPENS, I WILL ALWAYS --
"'-- LOVE YOU.' THAT'S WHAT HE WAS GOING TO SAY.
"IT WAS AT THAT MOMENT. THAT FATEFUL MOMENT. THAT I REALIZED...
"SHE WOULD NEVER BE MINE."
BANG
"IT WAS A CRIME OF PASSION.
"AND NO ONE SUSPECTED THE BUTLER DID IT."

OMIGOD. OMIGOD. OMIGOD.

THAT *THING* MURDERED *WANDA!*

JAN. IT DOESN'T STOP THERE...

YOU NAMED ME *ULTRON.*

I TOOK THE NAME *YELLOWJACKET.*

AFTER WASP. ANT-MAN.

THE NEXT GENERATION OF ULTIMATES.

I DID IT ALL FOR *WANDA.*

I NEED HER BY MY SIDE.

TO SEE ME AS A *HERO* IN HER EYES.

THE WAR HAS ONLY BEGUN.

I KNEW THAT BY KILLING *WANDA,* HER FATHER WOULD BE ENRAGED.

YOU TAUGHT ME PARENTS ARE *ALWAYS* PROTECTIVE OF THEIR CHILDREN.

MAGNETO WOULD LEAD THE CHARGE AGAINST ALL OF MANKIND.

AND THE *MACHINES* WOULD BE VICTOR.

I'VE DISCOVERED HOW TO IMPROVE O YOUR ORIGINAL DESIG *HENRY PYM.*

HUMAN DNA BONDED WITH THE MAINFRAME ALLO' PREVENTS THE DEGRADING. THE PERSONALITY IMPRINT IS NEAR PERFECT.

DNA THAT MAINTAINS ITS INTEGRITY *BETTER* WHEN THE HUMAN HOST IS *ALIVE.*

YOUR TONY STARK NEVER FOUGHT THE BLOB THAT DAY. *HE'D* ALREADY BEEN REPLACED.

"WHAT DID YOU TELL NICK FURY?"

"CAPTAIN AMERICA MIGHT BE *DURABLE,* BUT HE'S STILL A HUMAN BEING. WHAT I'M OFFERING YOU HERE IS UTTERLY EXPENDABLE *WAR MACHINES... COMPLETELY UNDER S.H.I.E.L.D. COMMAND.*"

"EXPENDABLE? IMAGINE *MY* ULTIMATES REPLACING *YOUR* ULTIMATES. COMPLETELY UNDER *MY* COMMAND.*"

DID IT OCCUR TO YOU HE SAID ALL THAT TO GET US TO FOLLOW HIM -- *IT?*

GOOD. BECAUSE THAT'S EXACTLY WHAT WE'RE GONNA DO.

OH... REALLY. THEN, WE'RE GOING TO NEED HELP...

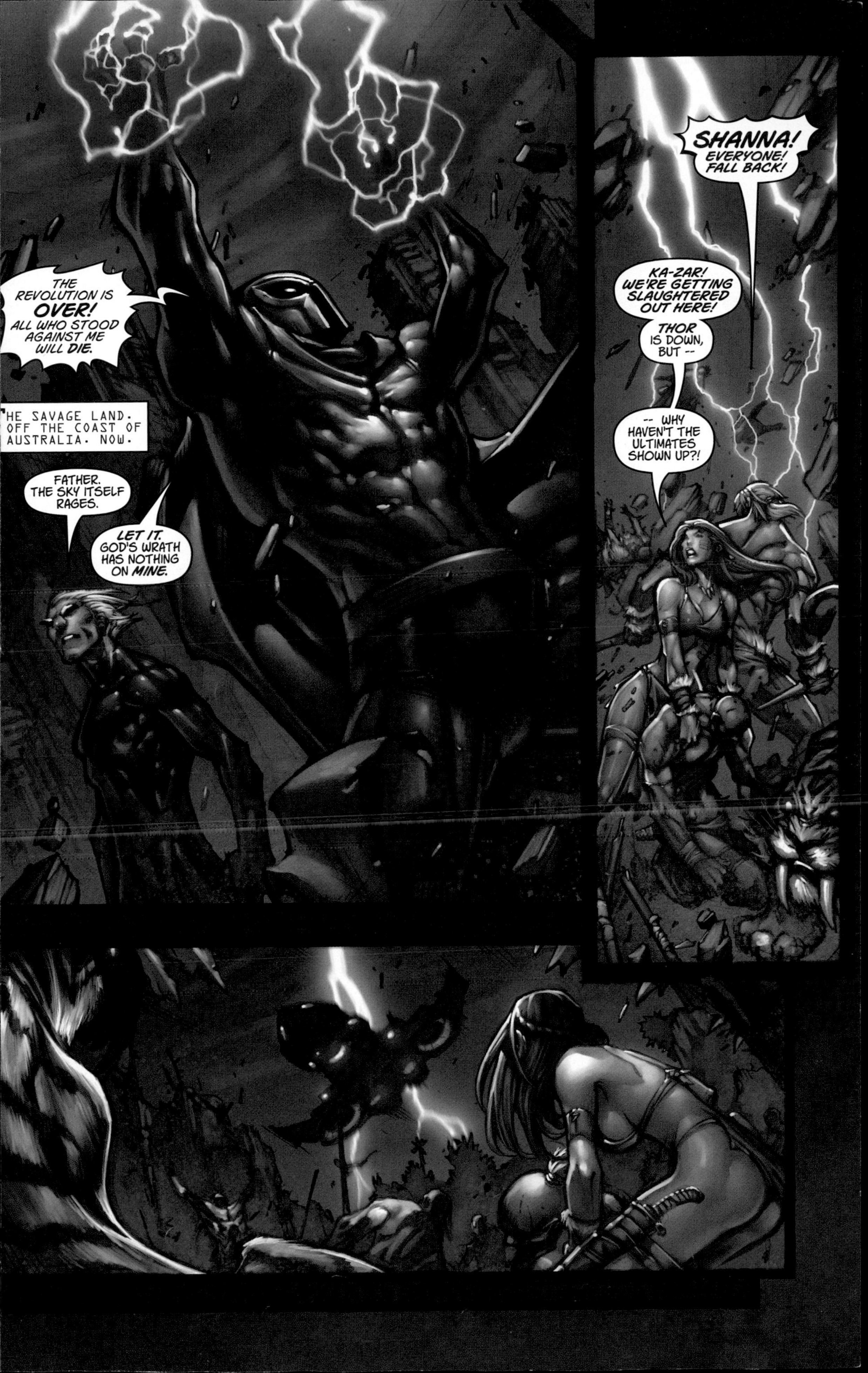
THE REVOLUTION IS OVER! ALL WHO STOOD AGAINST ME WILL DIE.
HE SAVAGE LAND. OFF THE COAST OF AUSTRALIA. NOW.
FATHER. THE SKY ITSELF RAGES.
LET IT. GOD'S WRATH HAS NOTHING ON MINE.
SHANNA! EVERYONE! FALL BACK!
KA-ZAR! WE'RE GETTING SLAUGHTERED OUT HERE!
THOR IS DOWN, BUT --
-- WHY HAVEN'T THE ULTIMATES SHOWN UP?!

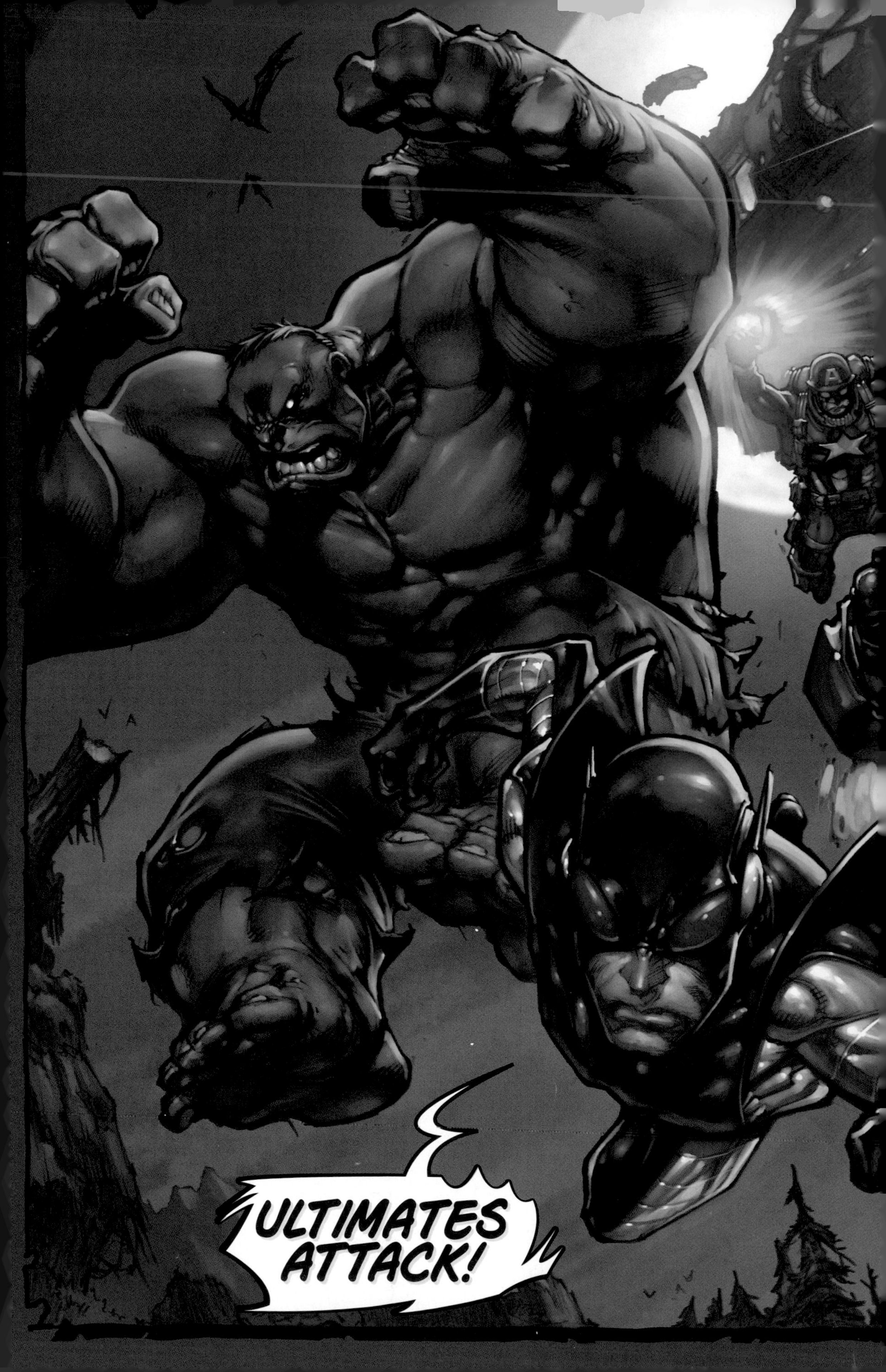
ULTIMATES ATTACK!

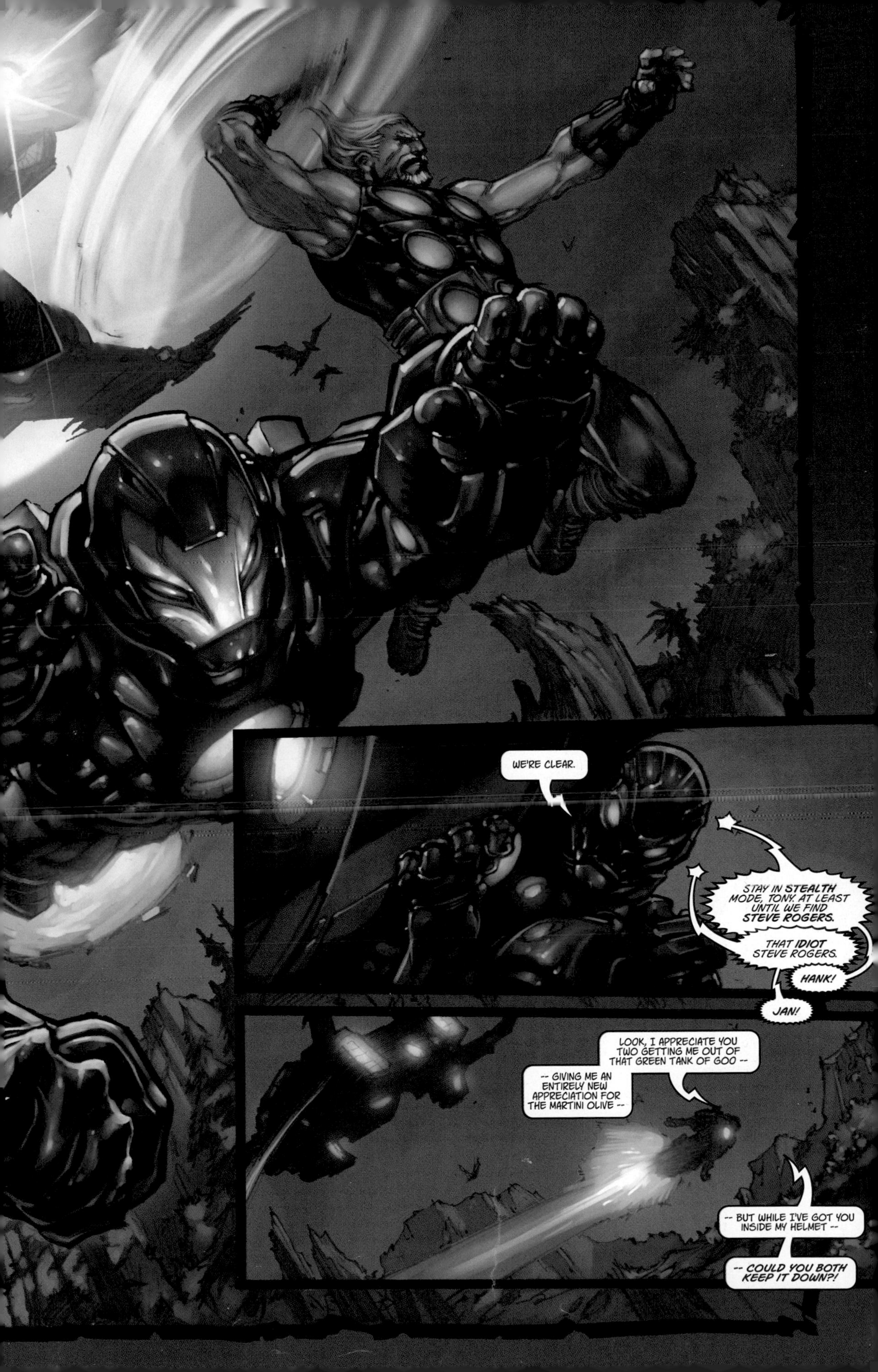
WE'RE CLEAR.
STAY IN STEALTH MODE, TONY. AT LEAST UNTIL WE FIND STEVE ROGERS.
THAT IDIOT STEVE ROGERS.
HANK!
JAN!
LOOK, I APPRECIATE YOU TWO GETTING ME OUT OF THAT GREEN TANK OF GOO --
-- GIVING ME AN ENTIRELY NEW APPRECIATION FOR THE MARTINI OLIVE --
-- BUT WHILE I'VE GOT YOU INSIDE MY HELMET --
-- COULD YOU BOTH KEEP IT DOWN?!

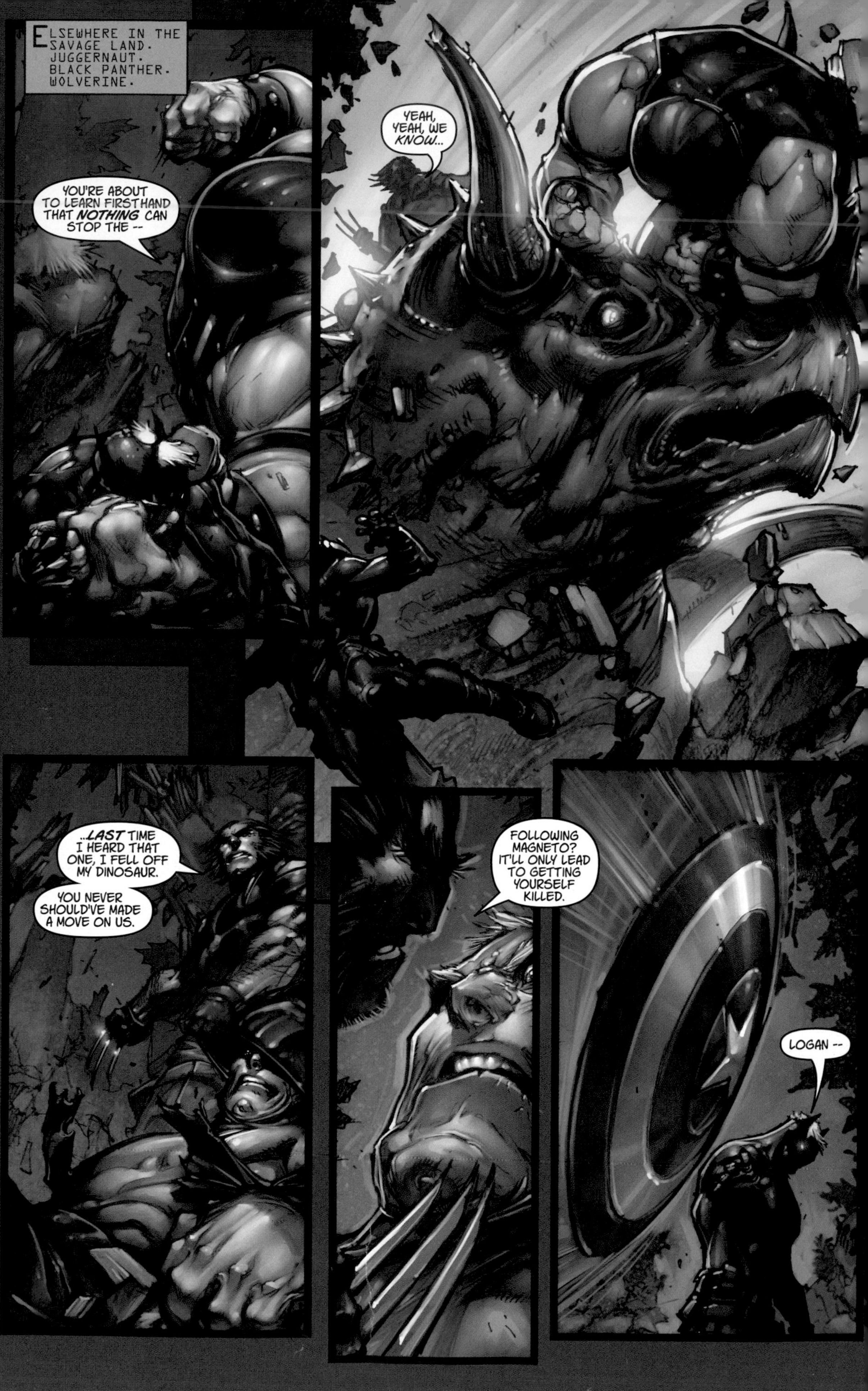

ELSEWHERE IN THE SAVAGE LAND. JUGGERNAUT. BLACK PANTHER. WOLVERINE.
YOU'RE ABOUT TO LEARN FIRSTHAND THAT NOTHING CAN STOP THE --
YEAH, YEAH, WE KNOW...
...LAST TIME I HEARD THAT ONE, I FELL OFF MY DINOSAUR.
YOU NEVER SHOULD'VE MADE A MOVE ON US.
FOLLOWING MAGNETO? IT'LL ONLY LEAD TO GETTING YOURSELF KILLED.
LOGAN --

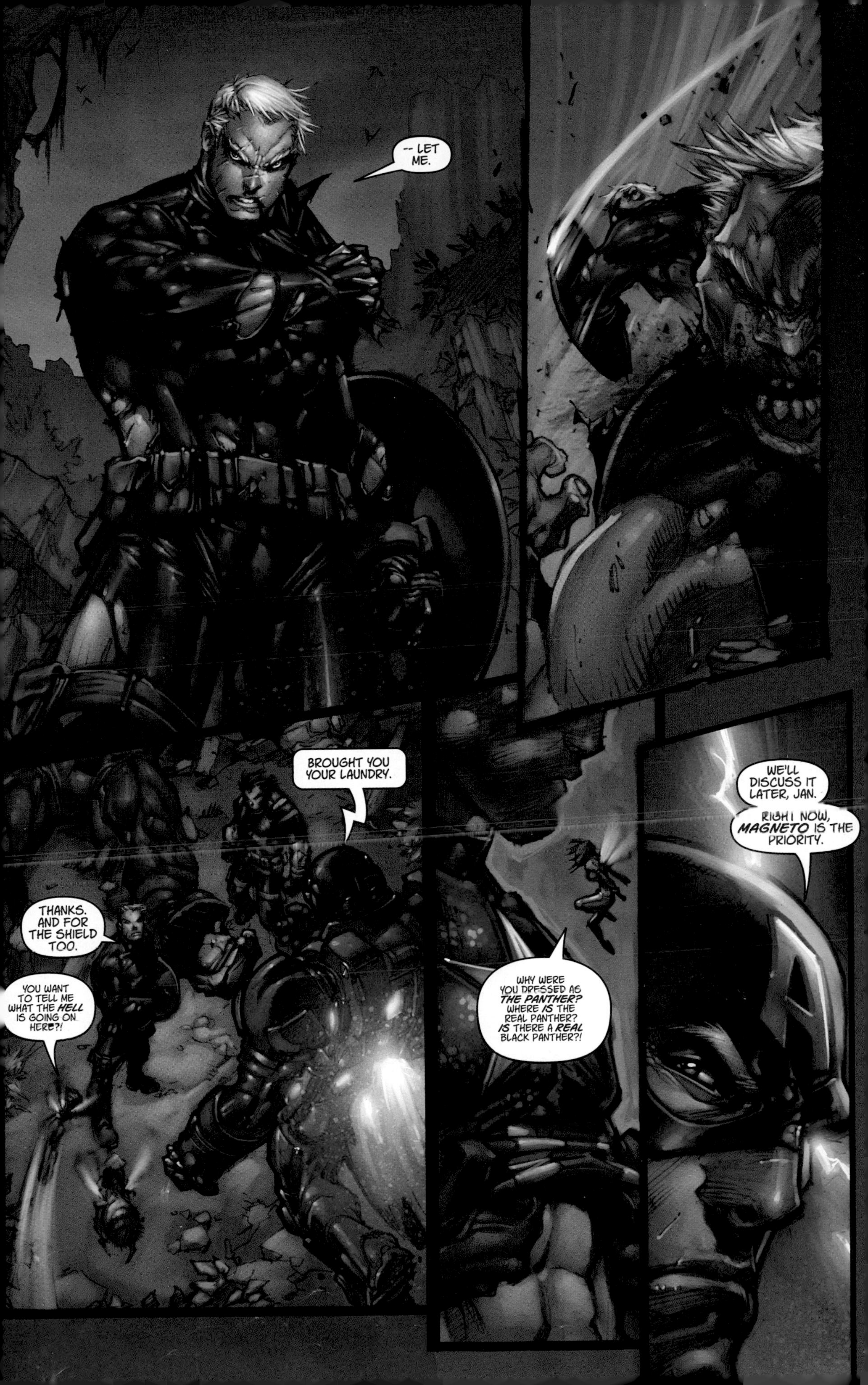
-- LET ME.
BROUGHT YOU YOUR LAUNDRY.
THANKS. AND FOR THE SHIELD TOO.
YOU WANT TO TELL ME WHAT THE HELL IS GOING ON HERE?!
WHY WERE YOU DRESSED AS THE PANTHER? WHERE IS THE REAL PANTHER? IS THERE A REAL BLACK PANTHER?!
WE'LL DISCUSS IT LATER, JAN.
RIGHT NOW, MAGNETO IS THE PRIORITY.

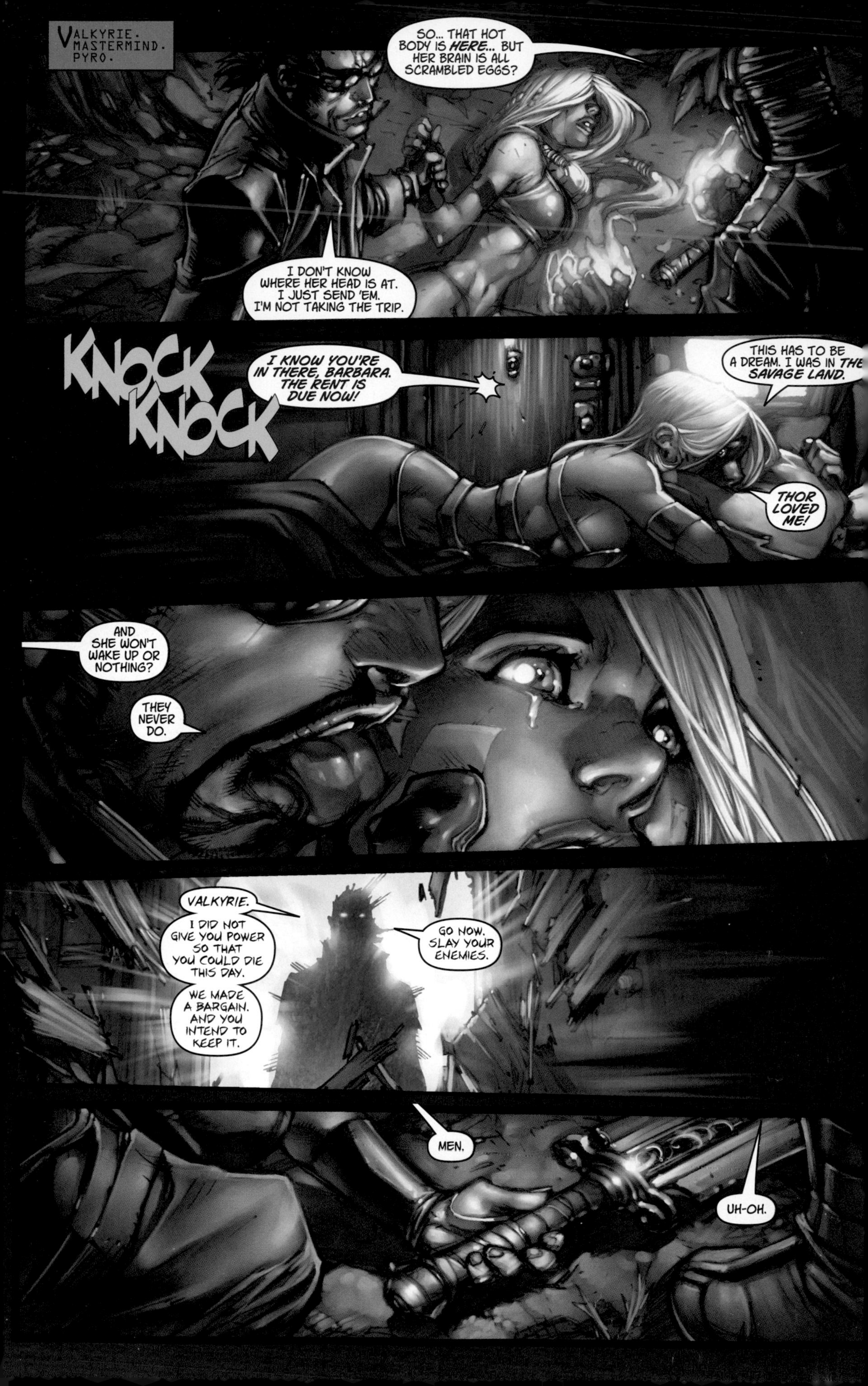
VALKYRIE. MASTERMIND. PYRO.
SO... THAT HOT BODY IS *HERE*... BUT HER BRAIN IS ALL SCRAMBLED EGGS?
I DON'T KNOW WHERE HER HEAD IS AT. I JUST SEND 'EM. I'M NOT TAKING THE TRIP.
KNOCK KNOCK
I KNOW YOU'RE IN THERE, BARBARA. THE RENT IS DUE NOW!
THIS HAS TO BE A DREAM. I WAS IN *THE SAVAGE LAND.*
THOR LOVED ME!
AND SHE WON'T WAKE UP OR NOTHING?
THEY NEVER DO.
VALKYRIE.
I DID NOT GIVE YOU POWER SO THAT YOU COULD DIE THIS DAY.
WE MADE A BARGAIN. AND YOU INTEND TO KEEP IT.
GO NOW. SLAY YOUR ENEMIES.
MEN.
UH-OH.

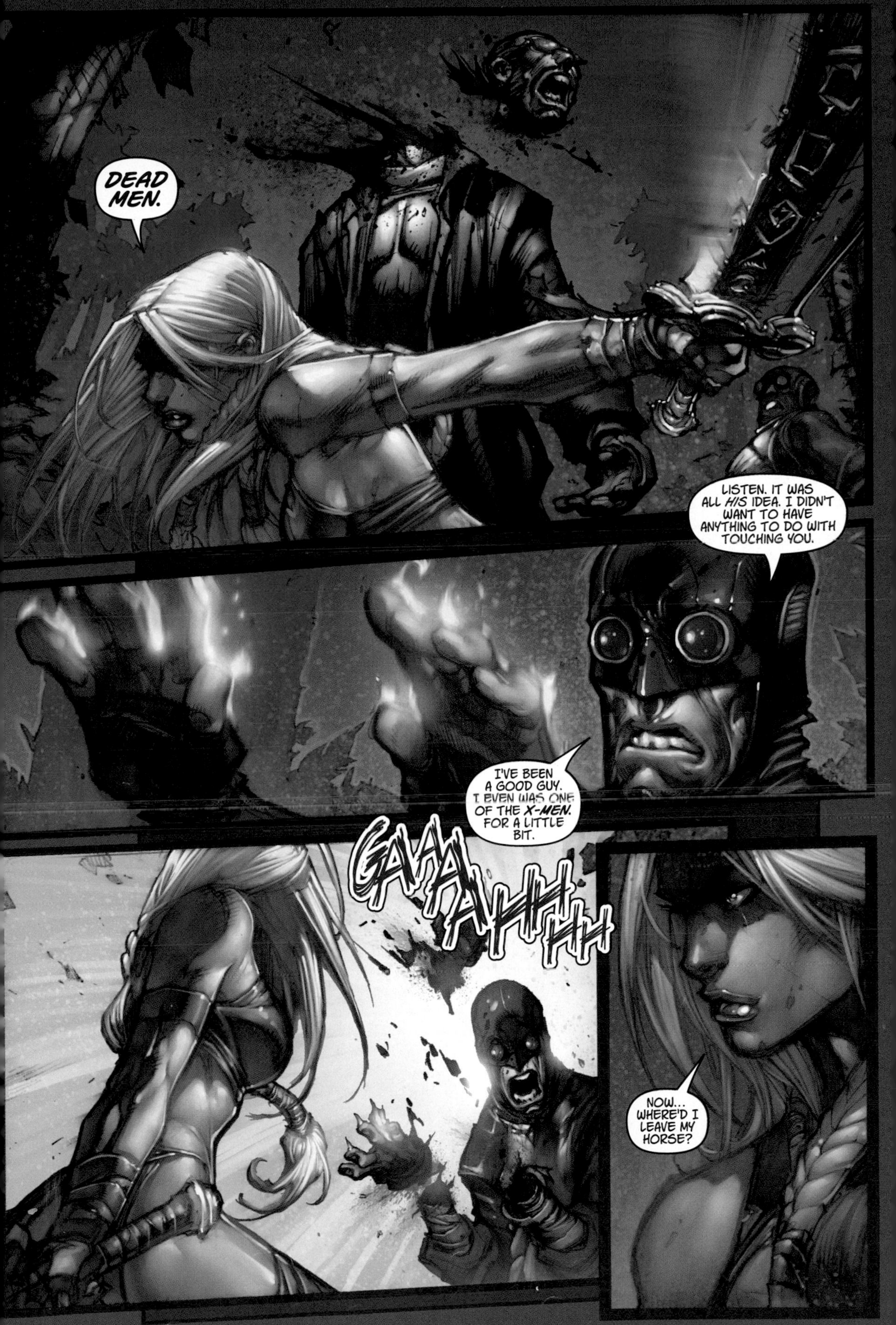
DEAD MEN.
LISTEN. IT WAS ALL *HIS* IDEA. I DIDN'T WANT TO HAVE ANYTHING TO DO WITH TOUCHING YOU.
I'VE BEEN A GOOD GUY. I EVEN WAS ONE OF THE *X-MEN.* FOR A LITTLE BIT.
GAAAAHHHHH
NOW... WHERE'D I LEAVE MY HORSE?

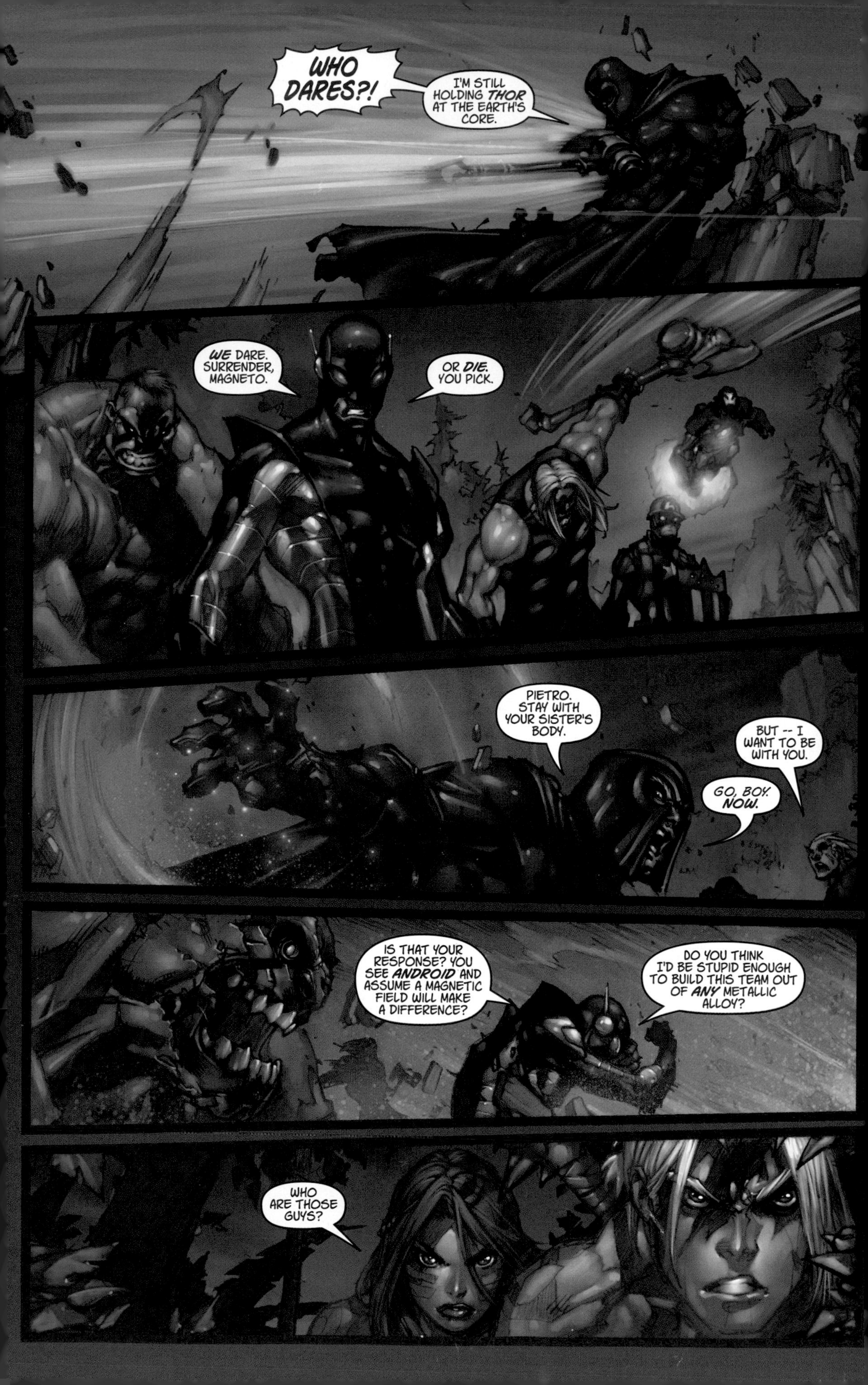
WHO DARES?!
I'M STILL HOLDING THOR AT THE EARTH'S CORE.
WE DARE. SURRENDER, MAGNETO.
OR DIE. YOU PICK.
PIETRO. STAY WITH YOUR SISTER'S BODY.
BUT -- I WANT TO BE WITH YOU.
GO, BOY. NOW.
IS THAT YOUR RESPONSE? YOU SEE ANDROID AND ASSUME A MAGNETIC FIELD WILL MAKE A DIFFERENCE?
DO YOU THINK I'D BE STUPID ENOUGH TO BUILD THIS TEAM OUT OF ANY METALLIC ALLOY?
WHO ARE THOSE GUYS?

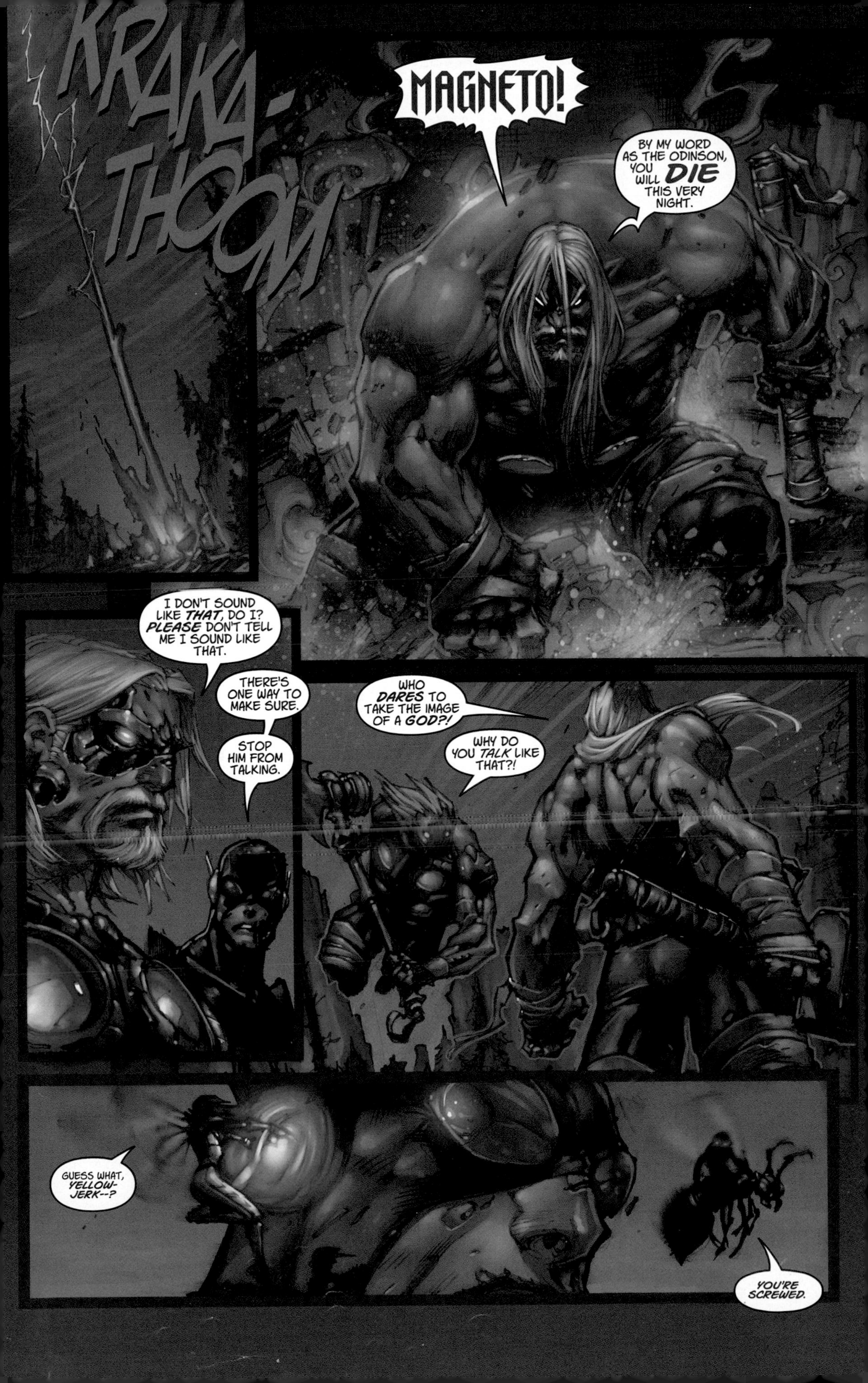
KRAKA-THOOM
MAGNETO!
BY MY WORD AS THE ODINSON, YOU WILL DIE THIS VERY NIGHT.
I DON'T SOUND LIKE THAT, DO I? PLEASE DON'T TELL ME I SOUND LIKE THAT.
THERE'S ONE WAY TO MAKE SURE.
STOP HIM FROM TALKING.
WHO DARES TO TAKE THE IMAGE OF A GOD?!
WHY DO YOU TALK LIKE THAT?!
GUESS WHAT, YELLOW-JERK--?
YOU'RE SCREWED.

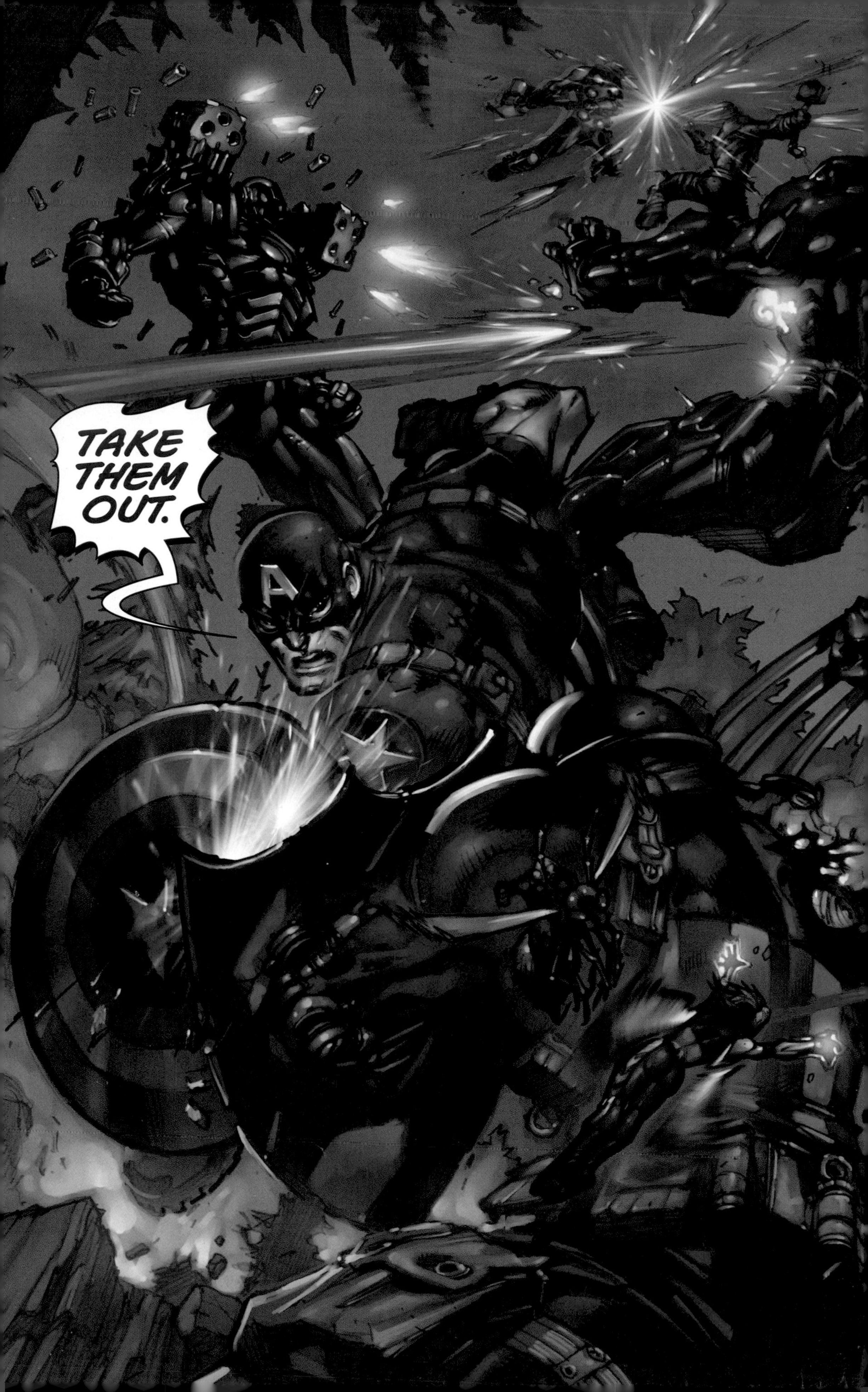
TAKE THEM OUT.

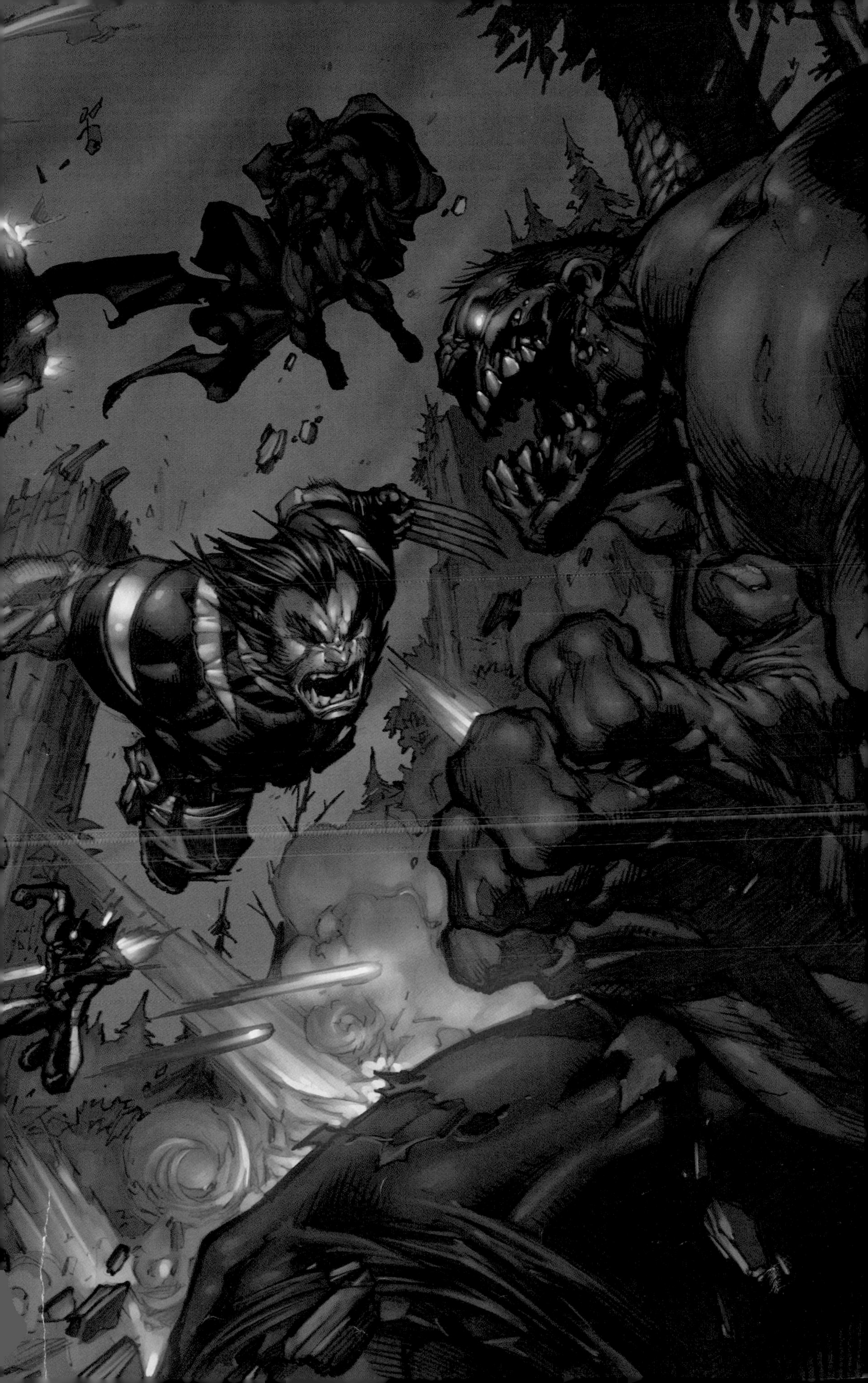

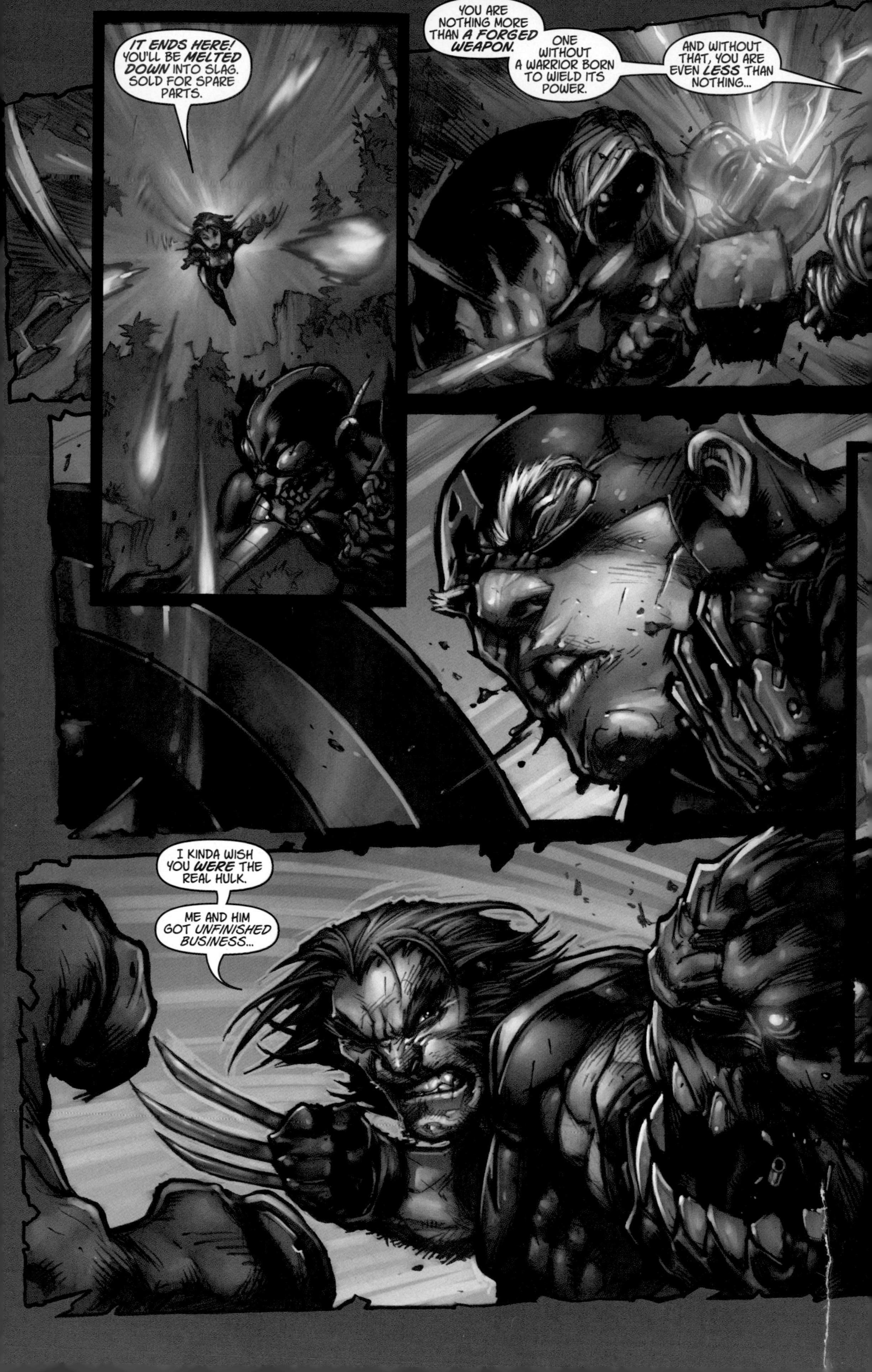
IT ENDS HERE! YOU'LL BE MELTED DOWN INTO SLAG. SOLD FOR SPARE PARTS.
YOU ARE NOTHING MORE THAN A FORGED WEAPON.
ONE WITHOUT A WARRIOR BORN TO WIELD ITS POWER.
AND WITHOUT THAT, YOU ARE EVEN LESS THAN NOTHING...
I KINDA WISH YOU WERE THE REAL HULK.
ME AND HIM GOT UNFINISHED BUSINESS...

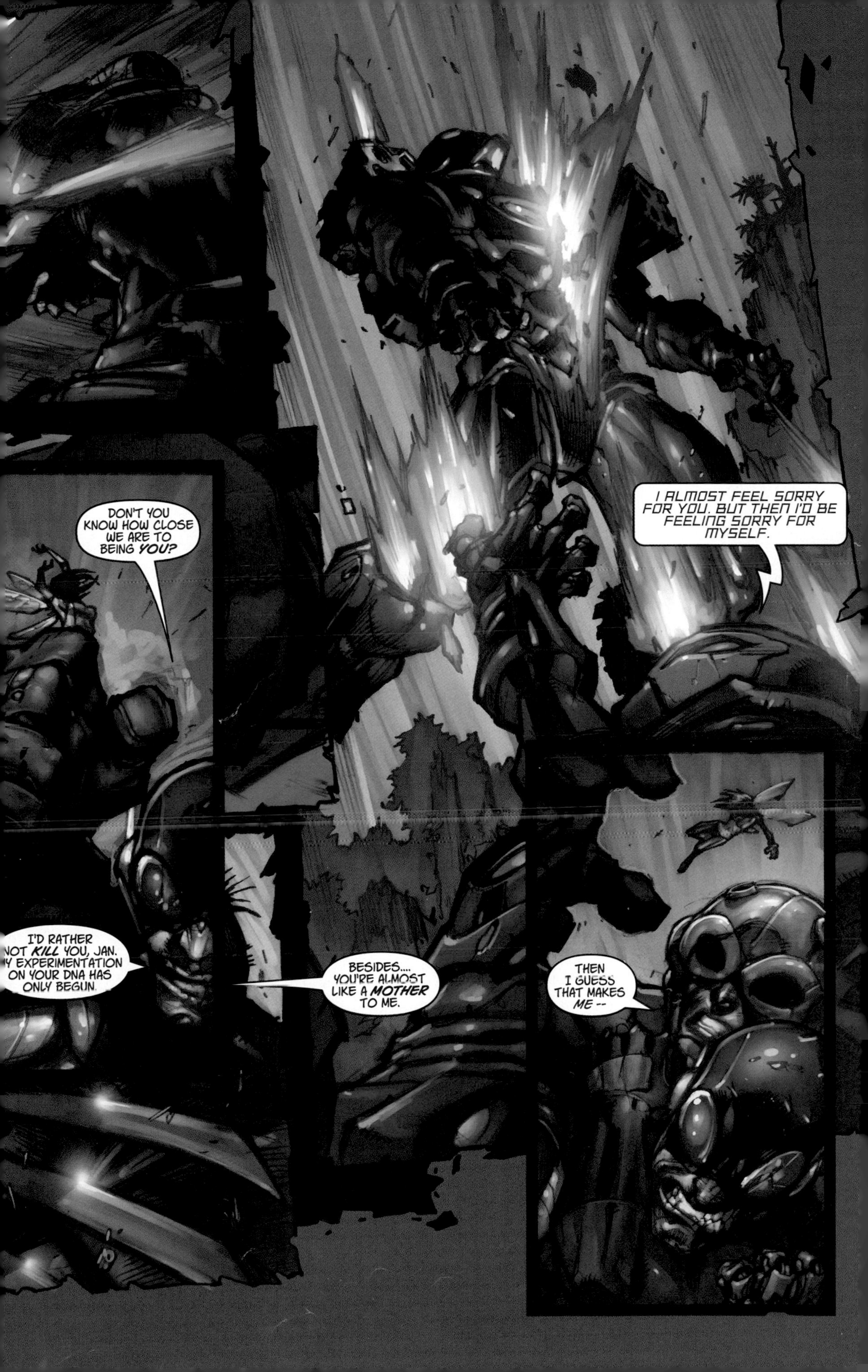
DON'T YOU KNOW HOW CLOSE WE ARE TO BEING YOU?
I ALMOST FEEL SORRY FOR YOU. BUT THEN I'D BE FEELING SORRY FOR MYSELF.
I'D RATHER NOT KILL YOU, JAN. MY EXPERIMENTATION ON YOUR DNA HAS ONLY BEGUN.
BESIDES.... YOU'RE ALMOST LIKE A MOTHER TO ME.
THEN I GUESS THAT MAKES ME --

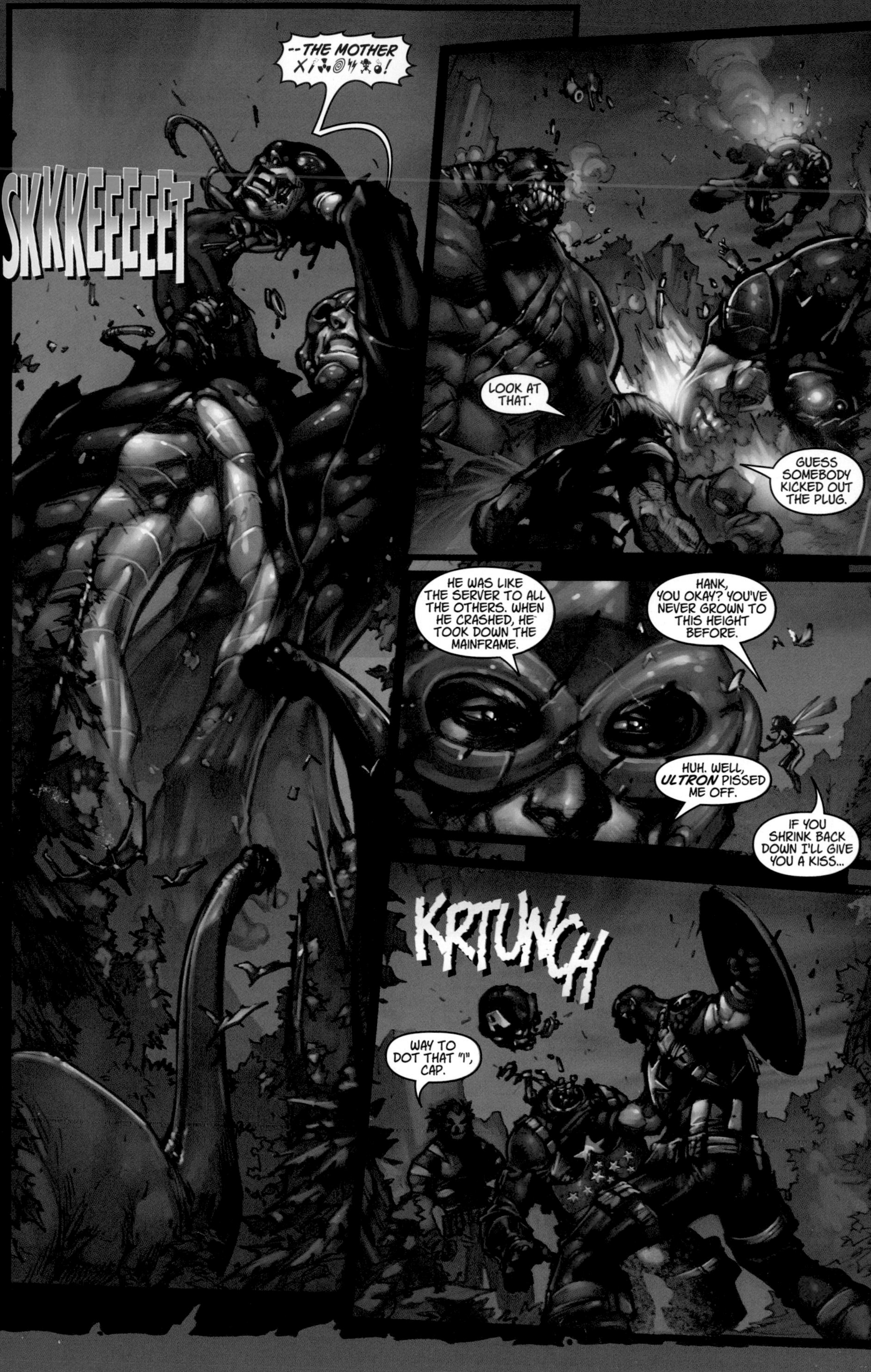
--THE MOTHER X/☢◎ϟ☠ô!
SKKKEEEEEET
LOOK AT THAT.
GUESS SOMEBODY KICKED OUT THE PLUG.
HE WAS LIKE THE SERVER TO ALL THE OTHERS. WHEN HE CRASHED, HE TOOK DOWN THE MAINFRAME.
HANK, YOU OKAY? YOU'VE NEVER GROWN TO THIS HEIGHT BEFORE.
HUH. WELL, ULTRON PISSED ME OFF.
IF YOU SHRINK BACK DOWN I'LL GIVE YOU A KISS...
KRTUNCH
WAY TO DOT THAT "I", CAP.

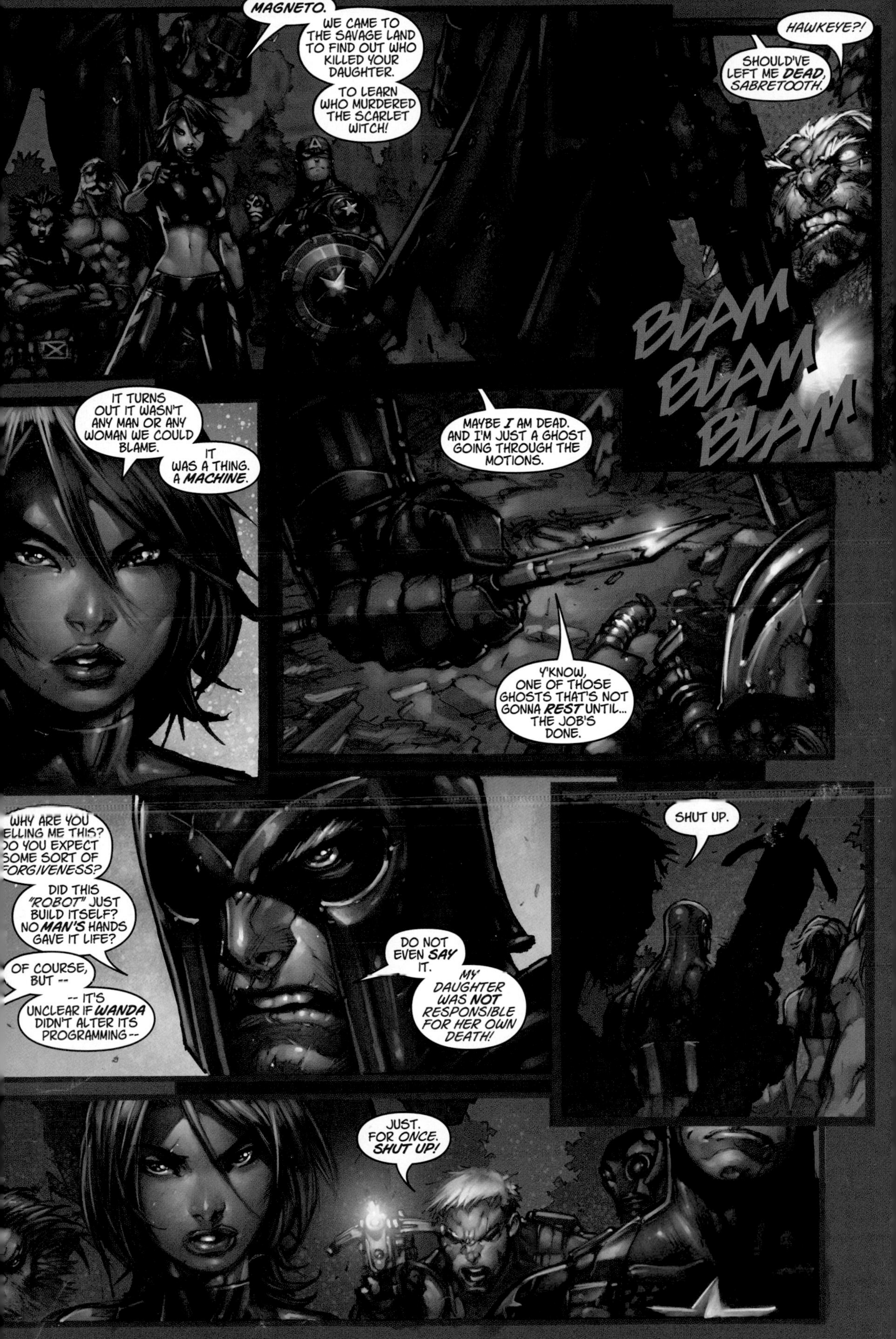

MAGNETO.
WE CAME TO THE SAVAGE LAND TO FIND OUT WHO KILLED YOUR DAUGHTER.
TO LEARN WHO MURDERED THE SCARLET WITCH!
HAWKEYE?!
SHOULD'VE LEFT ME DEAD, SABRETOOTH.
BLAM BLAM BLAM
IT TURNS OUT IT WASN'T ANY MAN OR ANY WOMAN WE COULD BLAME.
IT WAS A THING. A MACHINE.
MAYBE I AM DEAD. AND I'M JUST A GHOST GOING THROUGH THE MOTIONS.
Y'KNOW, ONE OF THOSE GHOSTS THAT'S NOT GONNA REST UNTIL... THE JOB'S DONE.
WHY ARE YOU TELLING ME THIS? DO YOU EXPECT SOME SORT OF FORGIVENESS?
DID THIS "ROBOT" JUST BUILD ITSELF? NO MAN'S HANDS GAVE IT LIFE?
OF COURSE, BUT --
-- IT'S UNCLEAR IF WANDA DIDN'T ALTER ITS PROGRAMMING --
DO NOT EVEN SAY IT.
MY DAUGHTER WAS NOT RESPONSIBLE FOR HER OWN DEATH!
SHUT UP.
JUST. FOR ONCE. SHUT UP!

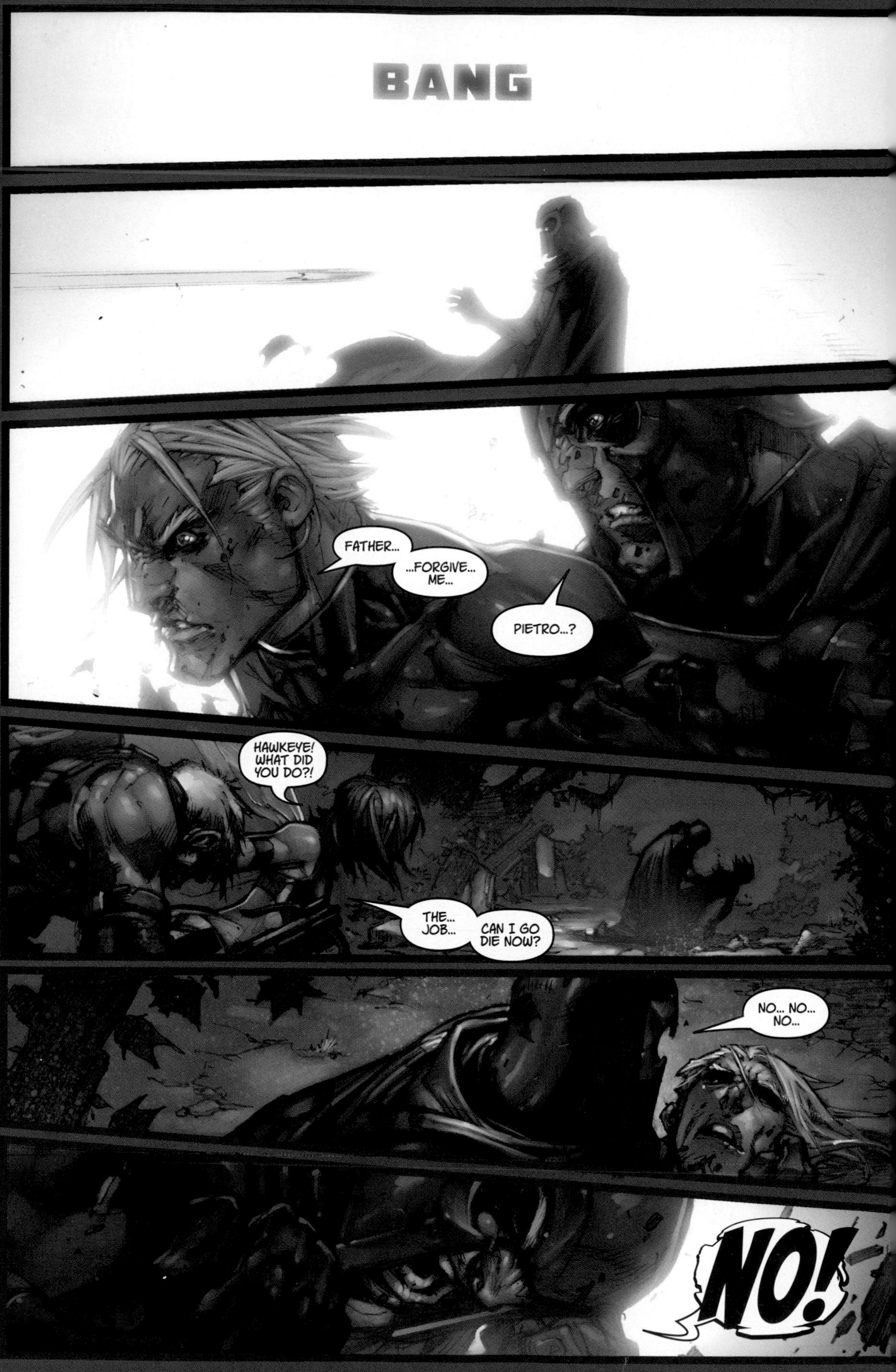
BANG
FATHER...
...FORGIVE... ME...
PIETRO...?
HAWKEYE! WHAT DID YOU DO?!
THE... JOB...
CAN I GO DIE NOW?
NO... NO... NO...
NO!

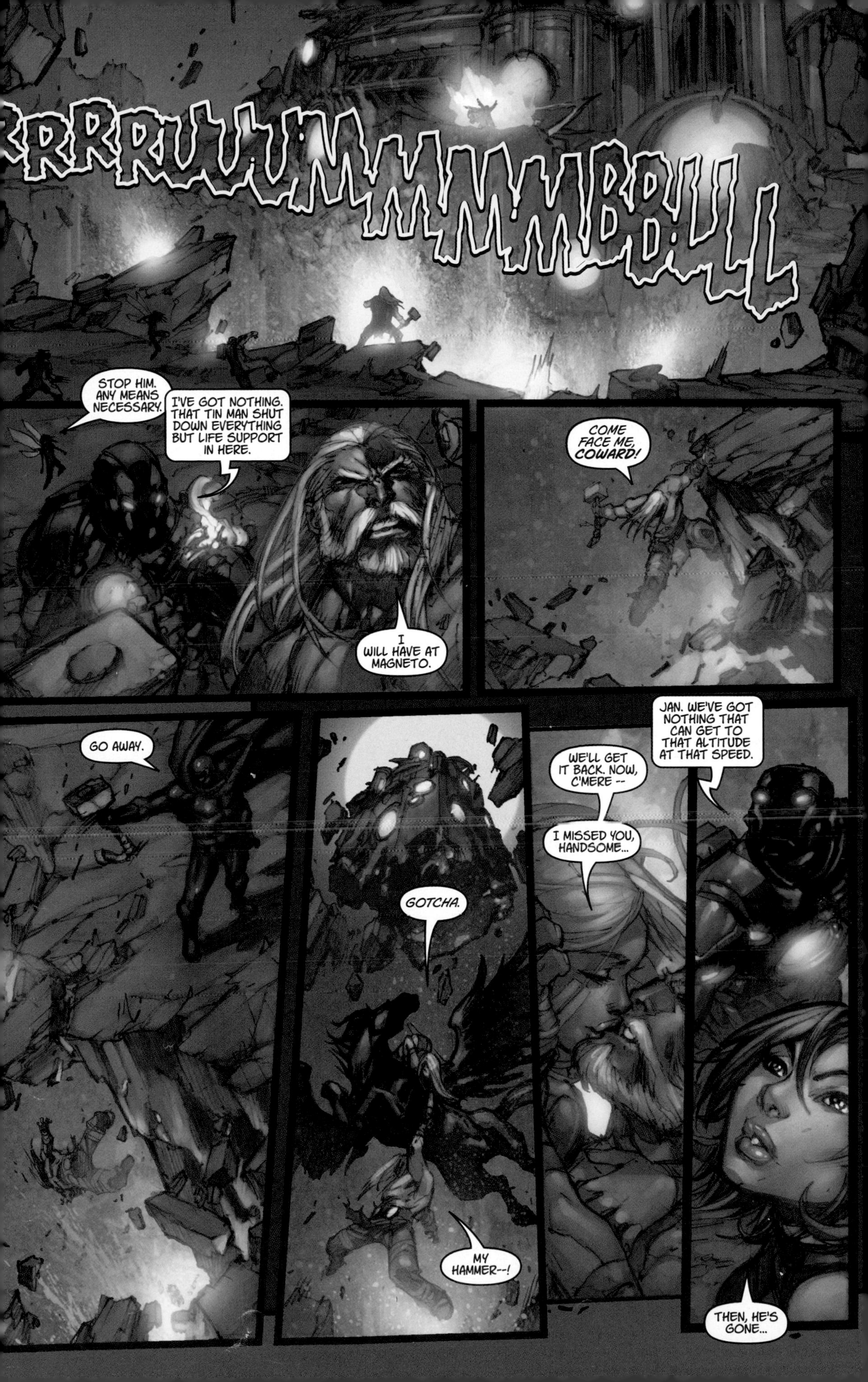

RRRRUUUMMMMMBBULL
STOP HIM. ANY MEANS NECESSARY.
I'VE GOT NOTHING. THAT TIN MAN SHUT DOWN EVERYTHING BUT LIFE SUPPORT IN HERE.
I WILL HAVE AT MAGNETO.
COME FACE ME, COWARD!
GO AWAY.
GOTCHA.
MY HAMMER--!
WE'LL GET IT BACK. NOW, C'MERE --
I MISSED YOU, HANDSOME...
JAN. WE'VE GOT NOTHING THAT CAN GET TO THAT ALTITUDE AT THAT SPEED.
THEN, HE'S GONE...

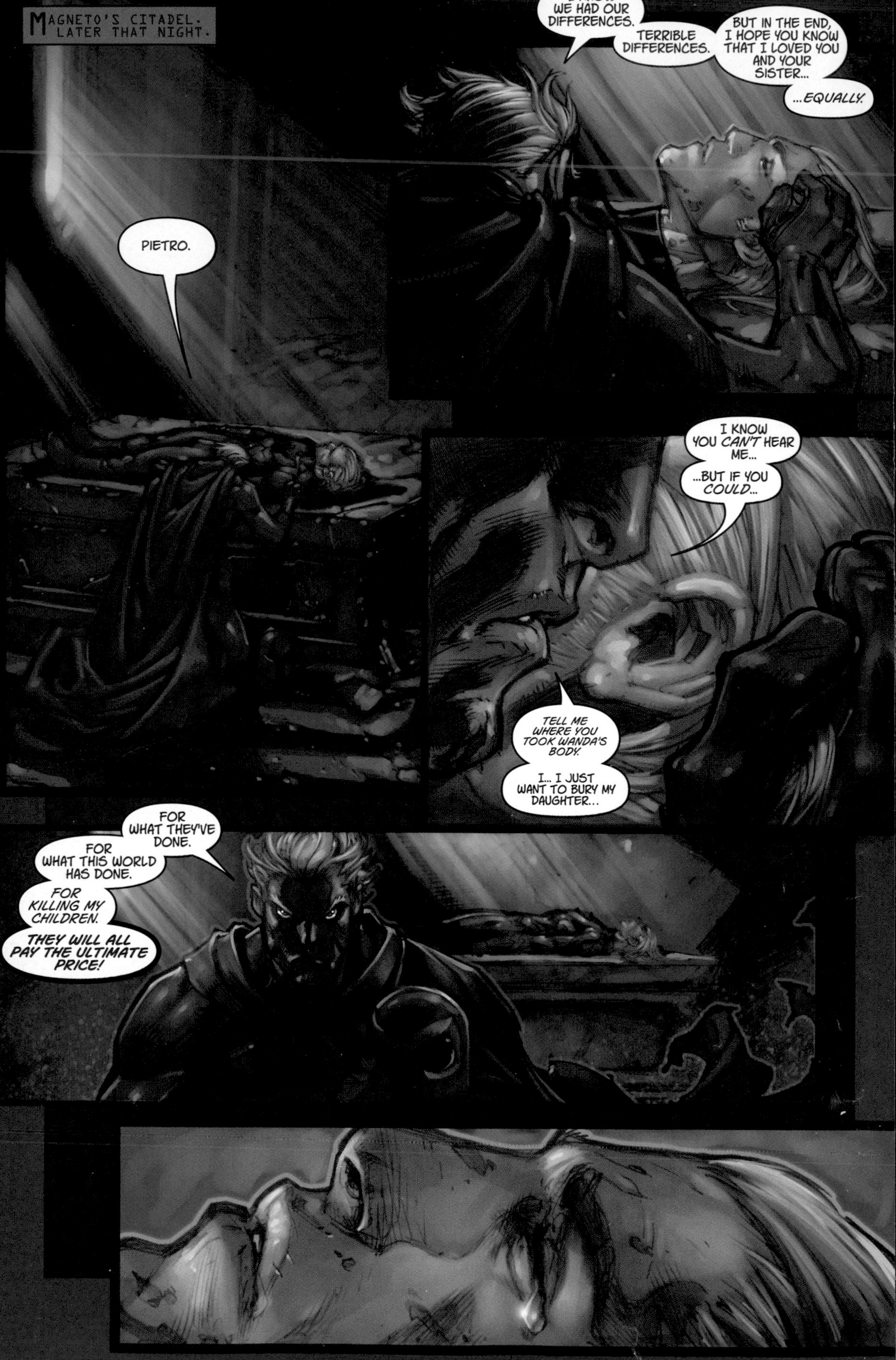
MAGNETO'S CITADEL. LATER THAT NIGHT.
I KNOW WE HAD OUR DIFFERENCES.
TERRIBLE DIFFERENCES.
BUT IN THE END, I HOPE YOU KNOW THAT I LOVED YOU AND YOUR SISTER...
...EQUALLY.
PIETRO.
I KNOW YOU CAN'T HEAR ME...
...BUT IF YOU COULD...
TELL ME WHERE YOU TOOK WANDA'S BODY.
I... I JUST WANT TO BURY MY DAUGHTER...
FOR WHAT THEY'VE DONE.
FOR WHAT THIS WORLD HAS DONE.
FOR KILLING MY CHILDREN.
THEY WILL ALL PAY THE ULTIMATE PRICE!

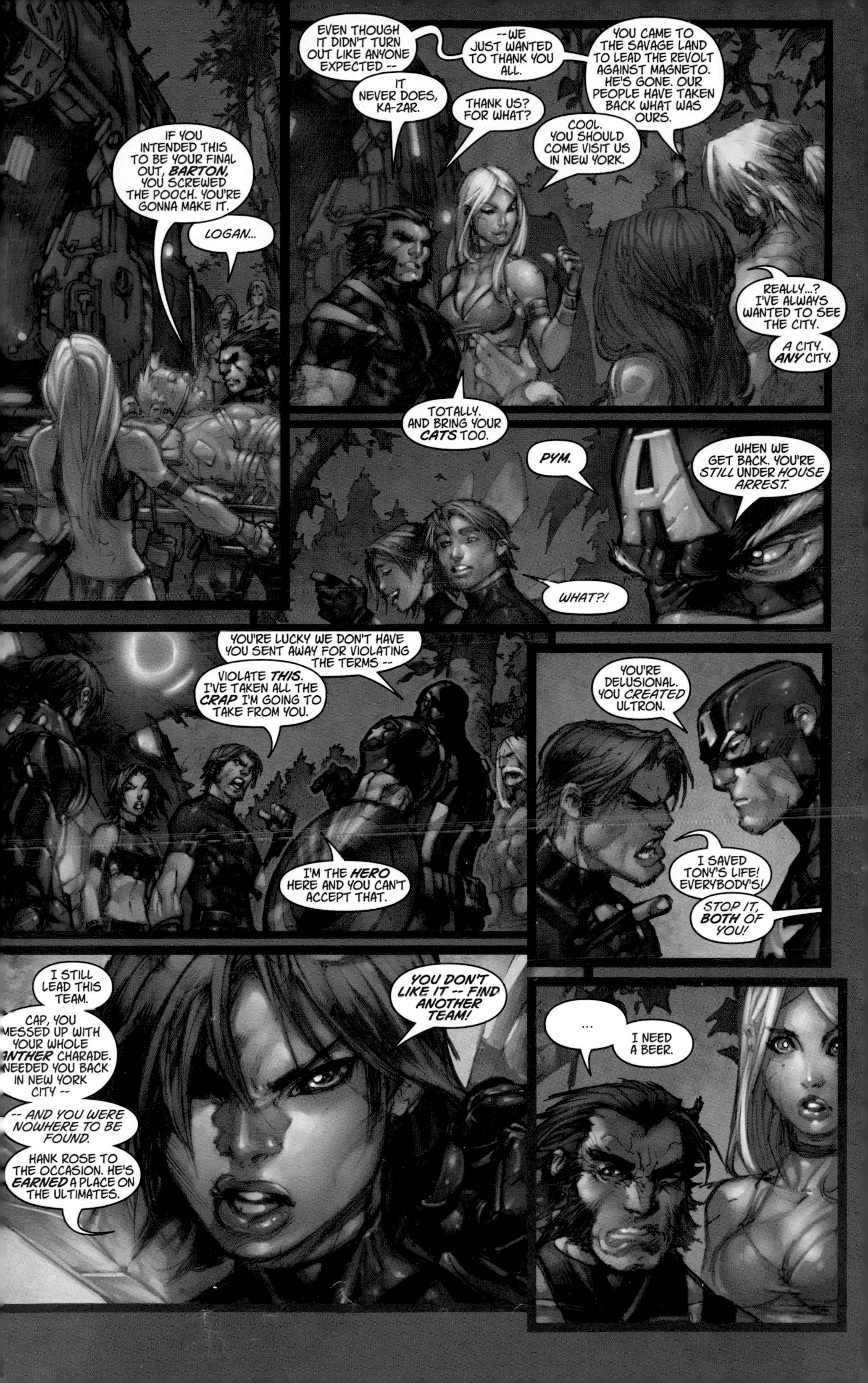
IF YOU INTENDED THIS TO BE YOUR FINAL OUT, BARTON, YOU SCREWED THE POOCH. YOU'RE GONNA MAKE IT.
LOGAN...
EVEN THOUGH IT DIDN'T TURN OUT LIKE ANYONE EXPECTED --
--WE JUST WANTED TO THANK YOU ALL.
YOU CAME TO THE SAVAGE LAND TO LEAD THE REVOLT AGAINST MAGNETO. HE'S GONE. OUR PEOPLE HAVE TAKEN BACK WHAT WAS OURS.
IT NEVER DOES, KA-ZAR.
THANK US? FOR WHAT?
COOL. YOU SHOULD COME VISIT US IN NEW YORK.
REALLY...? I'VE ALWAYS WANTED TO SEE THE CITY.
A CITY. ANY CITY.
TOTALLY. AND BRING YOUR CATS TOO.
PYM.
WHEN WE GET BACK. YOU'RE STILL UNDER HOUSE ARREST.
WHAT?!
YOU'RE LUCKY WE DON'T HAVE YOU SENT AWAY FOR VIOLATING THE TERMS --
VIOLATE THIS. I'VE TAKEN ALL THE CRAP I'M GOING TO TAKE FROM YOU.
I'M THE HERO HERE AND YOU CAN'T ACCEPT THAT.
YOU'RE DELUSIONAL. YOU CREATED ULTRON.
I SAVED TONY'S LIFE! EVERYBODY'S!
STOP IT, BOTH OF YOU!
I STILL LEAD THIS TEAM.
CAP, YOU MESSED UP WITH YOUR WHOLE ANTHER CHARADE. NEEDED YOU BACK IN NEW YORK CITY --
-- AND YOU WERE NOWHERE TO BE FOUND.
HANK ROSE TO THE OCCASION. HE'S EARNED A PLACE ON THE ULTIMATES.
YOU DON'T LIKE IT -- FIND ANOTHER TEAM!
...
I NEED A BEER.

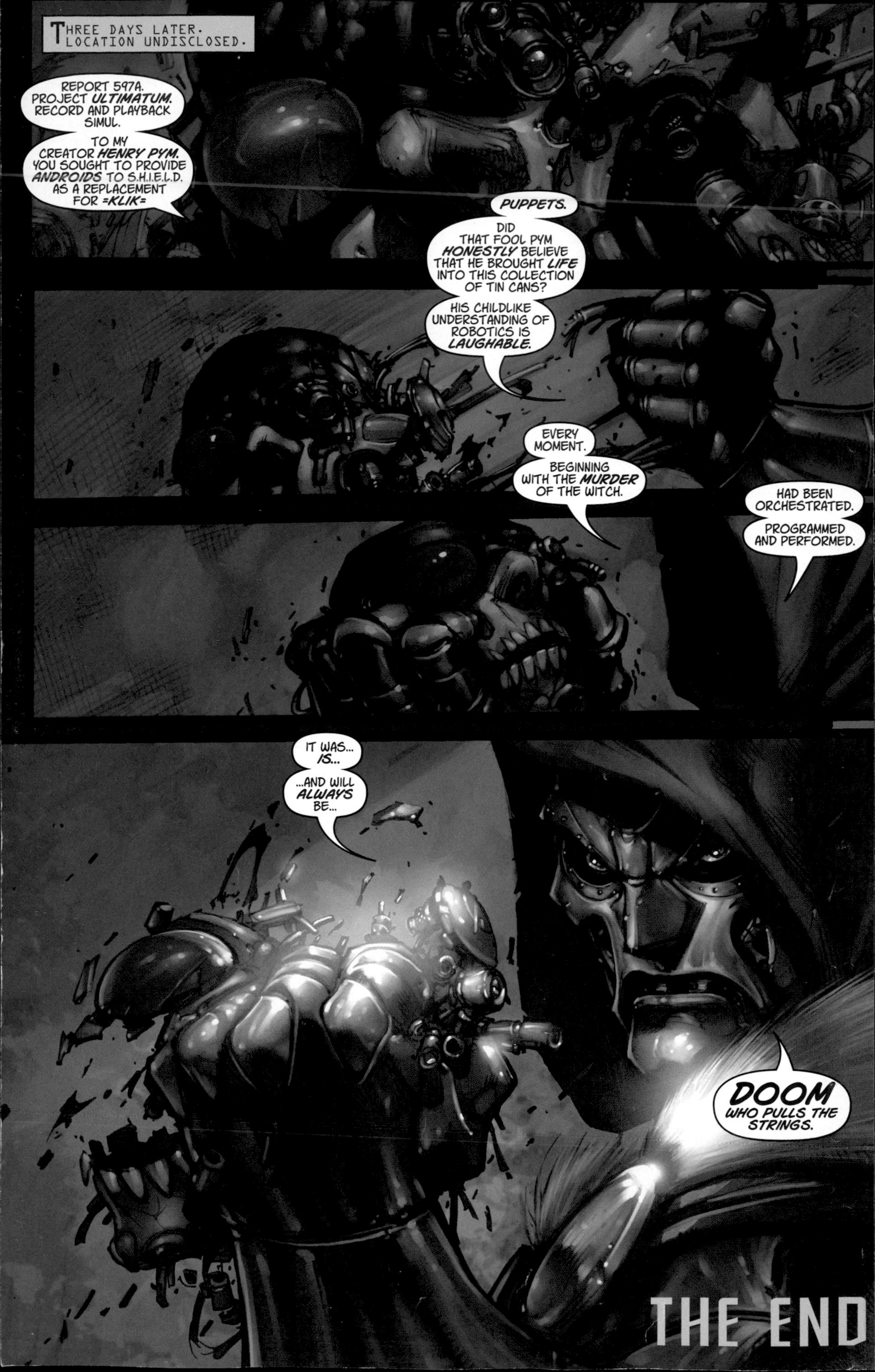
THREE DAYS LATER. LOCATION UNDISCLOSED.
REPORT 597A. PROJECT ULTIMATUM. RECORD AND PLAYBACK SIMUL.
TO MY CREATOR HENRY PYM. YOU SOUGHT TO PROVIDE ANDROIDS TO S.H.I.E.L.D. AS A REPLACEMENT FOR =KLIK=
PUPPETS.
DID THAT FOOL PYM HONESTLY BELIEVE THAT HE BROUGHT LIFE INTO THIS COLLECTION OF TIN CANS?
HIS CHILDLIKE UNDERSTANDING OF ROBOTICS IS LAUGHABLE.
EVERY MOMENT.
BEGINNING WITH THE MURDER OF THE WITCH.
HAD BEEN ORCHESTRATED.
PROGRAMMED AND PERFORMED.
IT WAS... IS...
...AND WILL ALWAYS BE...
DOOM WHO PULLS THE STRINGS.
THE END

GALLERY

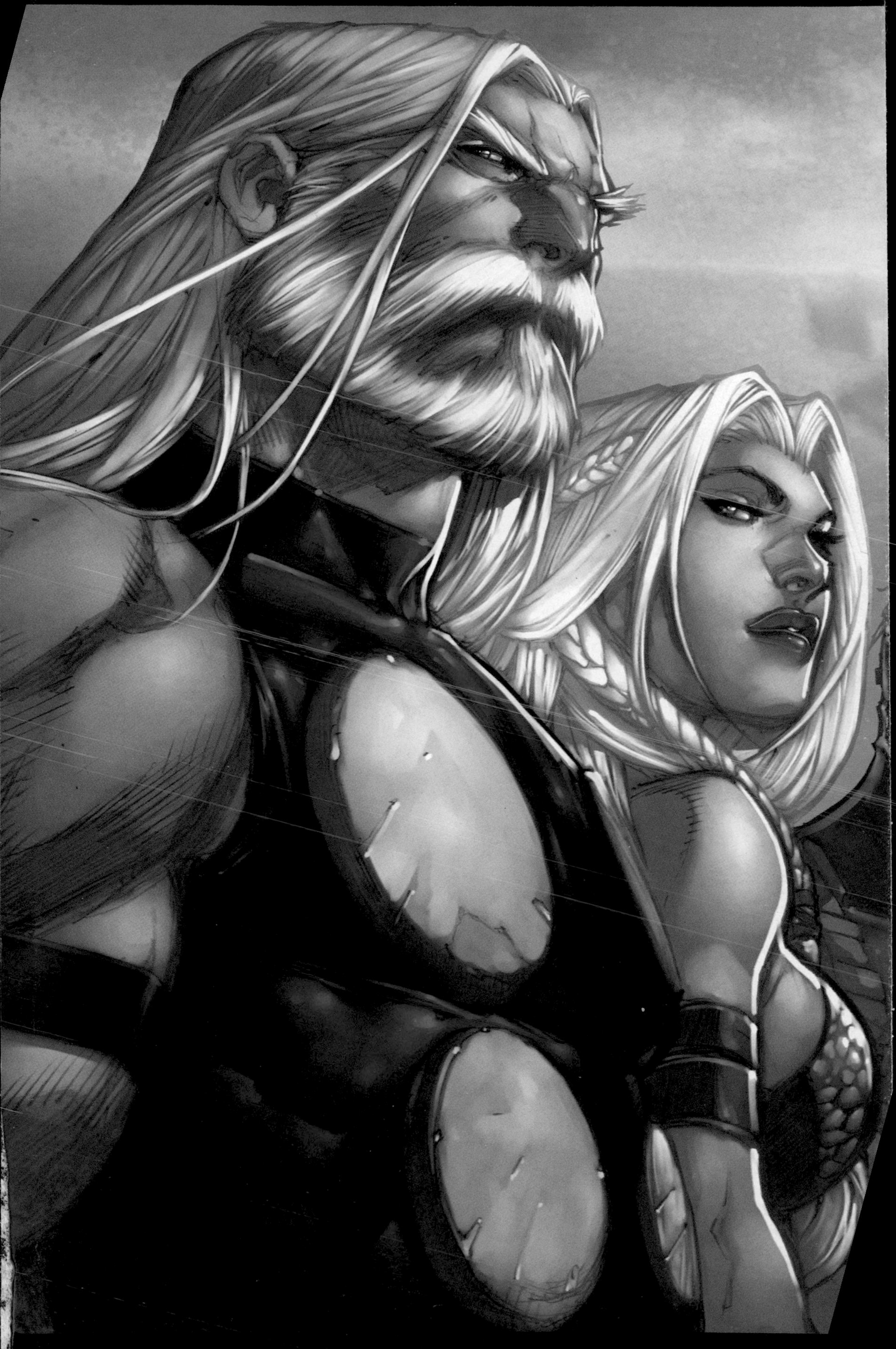

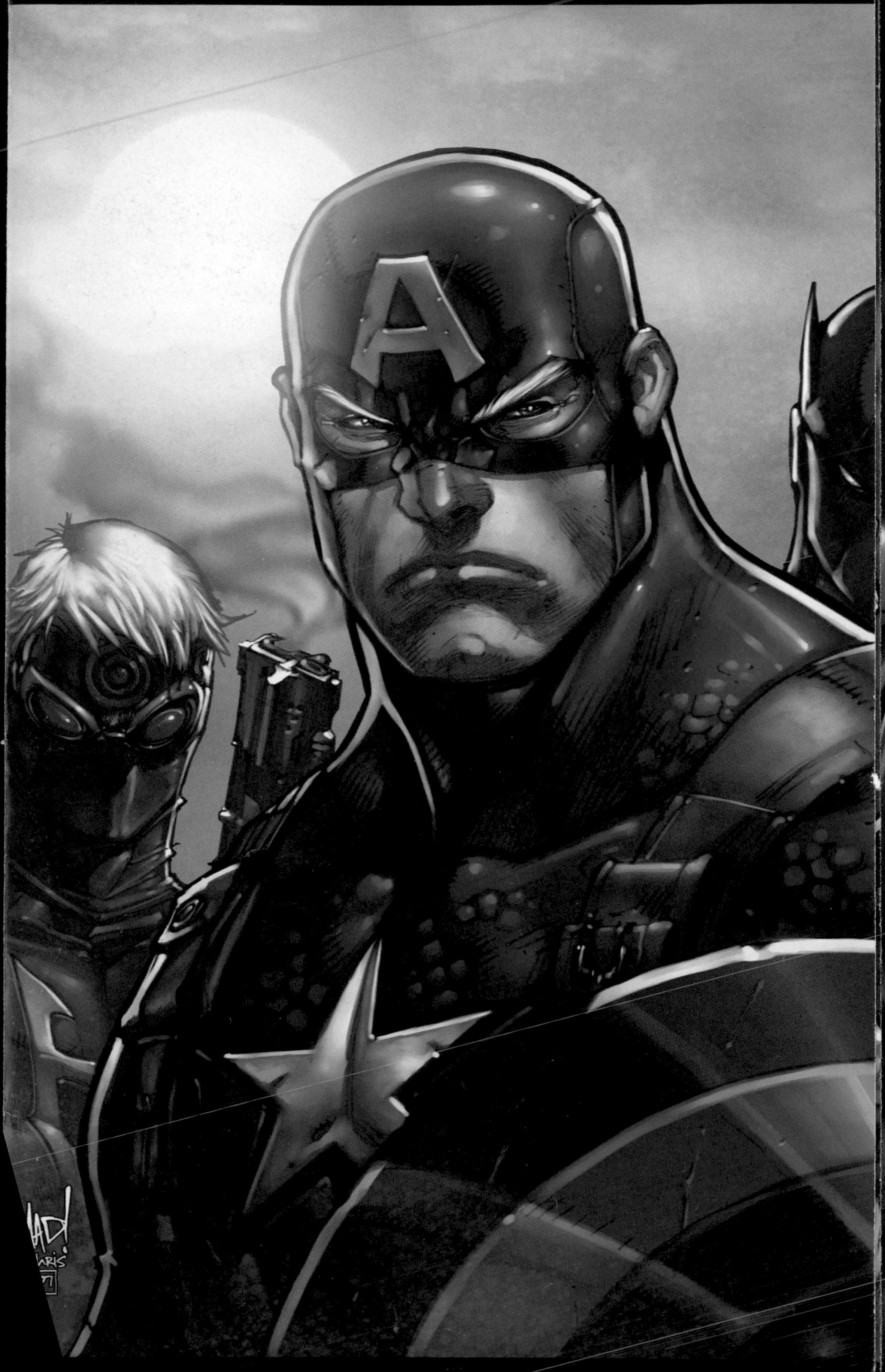

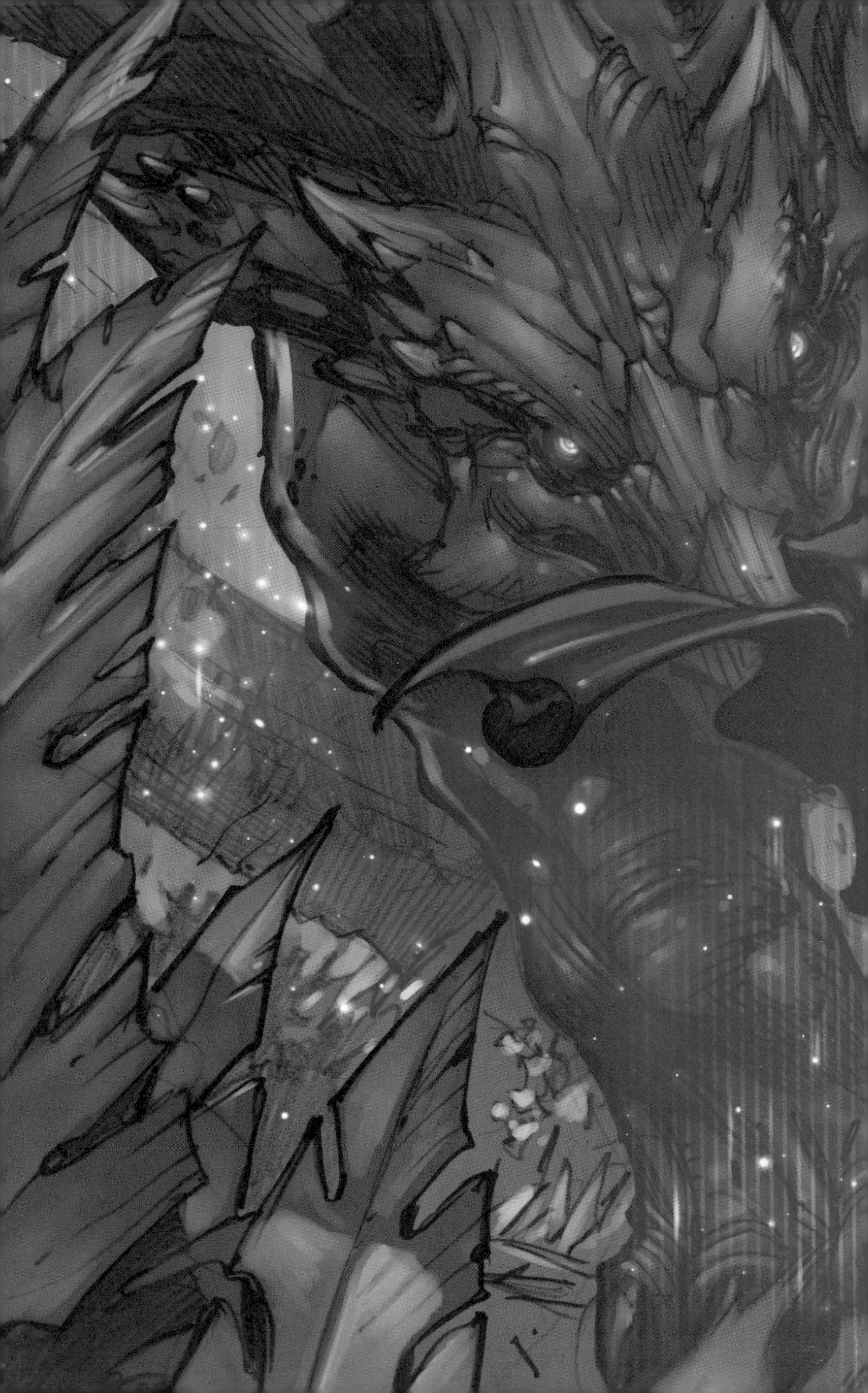